BRUNCH
in London

Dedicated to the
treasures of the world:
the children we serve.

BRUNCH
in London

A book by Thérèse Nichols

OnePlate

CONTENTS

FOREWORD

By OnePlate Co-founder & Director Thérèse Nichols

Welcome to the vibrant world of *Brunch in London*, where culinary traditions from around the globe converge in a delightful fusion of flavours. In this cookbook, we embark on a journey through the heart of one of the world's most dynamic cities, bringing the spirit of London's brunch scene directly into your kitchen. This book represents more than just a celebration of food – it embodies a powerful commitment to creating positive change in the lives of children through our charity OnePlate.

London, with its rich history and diverse cultural influences, has long been a melting pot of culinary creativity. From the traditional 'Full English' to delights from further afield, the city's brunch scene reflects its cosmopolitan spirit.

Brunch is more than a meal, it's an experience, allowing us to indulge in a luxurious pause and celebrate the art of slowness. This book is a homage to this delightful ritual, capturing the essence of London's culinary landscape and inviting you to experience the city's gastronomic treasures from the comfort of your own kitchen.

I have always loved brunch as it's a leisurely ritual celebrating the luxury of time, allowing us to enjoy meaningful moments with friends and rediscover the joy of simply being present. It's a deep breath of relaxation and connection. In a world that glorifies speed and efficiency, brunch reminds us to savour calm mornings and rekindle our love for life's unhurried, soul-nourishing periods.

Brunch is a cherished tradition that brings people together, celebrating the joy of good food and conversation. It is with this spirit of togetherness and generosity that we have embarked on a unique mission.

What makes this cookbook truly special is that, beyond its delicious recipes, every purchase contributes to funding OnePlate sustainable food projects for children in great need across Africa and Asia. The very essence of brunch is about sharing, and through your purchase, you are contributing to a cause that embodies that spirit of compassion and community.

The decision to focus our efforts on sustainable food initiatives was born out of a deep commitment to making a tangible difference. By supporting projects that promote agricultural education, community gardens, farms and access to clean, nutritious food, we aim to empower children and their families, breaking the cycle of hunger, so that every child has the opportunity to grow, dream and reach their full potential.

Through your generosity in purchasing this cookbook, you are not only enjoying culinary delights but also contributing to a global movement, sowing seeds of hope and nourishment.

I extend my heartfelt gratitude to London's cafés, restaurants and talented chefs who have contributed their recipes, expertise and creativity to this cookbook. Their recipes are a testament to the city's culinary brilliance and the endless possibilities that brunch in London has to offer.

We are so grateful to everyone involved in bringing this cookbook to life, from our photographers, food stylists and writers who have dedicated their time and skills to creating this special cookbook, to the generosity of our readers who believe in the power of giving. Together, we are creating a legacy of compassion, and paving the way for transformative change in the lives of countless children.

Thank you for joining us on this journey. With your support, we are turning the simple act of enjoying brunch into a force for good, planting gardens and farms to nourish children in need. In these farms and gardens children are taught how to plant seeds, to water them and to patiently watch them grow until those seeds bear fruit. May we never forget that if something is loved and not forgotten, it will grow.

So, whether you're a Londoner seeking new brunch inspiration or a visitor eager to bring a taste of London's culinary magic home, I invite you to dive into these recipes and immerse yourself in the delightful world of *Brunch in London*. May you be inspired to gather loved ones around your table, whether it be a cosy weekend brunch with friends or a grand family gathering.

OnePlate is a global charity
partnering with foodies, restaurants,
cafés and chefs to fund sustainable
food projects in Africa and Asia.

Our vision is to nourish and nurture
children in great need, offering love
and hope, one plate at a time.

FIVE HUNDRED HEARTS

The story of OnePlate.

The story of OnePlate began in Manila in 2015, when Thérèse Nichols was visiting from Australia. She was heartbroken after witnessing children abandoned on the streets, searching for food to survive. Thérèse was shocked to see children as young as two picking through rubbish bins for something to eat, and young children high on drugs to numb their stomachs from hunger.

During this time, Thérèse decided to volunteer at a foundation that cares for street children. On her first day, she found the doors to a simple building with a concrete floor and tin roof wide open, for a special day dedicated to bringing fun, games, play and food to the children. Here, the foundation lets every child be a child for the day because, for the rest of the week, the children have one simple goal – to survive. Day in, day out, their sole aim is to look for food, to survive another night on the streets.

Every Saturday, this organisation opens their doors, welcomes 500 children from the streets and provides them with lunch. This is not just about handing out plates of food, but providing a special experience for the children to sit down and share a meal together. The tables were beautifully decorated with tablecloths, cutlery perfectly laid, and food prepared on a plate like a piece of art, topped with a small heart carefully drawn in tomato sauce. Each child was honoured and served like a little king or queen, with dignity and love. The volunteers put effort into every detail and served each child one by one. Every single plate said: 'We love you. We care. And you are special.' These children, who spent their days searching for food to sustain them, suddenly sat up a little straighter and had smiles on their faces.

Five hundred plates, five hundred perfectly placed spoons, and five hundred hearts.

On this one day of the week, through the simple act of a beautiful, individually prepared plate of wholesome, nourishing food, these children felt cherished.

When Thérèse cast her eyes around the room to see the shining faces of the children, and the tables laden with 500 plates, she saw the power and possibility in each and every plate. Each individual plate of food, made and served with love, gave these children hope.

Deeply inspired, Thérèse was moved to celebrate Australia's beautiful food culture and partner with the hospitality industry to make a difference, and to have an impact on the lives of children in need, through gardens and farms created with in-country partners.

She went back home to Australia with the idea to begin OnePlate, asking three friends, Regina Wursthorn, Katarina Kelekovic and Joshua Lanzarini, to join her. Each was captivated by the vision and, alongside Thérèse, launched OnePlate in 2016. Together they began raising money to fund rooftop gardens, fruit orchards and farms to provide food to nourish children in need.

Since then, OnePlate has grown into a charity for food lovers, partnering with cafés and restaurants to fund sustainable food projects for children across the Philippines, Cambodia, Kenya, Uganda and Tanzania.

From farms and rooftop gardens, to orchards and bee hives, children are taught how to grow their own food and create sustainable food projects that not only provide nourishment, but teach them life lessons on leadership, patience, responsibility and love. At the heart of each project is the desire to give children great hope to dream about the future.

In 2020, Thérèse launched *Brunch in Melbourne*, a cookbook for impact that became a bestseller, with 100% of the profits funding OnePlate food security projects for children.

OnePlate was born from a desire to bring love, comfort and nourishment to children through the joy of food. To freely give the gift of hope; a chance for them to dream; to build a future.

OnePlate is so grateful, and humbled, that this powerful vision has captured the imagination of food lovers everywhere. Together, even in just the early years of the charity, a shared love of the joy of food is changing the lives of hundreds of children.

At OnePlate, we invest in hope and we deliver sustainable impact that nourishes children now and into the future. Through our farms, gardens, orchards and food projects we are planting seeds for tomorrow, enriching the land as well as the communities who tend it for generations to come.

We believe that providing nutritional food sources for children, and introducing them to the knowledge and skills needed to be self-sufficient in growing their own food, is a powerful means of transformation and hope.

THE ONEPLATE MISSION

Foodies for impact. Restaurants with purpose. Cafés with heart.

OnePlate is a global charity partnering with foodies, restaurants, cafés and chefs to fund life-changing sustainable food projects across Africa and Asia. We do this by empowering local communities to adopt, build and expand food projects and social enterprises that, over time, nurture and feed children in great need.

Our mission is to harness the deep passion for food culture in Australia and the UK, giving foodies and socially conscious consumers the opportunity to nourish children and communities.

Australia and the UK are both nations of foodies. It's a culture that brings communities together and happiness to our lives. A culture that celebrates the joy of food, flavour, fresh produce and sustainability. And it's a culture with the potential to create an enormous impact. It was this potential that inspired OnePlate to create unique partnerships with food-led businesses and, by doing so, create hope for a better future.

OnePlate began with a 'Foodies for Impact' campaign, by simply asking local cafés and restaurants to nominate a specific menu item, and donate $1 to OnePlate each time that dish was ordered. 100% of each donation went towards in-country food programmes, set up and run through our partners on the ground, to help children and communities break the hunger cycle. These high-impact projects empowered local communities to adopt, build and expand production of fresh produce and develop social enterprises that, over time, would continue to help feed children.

Our vision captured the hearts of the foodie community and inspired thousands of people. As OnePlate has grown, so has our loyal community and their commitment to our vision. A universal love of food, changing lives, one plate at a time.

From our 'Foodies for Impact' campaign grew a bold plan to create and sell beautiful cookbooks, filled with recipes generously donated by some of the most popular dining locations in the world. Once again, 100% of the profit from each sale would fund our food projects.

Following the huge success of our first cookbook for impact in Australia, *Brunch in Melbourne*, we reached out to foodie communities across London and have been greeted with a warm embrace. Now we dream of taking our impact even further through the sale of this cookbook, *Brunch in London*.

From the seed of an idea, a powerful, impactful partnership has developed; a global, grassroots movement within the hospitality industry that enables real change, creating a ripple effect that builds exponential support. United by a shared passion for food, the phenomenal OnePlate community is bringing nourishment and comfort, improved health and nutrition and, most importantly, dignity and hope to children. OnePlate's practical and sustainable projects are carefully created to help children who have been living on the streets, abandoned, or experienced trauma due to trafficking and child labour.

These projects also flow across entire communities. We believe that by providing highly nutritional, organic food sources for children and their families, we give more people the chance to learn the skills needed for lifelong self-sufficiency. Each project also brings significant social change: access to education, increased employment, entrepreneurship and skills in business, agriculture and food production.

OnePlate has always been a two-way exchange. In giving, we learn. We honour the children we care for and gently guide them to look beyond survival to dream about their future. And every day, the children inspire us with their resilience and quiet determination, and teach us patience, grace, acceptance and gratitude.

At OnePlate, we are all volunteers. All overheads and administration costs are covered by our generous angel donors. 100% of all donations go directly to funding our sustainable food projects for the children, creating flourishing orchards, farms and gardens that will impact generations to come.

In the words of Helen Keller, 'Alone we can do so little, together we can do so much.'

At OnePlate, we celebrate the power of joy through food, elevating the hospitality industry for impact.

We invite foodies everywhere to contribute meaningfully to our projects, making a difference through the power of our food culture. We believe in hope, not guilt.

Our work provides nourishment, love and support for children in great need through food security, and our projects enrich lives and communities.

TO NOURISH AND NUTURE

Growing food is a powerful means of transformation and hope.

A tiny seed, nurtured in the right environment, will slowly grow and thrive. So do the children we serve when they receive good food, the right support and unconditional love.

For these children, watching food grow from a small seed, and the transformation from seedling to tree, is truly magical. This is one of the reasons why at OnePlate we believe in creating sustainable food security solutions and projects for the children that will impact the whole community, through nourishing healthy food, skills training, creating local employment and opportunities for new enterprises, business and income streams.

Children supported by the generous OnePlate community have been living on the streets, in slums, have been abandoned and neglected or are from the most marginalised and impoverished communities. Most of the children have never seen or tasted fresh, nutritious food, grown at home or prepared for them by someone who loves them. Food they find on the streets simply satisfies their hunger; a means to an end.

Every project is created to nourish the lives of children – children who have only known survival. Our projects empower children, their families and entire communities, with the confidence and ability to grow their own food, develop sustainable enterprises and break the hunger cycle.

Every meal has the capacity to transform and enrich lives. The nutritious food from our farms, gardens, orchards and community projects gives children everything they need to build a happy, healthy life, from increased energy, improved cognitive and physical development and the ability to concentrate, to the desire to learn, love and hope.

Every planting teaches children that a different future is possible. A garden shows us the cycle of life, the power of nature, and the miracle of new growth. It shows our children they can look further than survival, and they can dare to dream. When these children are able to help plant, grow and nurture food, and taste the results, something amazing happens. They can look further than tomorrow. They can finally begin to dream about the future.

For OnePlate, gardening and farming are metaphors for life, reflecting new growth and beginnings. OnePlate's sustainable food security projects in the Philippines, Cambodia, Kenya, Uganda and Tanzania, are bringing hope to many children and communities, one plate at a time. Over the next few pages, we have featured just a handful of the many OnePlate projects across Africa and Asia that are changing the future for these children.

'To plant a garden is to believe in tomorrow.' Audrey Hepburn

ONEPLATE PROJECTS

THE PHILIPPINES

Urban Rooftop Garden

Nothing compares to the look of wonder in children's eyes as they watch plants grow from seed! OnePlate's inaugural project, the Urban Rooftop Garden in Manila, was born from a desire to show children living on the street how food is grown, and offer them fresh, organic fruit and vegetables they have never tasted in their lives.

Ripe red tomatoes, deep green calamansi (Philippine lemon), fresh, sweet spring onions, shining aubergines (eggplants) and the aroma of fresh herbs on the breeze... all of this can be found nestled within a thriving rooftop garden atop a four-storey building in the middle of Manila. Food from the garden provides sustenance for more than 100 children.

This is not just a garden, it is an educational and therapeutic space, too. Here, gardening is gradually introduced to children who arrive at the special community organisation housed in the building.

These are children who are traumatised after being abandoned and who know nothing but survival. The garden is a peaceful place where they learn to leave behind fear, and the ache of hunger and loss, and begin to hope and dare to dream. Many of the children are captivated by the wonder of horticulture and excited to pursue agriculture.

Due to Manila's tropical climate, plants can be grown continuously without dying off as they do in the cold seasons of the Australian and British climates, so the Urban Rooftop Garden is always bursting with nutritious food.

The Rooftop Garden was OnePlate's first ever food projects back in 2016, and continues to bring joy and wonder, as well as beautiful, healthy food for local children.

Tacloban Garden Farm Project

Creating a vegetable garden to eat and sell fresh, nutritious produce is one of the fastest and most affordable paths to food security, but without the skills to cultivate, and the means to purchase seedlings, for many it's a solution that's out of reach.

Many of OnePlate's in-country projects are targeted in areas where natural disasters and weather events have had a severe impact on children's wellbeing. After Tacloban in the Philippines was devastated by Typhoon Haiyan in 2013, communities struggled to recover, leaving children hungry and living on the streets.

To help, OnePlate provided training in the production and marketing of organic vegetables for 120 young people and women, along with the seeds, materials and tools needed to establish their own farm market gardens at home, in community spaces or rural areas.

The Tacloban Garden Farms are very special to us. The second project OnePlate established in 2017, the courses and programme have been accredited by the Philippines Education Department to run in local high schools and further education facilities. OnePlate's assistance has enabled training and new pathways for children living on the streets, enabling them to have access to nutritious, fresh food, gain employment or start their own social enterprises in the agriculture sector.

Agroforestry Project: Fruit and Nut Orchard

Heart-led, fruitful partnerships are at the core of OnePlate's achievements, and our Agroforestry Project in Manila is particularly special. It was the first time one of our partner cafés came on board to fund an entire project, from start to finish!

The Fruit and Nut Orchard in Manila supports the health and wellbeing of hundreds of street children every week. Thanks to the support of Warran Glen Café, OnePlate facilitated the planting of more than 1,500 trees: including mango, guyabano, rambutan, jackfruit,

grapefruit, star apple, banana, lemon, tamarind and mulberry. And nut trees: pili nut, coconut, pecan and walnuts.

OnePlate also funded the establishment of an agroforestry nursery to plant vegetables.

The produce is used firstly for food programs that support the children, then 60% of the produce is sold at market as an income-generating programme for orchard maintenance and paid staff.

Thanks to the generosity of Warran Glen Café and their customers, this is not just food for today, it's food for generations. This wonderful orchard will feed thousands of children for many years to come. Read more about this on page 343.

Fish Farm

We are overjoyed at the success of our Fish Farm Project in Manila, which today has many ponds filled with produce, and feeds more than 500 children who would otherwise be seeking food on the streets.

The project was established by digging fish ponds, then allowing them to be naturally filled during the rainy season. Vegetation was planted along the border of each pond to assist in stabilising the edges; date palms, coconut palms, taro and banana trees, with a dual role of stabilising the ponds and providing further food.

A few short months after the farm was established, the first fish harvest was planned for a community feast. Now there is a weekly harvest on Thursdays for a fresh meal every Friday for the whole community, and a special meal every Saturday for the street children. The whole community gets involved in the exciting fish harvest, and children and community members are being trained in fish farming.

Our original plan was to provide fish protein for 500 children and 350 people in the community, but the farm has been so successful, it has exceeded expectations. Every month, we harvest a total of 1,350 fish, each fish weighing 500g (18oz), from the carefully tended ponds. That is sufficient to provide 2.5 fish-based meals a week for 1,500 people! Read more about this on page 325.

Chicken Farm

Protein is essential as part of a balanced diet for growing bodies and minds, along with nutritious fruit and vegetables. Thanks to a wonderful OnePlate project, once a week, 300 street children in Manila eagerly sit down at a table to eat a delicious meal of chicken and rice from their very own plate. This is the highlight of their week.

Many of the children supported by OnePlate do not eat any protein at all. They spend their time in a perpetual hunt for food, looking in bins and rubbish dumps. To change this, OnePlate has worked with a partner organisation in Manila to fund a pilot program breeding chickens.

OnePlate has funded a purpose-built chicken farm with plenty of room for the chickens to graze and grow. Our pilot program began with 500 chickens that provided food for the feeding programme and is expanding to 1,000 chickens every 45 days.

The program has been such a success, with over 300 street children benefitting from nutritious protein meals. This project has also become a profitable enterprise generating income from the sale of chicken which in turn continues to develop more opportunities for the children.

Piggery

OnePlate is committed to developing unique, sustainable projects that enable us to feed disadvantaged children, employ local people and create new agricultural opportunities.

The prices of prime commodities including pork, chicken and vegetables have significantly increased due to the economic crisis in the Philippines, putting them completely out of reach of most families, and particularly children who have been abandoned and are homeless.

The vision for the Piggery is to feed as many children as possible, provide shelter, and train people in agriculture, thus encouraging families to earn a living.

Families, who previously lived on the streets, now live on the farm and are responsible for the care and feeding of the animals and management of the farm and piggery. These families are becoming niche farmers, being taught by specialists, and now earn a living with purpose. Their training can in turn be passed on to other family members as well as members of the local neighbourhood.

Chemicals and other harmful elements are not used as part of the farming project, with an emphasis on organic breeding and feeding. The pigs are fed from feed and fertiliser mills that have also been funded by OnePlate.

Beginning with one sow, the farming families have been able to raise 13 pigs, then through another pregnancy from those pigs, 27 piglets have been born. Fourteen piglets were recently sold, and the money invested back into the farm, buying more pigs and paying for maintenance and feed. Each pig is pregnant for 114 days and now with 10 sows, the plan is to have 100-300 new pigs born each year, which will be sold. This high-quality protein will feed more than 500 local street children per week.

The Piggery has already demonstrated significant income-earning potential. The facility can process the meat and sell directly to consumers; meat can be supplied to local restaurants, and also sold at markets.

KENYA

Fruit Orchard

Picking fresh fruit direct from a tree is something quite wonderful, especially when you have watched the tree slowly grow bigger and bigger, day by day. And seeing a small child excitedly pick a flavour-packed banana in their very own orchard is one of the reasons OnePlate was born.

OnePlate's beautiful Fruit Orchard project in Kenya, bursting with ripe, juicy fruit on thriving trees, has simultaneously solved many problems. Within Kenya there are far too many children suffering from malnutrition and poor growth, due to disadvantage, abandonment and exploitation.

An organisation has been set up in the region, with a village to provide care, shelter, education and, most importantly, food for over 300 children. This orchard not only provides fruit for the children and staff but provides income from the sale of excess produce. Food trees are such an important part of a diet, offering fruits, leafy vegetables, nuts, seeds and edible oils, increasing micronutrients (mineral and vitamins) and also macronutrients (protein, carbohydrates).

Local labourers were employed to establish the orchard, ploughing and undertaking weed control, before planting seedlings, small trees and banana tissues. Fast-growing vegetables were planted between trees over subsequent months to control weeds and increase the diversity of produce.

Today, the Fruit Orchard holds oranges, bananas, avocadoes, lemons and mangoes. Often the children walk past the orchard on their way to lunch and they like to guess on what tree they will see fruit next.

The Bakery Project

The irresistible aroma of piping hot, fresh bread straight from the oven is one of life's simple pleasures... especially savouring that first mouth-watering bite. OnePlate's self-sustaining Bakery Project has given the simple goodness of fresh bread rolls to hundreds of children in north-west Kenya.

For many years, bread has been missing as a staple food in the diets of children and families in south-west Kenya, due to extreme poverty and food insecurity. A staggering number of abandoned children struggle to find food each day.

OnePlate's Bakery Project was established alongside an eco-village and school, specially created for vulnerable children. The project immediately delivered a daily supply of 300 nutritious fresh bread rolls.

The enormous success of the bakery has led to an exciting expansion to a full-scale commercial enterprise; new larger premises, a fit-out with commercial ovens and mixers, and a small delivery van.

The Bakery now produces bread products for entire communities as well as products to sell at local markets. This fully sustainable food security project provides food for the children and school staff, baking instruction for the children, income for the school and employment for local people. The Bakery is also now part of a local Vocational Skills Training Centre. Read more about this on page 169.

The Avocado Project

Loaded with 'good' fats, creamy, buttery and nutty avocados are simply bursting with goodness, and synonymous with brunch! OnePlate's Avocado Project goes hand-in-hand with The Bee Project (see overleaf). Together, these two fully self-sustaining initiatives are creating nourishing, healthy food for children in need.

Many children in Kenya have grown up on the streets, abandoned, and seeking food in rubbish bins and dumps. They have no foundational knowledge of how healthy food is grown or the joy of its fresh, clean and inviting taste.

With assistance from OnePlate, these vulnerable children are now well cared for by a compassionate organisation dedicated to providing safe housing, education and nourishing food from our Avocado and Bee Projects.

An enthusiastic team prepared farmland, dug holes and planted more than 300 avocado seedlings. The flowering trees will provide pollen and nectar to help our bees do their work producing honey in neighbouring hives.

When fully mature, this flourishing orchard will provide avocados to feed hundreds of children and currently provides employment for local people, who are maintaining the orchard. Excess avocados, not used for school meals, will be sold at market with all profits used to fund educational opportunities and buy supplies for the children. Read more about this on page 134.

The Bee Project

Bees are truly tiny miracles. Did you know that almost 90% of wild plants and 75% of global crops depend on pollination by animals? One out of every three mouthfuls of food depends on bee pollination!

Our Bee Project in Kenya has been transformational for so many children and communities. Alongside our partner organisation, OnePlate has funded a Bee Farm. Expanding to 300 beehives and over 1,300 tree and flower seedlings, this project has created a complete eco-system for a new bee population.

Calliandra trees, bottle brush, sunflowers and sesbania plants have been planted to attract the bees and encourage pollination, along with *Moringa oleifera*, commonly known as the 'miracle' tree.

Every part of the nutrient-rich Moringa tree – seed pods, fruits, flowers, roots and bark – is edible, offering unlimited social enterprise opportunities from sale of tree products, including leaves and pods for food, cattle feed and biofuel.

The hives alone, filled with thousands of bees, produce an amazing 16kg (35lb) of honey per year, per hive.

Along with improved nourishment from consuming honey, as well as the bee pollination of plants on the property, the Bee Project is ensuring increased production of essential medicine and natural therapies, employment and new commercial opportunities, and funds invested towards schooling for the children. Read more about this on page 407.

Water Sustainability Project

Fresh water is critical for flourishing fruits, vegetables and produce like honey, all over the world but nowhere is it as crucial as in countries like Kenya, which have struggled to improve water quality for many years. Now a special OnePlate project has secured a high-quality bore water system and turned orchards into a wonderful and nutritious bounty for children and their communities.

About 80 percent of people who end up in hospitals in Kenya have preventable illnesses. At least 50 percent of these illnesses are related to water, sanitation and hygiene, caused through the use of untreated water for washing and watering food.

OnePlate was working in partnership with an organisation supporting vulnerable children, when a local horticulturalist discovered a serious problem. Planning had begun for fruit and vegetable planting, with the site reliant upon a three metre well. However, the level in the well indicated a water shortage, which meant there wouldn't be enough to support our projects.

After brainstorming several options, OnePlate was able to fund a water bore which will nourish all future agricultural projects at this site. The borehole was drilled to a depth of 150 metres, a water pump was installed, and repairs carried out on the existing water stand. This fully sustainable irrigation system now has the capacity to provide water for our food projects without the worry of running low on water supply.

The water bore will improve yield for nearby avocado, passionfruit and kitchen garden plantings, and also improve the success of the Bee Project.

Thanks to this sustainable water bore, these projects will provide fresh fruits and honey to over 300 children and the local community. Care and maintenance of the bore and plantings will provide employment for local community members. Profits from the sale of produce will help supply education scholarships for 120 children and young adults.

CAMBODIA

Children's Fruit Orchard

The delight of a juicy mango, citrus tang of fresh orange, and sweet, succulent longan! Each of these fruits now flourishes in the Children's Fruit Orchard in Cambodia, alongside trees laden with beautiful jackfruit, rambutan, guava, coconut and avocado. This is life-changing food, now savoured by children who had never before tasted fresh fruit.

The Children's Fruit Orchard is a wonderful OnePlate initiative delivering nutritious, vitamin-packed fruit to underprivileged children. The orchard was planted adjacent to a purpose-built village and school, developed to care for more than 75 at-risk children who would otherwise be unable to leave a cycle of poverty. The children now live in a place of care, protection and nourishment.

Developing the orchard took incredible patience and hard work. After many weeks removing shrubs and preparing and ploughing soil, the team had to travel to different provinces to source seedlings, then adjust watering and planting to ensure thriving trees.

The orchard is completely sustainable, increasing access to nutritious fruit for the children and generating

income. Excess produce is sold to the local markets. As part of the school curriculum, children also take part in practical lessons on care and cultivation of the fruit crops and learn how to make fruit products such as dried fruit, juices, jams and preserves.

School Nutritional Gardens Project

When children are still growing, the need for nurturing is extremely high; mind, body and soul. Creating a place where they receive plentiful food, unconditional love, encouragement and education is the perfect solution, and the School Nutritional Gardens project in Cambodia has had an enormous impact.

When work and food is scarce, and there are little to no existing skills in cultivating food, children are often left behind or abandoned completely while their parents seek out a way to earn a living. In Cambodia there is a whole generation of children who are severely malnourished due to lack of food, and at risk of abuse and child trafficking due to being left all alone.

OnePlate has partnered with an organisation in Cambodia to address the lack of nutrition and build farming skills through the creation of school gardens. The project now provides not only nutrition, but an opportunity to learn about plants and the environment, basic farming skills and further agricultural training programs in the future.

There are 148 children in this school in Cambodia, many of whom are staying the full day at the school for safety and care, because their parents leave for work early morning and come back at night. The children are aged from just a few months old up to nine, where the older siblings are responsible for caring for baby brothers and sisters.

It was exciting to work with local experts to find creative techniques to maximise any space in the school grounds, such as trellis gardens along walls and pergolas with climbing plants that provide shade during the day. Chickens were purchased and incorporated into the limited space to provide eggs for the children as well as fertiliser for the gardens. Rotary compost bins are used to turn organic vegetable waste into valuable fertiliser.

Vegetables including aubergines (eggplants), pumpkins, broccoli, cucumber and mushrooms are now plentiful in the garden, and a worm garden – which the children love – adds to the abundance. In the school cook house, local cooks are providing a nutritious hot meal to more than 100 children every day. Without this support, these children would not have a meal for days on end.

Mushroom Farm Enterprise Project

Mushrooms are a simple and tasty source of nutrition, rich in vitamins B and D, fibre, protein and antioxidants. They're also a highly sought after staple food, easily cultivated and a favourite at market stalls in Cambodia.

With the assistance of a passionate and skilled local agriculturalist in Cambodia, OnePlate has funded the establishment of a wonderful Mushroom Farm Enterprise, giving dozens of families in need not only a highly nutritious source of food, but a fully sustainable micro-enterprise of their very own.

Communities on the Cambodia-Thailand border have struggled with social and economic difficulties for many years, with families unable to find work or source food. Hundreds of children have been unable to attend school and experienced severe malnutrition.

Through the Mushroom Farm Enterprise Project, OnePlate was able to gift families starter mushroom kits and mushroom farming training, empowering them to cultivate mushrooms in their own homes for consumption and sale. Cultivating mushrooms requires little space and minimal light, making fungi the perfect food for these families to grow. Families in slum areas who were going without food have created their own small businesses and, after only a few months, achieved a high yield of mushrooms for sale at markets and to fill their children's hungry tummies. Read more about this on page 153.

Aquaponic and Hydroponic Garden

Using hydroponics and aquaponics, OnePlate has funded a full 'cycle of life' garden project that feeds, nurtures and educates more than 100 seriously disadvantaged children in Cambodia.

The garden has been established in a space within a centre that provides a home, education and therapeutic counselling to more than 100 children. This multi-pronged project not only provides food and education, but a calming, enriching environment and distraction from the many traumas they have been through

The Aquaponic and Hydroponic Children's Garden includes an aquaponics area with fish, together with plants and hens adjoining the garden. The garden demonstrates and follows the full cycle of life, starting with organic waste to feed fly larvae and chickens, followed by a water life cycle from larvae to fish, that flows to the plants, and back again to the fish.

The garden is entirely chemical free and all the children in the centre learn how to work here. Every day they excitedly watch over and care for the fish, plants and hens, eager to see them thrive and grow. The produce flows into the centre, providing nutritious food, reducing the cost of daily living and becoming fully sustainable.

The cycle of life is fascinating to the children, who love to watch the changes and growth in all the areas of the project from day to day.

Community Food Gardens

A community garden is a wonderful place; somewhere children and families can come together, cultivate and enjoy wholesome food and share their knowledge and produce. But in Cambodia, entire communities living in extreme poverty have never had encouragement, motivation or access to the materials, tools and skills needed to make community gardening a success.

Vulnerable children in Cambodia don't have access to a healthy, safe and caring home and, from a young age, many children turn to begging on the street to gain income and provide for their families.

To help change the future for these children and their families, OnePlate has funded several community gardens and also provided families that have space at home with everything needed to plant and grow their own fruits and vegetables for eating and for sale.

Training parents and school children to grow their own nutritious food and understand the importance of food variety will empower more families to provide for their children, introducing a new healthy lifestyle and building a better future.

As part of the project, a number of hectares of land were purchased further away from the city to prevent the influences of drugs, begging, gambling and child trafficking. Owning this land also enables the establishment of an integrated food production market and farm as a training facility to develop skills.

Large permanent raised bed systems have been used for land cultivation, and 15 families who did not have their own land were trained in vegetable production. Families were trained in how to harvest and store seeds so they can continue planting vegetables without the need to keep repurchasing seedsand seedlings.

In the future, additional food production will be introduced to the community food gardens, like cattle, fruit trees, chickens, ducks and fishponds. This is a wonderful sustainable project with a positive impact on local communities for many years to come.

Fish Farm

Enjoying fish as a staple part of diet delivers satiety and nourishment; an excellent source of vital omega-3 fatty acids, vitamin D and B12. But for many communities in Cambodia, finding such a rich source of protein has been out of reach.

More than 70% of Cambodians survive on less than $3 a day. Entire communities are dependent upon subsistence farming of crops and livestock that only thrive in ideal weather conditions. One poor season means a cycle of poverty that is difficult to reverse. And with hundreds of families out of work, many more children have experienced the trauma of abandonment, abuse and neglect, hunger, and loss of access to education.

To provide a simple, sustainable food solution, OnePlate has worked closely with a centre in Cambodia housing vulnerable children, to establish a Fish Farm. The project involved the creation of three ponds large enough to hold excess water in the wet season and stocked with omnivorous fish that will eat any mosquito larvae in the water.

Fish grow quickly in the wet season for harvest in the dry season, then are easily caught with nets and buckets for a fast, delicious pan-fry meal with available herbs or vegetables.

These three large ponds, with two different breeds, now produce thousands of fish and more than 60 children as well local community members are benefitting from this wonderful source of protein. The children can catch them to eat whenever they want.

The Fish Farm project has provided a high-protein, daily food source, new skills and recreation for the children and a natural reduction in the incidence of mosquito-borne diseases.

Wicking Bed Vegetable Project

In Cambodia, as with all in-country projects, OnePlate's goal is to provide a plentiful, nutritious diet for children in great need, all year round. To nourish growing bodies and minds, maximise learning and bring happiness back to little lives, children need fresh vegetables, packed with energy, fibre, vitamins and minerals, every day.

Consistent, high-quality harvests are dependent on many factors, but extremes of climate, plant viruses and pests have a major impact. OnePlate's innovative project to establish a shade house with a wicking bed has made an enormous difference to the quality and frequency of vegetable harvests for children living at a special village and school in Cambodia who otherwise would have no home and would be living on the streets begging for food just to survive.

Wicking beds use water very efficiently – the plants have continual access to water in the reservoir below the bed and evaporation is reduced via a top layer of mulch. Plants grow quickly because they are not lacking in water or nutrients.

A shade house was constructed to completely enclose the wicking beds, reducing stress on the plants from the intense dry season sun and shutting out insects that can spread disease and damage vegetables.

A watering system was installed at the bottom of the beds and attached to a water tank, with a trellis along the length of each bed to encourage climbing vegetables. Vegetables requiring pollination are now pollinated by hand.

A consistent, disease-free and high-quality harvest from the wicking bed project now provides nutritious vegetables and seeds for the children throughout the year, which are also distributed to families in the community to grow, sell and enjoy.

UGANDA

Food Security Project

Gazing across the 9.5 acres of land of our Food Security Project in Uganda is an incredibly uplifting experience. Fertile land bursting with produce and possibility, and all created to ensure that local street children and communities have fresh, organic food.

The goal of the Food Security Project is to support 50 children and their families in great need, and every one of them receives fresh food directly from the farm. Their families are either unable to provide for them, or they have been abandoned and turned to living on the streets.

Since OnePlate began funding the farm, the land has been completely transformed. Plants on this farm include soya beans, rice, collard greens, cabbages, tomatoes, oranges, mangoes, avocados, maize and

peanuts. OnePlate has also funded a 100,000 litre water reservoir, pumps and two 5,000 litre tanks that water the crops. The farm is now approaching six acres of ground nuts, with every acre able to harvest an incredible 300–350kg (10½–12oz) of nuts, and just one acre of rice results in a 1,000kg (just over 2,000 tonnes) yield.

As well as eating food regularly from the farm during the school term, generous food hampers are sent home during school holidays to ensure there is always plenty for the children to eat.

There are exciting plans to develop the project further, with the possible addition of passionfruit, dairy, poultry, a piggery and bee hives.

Ugandan Farm

The burnished red earth of Uganda is iconic, and you might assume the rich red and orange colours indicate the soil is incredibly fertile. In fact, it's quite the opposite. That's why the abundance produced daily from OnePlate's Ugandan Farm project means so much.

The farm was established to meet the nutritional needs of children who have experienced extreme poverty and live in a nearby community. More than 50 children and their families now benefit from the wonderful produce of the Ugandan Farm. As the farm continues to flourish, our hope is this will ensure hundreds of children receive wholesome, healthy food.

The 10-acre farm was carefully planned to deliver a diverse mix of nutritious food for the children as well as create a series of income-generating food sources. Rather than solely focusing on a single crop or livestock, our hope is to expand in diversification by introducing dairy, poultry, fruit and vegetables.

Significant work was required to improve the soil quality. After many years of poor soil management, Ugandan soils are highly weathered, over-harvested and have low fertility. The soil lacks nitrogen, organic and phosphoric acid, is highly porous and has low moisture retention. With expert help, the soil has been well prepared, properly irrigated and cared for to ensure excellent conditions and harvest.

The diversified farm has also allowed a series of social enterprise opportunities, bringing year-round income sources and education for local farmers. This is a farm for generations, with a perpetual income, bringing hope and comfort to children. Our goal in time is that the farm will produce 164,000 meals every year. Read more about this on page 267.

JOSEPH'S STORY

'If not for you, I could be nobody.'

Joseph* has overcome significant trauma for one so young. But this humble 17-year-old young man is determined to make something of his life.

Joseph vividly remembers running and hiding with his mother, brother and sister when the post-election violence in Kenya began in 2007. Their home was destroyed, so they could not go back. They didn't know where to go, so they took to the streets, and hid when they heard gangs going by.

'There were many explosions. My brother, sister and I got separated from our mother, because we all ran in different directions to escape.'

Joseph and his brother found their way to the city showground, where a makeshift refugee camp was set up by the government to help displaced families, children and elderly people. By 2008, there were over 14,000 displaced people living at the refugee camp.

As the eldest, Joseph took charge. He looked in vain for their mother and sister, but could not find them. He was relieved to find his grandmother, and the three of them lived together in one tent.

'At the refugee camp we had a lot of problems. We did not have food to eat. We used to cry because we were hungry and starving.

'The tent was very small, it could not fit my grandmother and us. We did not have clothing to change, we could not take a shower because there were no soap basins or even water. We did not even have a blanket or a mattress. When it was raining we squeezed into the corner of the tent. We just had to sit until morning. Inside the tent, life was so hard.'

Then some volunteers came to the refugee camp to give Joseph and his family food. It was the moment everything changed in Joseph's life. The volunteers took Joseph and his brother in and gave them shelter and a home.

'They promised to be a family to us. They gave me food, a home, shelter, medication, education, all the things we had lost hope about. If not for this organisation, I don't know where I would be. I would be on the streets begging. I could have died at the refugee camp, due to cold or pneumonia or other diseases. Through simply giving us food, our lives changed forever.'

Joseph has now completed high school and aspires to join college. He wants to pursue a course in information communication technology.

'I am so grateful for the support, so grateful. If not for you, I could be nobody. Thank you for caring about young people like me and helping us dream about a career and a new life ahead.'

Names have been changed to protect identities.

ABIGAIL'S STORY

'I want to be Kenya's best criminologist.'

We first met Abigail* when she was just 10. A softly spoken young girl with eyes that tell of wisdom beyond her years, she was so grateful to be one of the 37 children taken in by the beautiful Mama Jackie (opposite) when she was aged four.

Abigail loves her life. Having started out with so little, and no adult to care about her, she flourished under the wing of Mama Jackie, who has created a home for abandoned children in south-west Kenya. From a young age, Abigail loved to talk about school, all the things she was learning, and how wonderful it was to live with 'all her brothers and sisters'.

Abigail is just one of many abandoned children who Mama Jackie so lovingly looks after. When she was just three, she took on more responsibility than a three-year-old should ever have to bear. She became the sole carer for her one-year-old brother while her siblings went out on the street to find food.

Her father had been arrested for sexual assault and sent to prison. Her mother stayed with the four children for a short time, but then became overwhelmed with the responsibility of raising the children alone. One morning she left home and never returned.

Hunger drove the children out onto the street. Every day, Abigail's big brother and sister would set out from their shanty home in south-west Kenya to find work and food.

'...they would sometimes be labourers on people's farms. As we were so young, the people they worked for would take advantage of them. Sometimes, when jobs were unavailable, my brother and sister were forced to steal. Sometimes they were caught and beaten up, while at other times they just got lucky. They had to do all they could to find food.'

'Then one day, we were rescued and given a home full of love and care. Coming to live with Mama Jackie was such a blessing. We became part of a family that never stopped growing, and formed special bonds with our new brothers and sisters.'

Abigail remembers clearly the first time Mama Jackie gave them food.

'It was good, healthy food that we didn't have to look for on the street. It came from a farm that was right next to our new home and I could not believe how good it tasted. I had never tasted food so clean and fresh before.'

Abigail has taken every opportunity she has been given with grace and gratitude, and has become a highly successful student.

Starting school at age six and working hard on her studies, Abigail was a natural learner with curiosity and drive. As time went on, it was clear to Mama Jackie and her teachers that Abigail was determined to be the very best student she could, to show those who now loved her that she could make them proud.

'With the right environment, the right focus and ultimate dedication, I did great in primary education and got to join high school. After many sleepless nights of working harder and smarter every day, I eventually got a B+ in my end of high school examination and earned direct entry into university!'

Now 18, Abigail hopes to take a bachelor's degree and later, a master's degree in criminal law and forensic science – and become Kenya's best criminologist.

'Despite knowing that I was a bright student, in the big wide world that is not enough. Without support, guidance and encouragement from Mama Jackie and all the kind people who run this organisation, I couldn't have become a success. I have only been able to achieve what I have because of the support I have received. It means so much to have someone believe in you, to encourage you and to love you. Thank you to this organisation that touches, heals and nourishes souls.'

OnePlate is dedicated to helping children like Abigail realise their dreams. Our in-country projects give hope to more children like Abigail, offering nourishment, new opportunities and the chance to thrive.

Names have been changed to protect identities.

THOMAS' STORY

'Life is now good because of the love, care and protection, and I never have to worry about food again.'

Eleven-year-old Thomas* is a kind, compassionate and creative young man with big dreams. He has incredible strength, and such a positive attitude. Talking with Thomas is uplifting. It is so wonderful to sit and listen to him talk about his passion for music and his love for picking fruit in the OnePlate garden.

Although he is only young, Thomas has already walked a difficult path. After being abandoned by his own family three times over, and walking the streets of north-west Kenya late at night searching for someone to care for him, he now lives in a compassionate home dedicated to caring for children like him.

Thomas knew everything was not good with his parents, but as a young boy, he had no choice but to stay. The eldest of four children, he felt responsible for caring for his siblings and often provided reassurance to the younger ones. His mother soon abandoned the children, leaving Thomas' dad to look after them.

'Dad never bothered about us. He left us at home without food, we could not go to school because we had to go to work at that tender age, so as to have something on the table.'

'He would go out to drink and come back very abusive. One day he drank to excess. He was vomiting, coughing and his nose was bleeding, and then he died.'

Thomas' aunt came to their rescue, taking in Thomas and his four siblings to live with her. But before long, he was abandoned yet again.

'We came home from school not long after we went to her place and she was gone. We asked neighbours but no one had seen her. We decided to go look for her, but we could not find her. There was no food, nothing was left behind for us. Our dad had died and our aunt had run away from us – we were left all alone.'

Thomas remembered they had another aunt in town and went looking for her. It was late at night and they were walking the streets, alone and hungry, when a kind person took him and his siblings to a rescue centre. Soon they were welcomed with love to an organisation that freely gives Thomas the comfort and care he needs.

This organisation is supported by several OnePlate in-country projects in Kenya that provide fruit and vegetables to feed children. Thomas is no longer afraid and is a confident young man with a big, beautiful smile. He can go to school, and loves to spend time in the OnePlate orchard and garden.

'I love the farm and garden. I go there every day and pick produce. I like it because after you plant and prune you get rewarded. I love the digging, planting, pruning. Food and gardens makes me happy. My dream is to be a musician. And I would like my own vegetable garden. I want to grow kale, cabbage and carrots. I have joined the scouts and have written two songs I hope to record soon.

'Thank you for the love, support and effort to make us comfortable. I love you.'

*Names have been changed to protect identities.

THE CULINARY CAPITAL

by Dylan Jones OBE

A wander down memory lane, celebrating the vibrant London food scene, with the revered English journalist and author Dylan Jones.

Honestly, all this looking back plays tricks with the mind. The Sixties had barely ended before we started referring to the decade in the way that a previous generation had referred to the Blitz: in the past. Rather quickly, the Sixties became a foreign country, a Valhalla of the mind, a former republic. But it wasn't like that at all. In her memoir *Dear London*, the New Jersey-born writer Irma Kurtz said that when she first came to the city, in 1963, it was less like an American city than any she knew of. The town reeked of 'wet wool and river mud, coal smoke, boiled cabbage' and she complained that 'everything from turning on a bedsit gas fire to buying a cheap cup of watery coffee seemed to require a pocket-full of large copper coins.' The city was often clouded by pea-soupers, the sulphurous coal-gas air that turned everything soot black.

If you blinked, it wasn't so different in the Seventies, not really, and while it is easy to look at photographs of the city mid-decade and see a cavalcade of colour, with punks with peroxide hair, red leather bondage trousers and blue suede shoes larking about for tourists, London's actual backdrop was grey, analogue, and rather uninspiring. For the sake of authenticity, and an appropriation of working class cool, punk rock needed to imagine itself in a hastily assembled montage of tower blocks, urban deprivation and Eastern European dystopia. While this was largely a stylized myth, the London it was trying to reinvent was fairly monochrome anyway. Black and white and clunky and slow, a city that went to bed at ten-thirty, with hardly enough good restaurants to fill a guide-book. It's been said that the Fifties were but a smear on the horizon, and London in the Seventies wasn't much more defined.

It used to be said that while on the continent people have good food, in London they have good table manners; now it's probably safe to say that London has the best restaurants in the world. We also have a far more relaxed attitude to dining. These days, London is not just the cultural capital of the world, it's the culinary capital too, a hotbed of everything from the very finest dining to the latest pop-up street food. Forty years ago – possibly even thirty – I couldn't have made this claim; indeed no one in London could have made this claim, as the city was still reliant on outliers to bolster its international reputation. Now, though, we could take on anyone and win. Give us your best shot – Copenhagen, New York, Mexico City, Barcelona, Los Angeles – and we'll win every time.

Back in the Eighties, there were slim pickings in the city. There were the big, old grandee restaurants, and the sprightly little trendy ones – I distinctly remember somewhere called The California Pizza Company (I think, although I distinctly recall the novelty of eating exotic fruit in a calzone), Alastair Little and the Indian nouvelle cuisine place in Charlotte Street that was fashionable for about 72 hours in 1989. And while we were quickly indoctrinated in the continental way of eating – in the middle of the decade I spent most of my hard-earned cash (and back then it really was cash) in The Soho Brasserie on Old Compton Street, which at the time we all thought was the most sophisticated place in the world. It wasn't, of course, but we loved it anyway.

Then, good food was really only available to those with money or access. At the other end we had to put up with fast-food stuff like Spud-U-Like and American imports, while the only real street food was in Brick Lane market or Drummond Street in Camden.

But London today is a city limned, its edges illuminated in colour, like its restaurants. We now have as many hooded outdoor cafés as Paris. London restaurants these days are vast, café-style places converted from banks, modernist French brasseries that look as though they were designed in Berlin and built in New York. Every new eatery appears to have a slab of neon above the door, like a prized swordfish, announcing itself proudly. Imagine Shinjuku or downtown Seoul at night, juxtaposed with the backstreets of Mumbai or the regal finery of Paris, squared – this is the soup that we swim in.

It is a great privilege that I'm able to introduce the following pages, overflowing with recipes from every corner of this thriving city. And all for such an important cause. By their nature, Londoners have always been do-gooders, and this book is evidence of that in forkfuls.

THE LONDON BRUNCH SCENE

Why not a new meal, served around noon, that starts with tea or coffee, marmalade and other breakfast fixtures before moving along to the heavier fare?

THE HISTORY OF BRUNCH

Sometimes mistaken as an American-born concept, thanks to their impassioned uptake of the tradition, this liminal meal in fact has its roots in the United Kingdom. An 1896 edition of satirical magazine *Punch* defined brunch as a 'combination meal' and credited the coinage of the term to the British writer Guy Beringer, who reportedly first introduced the idea in an essay for *Hunter's Weekly* in 1895, in an article concisely entitled 'Brunch: A Plea'. Beringer implored readers to consider it as an alternative to a more substantial Sunday lunch after church, declaring that it: 'puts you in a good temper, it makes you satisfied with yourself and your fellow beings'. He went on: 'Why not a new meal, served around noon, that starts with tea or coffee, marmalade and other breakfast fixtures before moving along to the heavier fare? By eliminating the need to get up early on Sunday, brunch would make life brighter for Saturday-night carousers'.

His plea didn't go unheard: not long after, the term was picked up by a Pennsylvania newspaper which described it as 'the latest fad'. By the 1930s, Americans and Antipodeans had made 'brunch' their own, adopting the notion with unfettered enthusiasm and giving it permanent status as a ritualistic weekend indulgence. The custom became ingrained in restaurant and café culture among the upper classes and elite, and the habit of accompanying boozy libations soon took hold. Egg 'n' avo was born and the rest is delicious history.

Without a doubt, London is clearly up there with the greatest culinary cities, and no matter what time of day you decide to indulge in a meal out in the big smoke, brunch is surely one of the best places to start.

BRUNCH IN LONDON

From the outset, brunch has encompassed a wide spectrum of dishes, from sweet to savoury, with eggs and bread being almost always a prerequisite. Beyond this, brunch menus diverge magnificently: on one street corner in London you might find a café serving smørrebrød every which way, on another there'll be fried chicken and waffles, buttermilk pancakes or Mexican huevos rancheros, or a pub doling out eggs Benedict and pain perdu (and açai bowls and green smoothies for the virtuous).

Any self-respecting Londoner recovering from a night of revelry, or simply taking things slow at the weekend, knows that there'll be at least a dozen purveyors of good food in their neighbourhood, or at least a short tube ride away. From idiosyncratic cafés to salubrious hotels – London establishments are plating up exactly what the city dwellers crave (some even sticking to classic eggs on toast or a good old British fry-up). And there's always someone bringing something new to the party, maybe mutton keema sloppy joes or a cutlery-free feast of gözleme, or an elevated egg and soldiers. The plethora of brunch options reflects the diversity of the city's cultural influences, the ever-changing food scene and regionality that makes it such a special place to be.

What was once rolled out as a weekend indulgence is now a daily temptation across the city, especially since London's artisan and speciality coffee scene has burgeoned and boomed. With third-wave coffee culture now properly embedded into Londoners' caffeine-fuelled psyches and café geography, brunchers expect some serious brews with their fare. Besides the coffee, brunch menus offer venues ample opportunity to get playful: alongside classic revivers – mimosas, spritzes and fruit-based cocktails – the capital's finest brunch spots go the extra mile with their drinks lists, coming up with giddy concoctions and something special for the 'no and low' crowd, and perhaps swerving prosecco for a refreshing pet nat. The city's brunch scene has never been more enticing and exciting.

Basics

FEEDING AND MAINTAINING A SOURDOUGH STARTER

TOP TIPS FROM E5 BAKEHOUSE – FIND THEIR RECIPE
FOR SOURDOUGH FLATBREADS ON PAGE 142.

The biggest challenge when making sourdough is keeping your starter alive and well. In fact, the success of your bread depends greatly on the liveliness of your starter. If you leave a starter without feeding it for too long, two things will happen: it will run out of food (sugars) and become too acidic. Both these things will slowly kill the yeast and the bacteria. In most sourdough bakeries the bakers will feed their starter at least once a day (often twice!), every day, so it stays happy. If you do that at home, your starter will be in very good shape but, unless you are planning to bake every day, that process will be quite demanding and wasteful. So, in order to lower the frequency of feeding your starter, we recommend keeping it in the fridge. This slows down the activity of the yeast and bacteria, meaning you won't have to refresh it so often. Once a week feeds will be will be good enough.

Once a week feed
Transfer 10g (⅓oz) starter into a new bowl, add 50g (2oz) lukewarm water and 50g (2oz) wholemeal rye flour (or other wholemeal wheat flour) and mix well. Discard the remainder of the previous starter (you won't need this any more) and give the starter container a quick wash with water. Put this 'new' starter in the container, cover and leave at room temperature for about 8 hours to kick-start the fermentation, then return it to the fridge.

Preparing the starter for making bread
When you are ready to make sourdough bread you will need to first refresh your starter. To do this, follow the above instructions but rather than leaving the starter at room temperature for just 8 hours, wait until it has nearly doubled in size and is visibly bubbly – if you taste it, it should have a fruity but not overpowering acidity. This could take up to 12 hours and these visual and flavour cues indicate that the yeast and bacteria populations are at their peak. We describe this as the starter being 'active'. You can then use this starter to create your leaven following the instructions in our flatbreads recipe on page 142.

Note
Our flatbreads recipe intentionally leaves you with a little extra leaven, so after you take the amount of leaven you need for the dough, you can keep the leftover leaven as your new starter. Get rid of your old starter, give the container a quick rinse with water and put the leftover leaven in. This is your new starter, which you can now put in the fridge.

POACHED EGGS

SERVES 4

8 eggs
Splash of vinegar

Bring a wide, shallow saucepan of water and a splash of vinegar to the boil.

Reduce the heat to a bare simmer and carefully crack in the eggs one at a time. Leave the eggs to poach for about 2 minutes, then remove using a slotted spoon and drain on kitchen paper.

Serve immediately.

SCRAMBLED EGGS

SERVES 4

8 eggs
25g (1oz) unsalted butter
Sea salt and ground black
  pepper

Whisk the eggs in a bowl with a large pinch each of salt and pepper.

Melt the butter in a large frying pan over a medium heat. Add the egg and let it sit for 30 seconds, then use a spatula to gradually bring the edge of the egg into the middle. Gently push and stir the egg as it starts to scramble, then remove from the heat just before it completely sets. The residual heat from the pan will finish cooking the egg.

Serve immediately.

CLASSIC OMELETTE

SERVES 1

2 eggs
10g (2 tsp/⅓oz) salted butter
Sea salt and ground black
  pepper
Snipped chives, to serve

Very lightly whisk the eggs in a bowl until just broken up. Season with a pinch each of salt and pepper.

Melt the butter in a small non-stick frying pan or omelette pan over a medium heat. When the butter is foaming, pour the egg into the pan and tilt the pan so the egg coats the base. Leave the egg for 30 seconds, then use a spatula to bring the edges of the egg into the middle. Gently stir the egg as it starts to scramble, then leave for another 30 seconds until the egg is mostly set.

Shake the pan back and forth to spread out the egg, then tilt the pan to one side and gently fold the omelette in half. Slide the omelette onto a plate and sprinkle with snipped chives.

Serve immediately.

FLUFFY PANCAKES

BY THE SAVOY

SERVES 8

130g (4½oz) plain flour
2 tsp caster sugar
1½ tsp baking powder
Pinch of fine sea salt
35g (1¼oz) yoghurt
1 egg
120g (4¼oz) whole milk
20g (¾oz) unsalted butter,
  melted

The day before you wish to serve these, combine all the ingredients in a blender or a food processor until smooth. Transfer to a bowl, cover and leave to rest in the fridge overnight.

Lightly grease a frying pan and an 8cm (3¼in) cake ring with oil. Heat the frying pan over a medium heat and add the cake ring. Pour a 1cm (½in) depth of pancake batter into the cake ring and cook for 2 minutes, then remove the ring and, using a flat spatula, carefully flip the pancake. Cook for a further 2 minutes or until the underside is golden brown. Remove to a plate and repeat to make 8 pancakes.

GLUTEN-FREE PANCAKES

BY VICTORIA SHEPPARD, QUEENS OF MAYFAIR

MAKES 8 SMALL
   PANCAKES

150g (5½oz) gluten-free
   self-raising flour
30g (1oz) caster sugar
1 tsp gluten-free baking
   powder
¾ tsp fine sea salt
185ml (6¼fl oz) whole milk
1 large egg
2 tbsp neutral-flavoured oil
   (sunflower, vegetable), plus
   a little extra to cook the
   pancakes

Combine the flour, sugar, baking powder and salt in a bowl. In a separate bowl, whisk together the milk, egg and oil. Pour the wet ingredients into the flour mixture and whisk until you have a smooth batter. Set aside to rest for 10 minutes.

Lightly oil a large frying pan over a medium heat. Ladle 8 small dollops of the batter into the pan (cook in batches if necessary) and cook for 3 minutes until golden on each side.

Serve, with crème fraîche and maple syrup and/or your favourite toppings.

FRENCH TOAST

BY NOPI

MAKES 6 SLICES

5 eggs
200ml (7fl oz) whole milk
400g (14oz) brioche loaf, ends
   trimmed, cut into 6 slices,
   3cm (1¼in) thick
80g (2¾oz) cold unsalted
   butter, cut into 2cm (¾in) dice

Crack the eggs into a medium bowl and whisk well until pale, light and fluffy. Continue to whisk as you slowly pour in the milk, then transfer to a dish which is large enough to fit the slices of brioche lying flat and not overlapping – use 2 dishes if you need to. Add the brioche slices and set aside for 5 minutes, turning them once or twice. It will seem like a lot of liquid for the bread to absorb, but it will do; just be careful when you are turning it, as it gets very soft.

Preheat the oven to 240°C (220°C fan/475°F/gas mark 9).

Place a large non-stick frying pan over a medium-high heat with 20g (¾oz) of the butter. When the butter starts to foam, lay 3 pieces of brioche in the pan and fry for 1–2 minutes. Flip the toast over, add 20g (¾oz) more butter to the pan, and continue to fry for another 1½ minutes until golden-brown on both sides. Remove from the pan and set aside on a baking tray while you wipe the pan with some kitchen paper and repeat with the remaining brioche and butter. Once all the brioche is on the tray, transfer to the oven and bake for a final 4 minutes until the toast has puffed up and is golden brown. Serve at once.

QUEENS
MAYFAIR

SCRAMBLED TOFU

BY LINNEAN

SERVES 2

125g (4½oz) firm tofu, drained
12g (½oz) nutritional yeast
Small pinch of ground turmeric
Small pinch of fine sea salt
1 tsp vegan butter
Pinch of kala namak (black salt)

Crumble the tofu into a bowl or use a fork to roughly mash it. Add the nutritional yeast, turmeric and salt, and mix to combine.

Melt the vegan butter in a saucepan over a medium heat and add the tofu mixture. Cook, stirring constantly, for 5 minutes or until the water from the tofu has nearly evaporated and the mixture resembles scrambled eggs. Turn off the heat and season with the kala namak, to taste. Serve at once on toast.

HASH BROWNS

BY SEABIRD

SERVES 4–5

1kg (2lb 3oz) Maris Piper
  potatoes, peeled and grated
1 tbsp salt
125ml (4½fl oz) melted butter
90g (3¼oz) plain flour
Oil, for pan-frying
Cracked black pepper

Rinse the grated potato until the water runs clear (this removes the starch). Dry the potato, place it in a bowl with the salt and mix thoroughly. Allow the potato to stand for 10 minutes to soften and release more water.

Squeeze the excess water away and dry the potato again. Return the potato to the bowl and stir through the melted butter, followed by the flour and some cracked pepper. Pile 200g (7oz) portions of the hash brown mixture into 10cm (4in) ring moulds and place on a baking tray, pressing down on the potato to compress it (you should get 4–5 portions). Transfer to the oven and bake for 30 minutes.

Heat a little oil in a frying pan over a medium-high heat. Add the hash browns and fry for 1½ minutes on each side until crispy and golden.

FLATBREADS
BY KURO EATERY

MAKES 5

200ml (7fl oz) lukewarm water
12g (½oz) fresh yeast
1 tbsp good-quality olive oil
15g (½oz) caster sugar
300g (10½oz) strong white
  flour, plus extra for dusting
15g (½oz) fine sea salt

Combine the water, yeast, olive oil and sugar in the bowl of a stand mixer until everything is dissolved. Combine the flour and salt in a separate bowl, then add this to the yeast mixture. With the dough hook attached, knead on low speed for 10 minutes, making sure the dough doesn't overheat.

Tip the dough onto a floured work surface and form into a ball by tucking the sides underneath the dough. Transfer to a greased bowl and prove in the fridge for at least 2 hours but ideally overnight.

Divide the dough equally into 5 pieces and shape into balls. Place on a floured tray until ready to use. (The dough can be prepared in advance and kept in the fridge for up to 2 days.)

Heat a cast-iron frying pan that has a lid over a high heat until scorching hot. Roll out one of the dough balls on a floured surface into a 15cm (6in) disc. Drop the flatbread into the hot pan and cover with the lid. Cook on each side for 2 minutes, then transfer to a plate and repeat to cook the remaining flatbreads. Serve warm with your choice of brunch toppings.

HOLLANDAISE
BY THE BEAUMONT HOTEL

SERVES 2

150ml (5fl oz) white wine
50ml (1¾fl oz) white wine
  vinegar
1 small shallot, finely sliced
1 tsp black peppercorns
1 tarragon sprig
1 egg yolk
250g (9oz) clarified butter,
  melted and cooled slightly
  (see page 242)
Lemon juice, to taste
Flaky sea salt

To make a white wine vinegar reduction, combine 50ml (1¾fl oz) of the white wine, the vinegar, shallot, peppercorns and tarragon in a small pan. Bring to a simmer over a low heat and reduce by half. Set aside to cool completely, then strain into a clean container. You will need 50g (1¾oz).

Whisk the egg yolk with the vinegar reduction and remaining white wine in a heatproof bowl set over a pan of just simmering water, until the mixture stops looking frothy and starts to thicken (about 70°C/158°F on a kitchen thermometer). Once it has thickened, whisk in the melted clarified butter slowly and steadily (ensure it is not too hot or the hollandaise will split), then season with salt and lemon juice. Remove from the heat and serve.

Savoury

TOASTED CRUMPETS WITH MARMITE & POACHED EGGS

BY 45 JERMYN ST

SERVES 2

50ml (2fl oz) white wine
  vinegar
4 crumpets
4 eggs, at room temperature
  (we use Burford Browns)
Unsalted butter, for spreading
Marmite, for spreading
Ground black pepper

This dish was created for the opening of 45 Jermyn St. There's some lively debate as to who invented this mightily British combination of butter, crumpet, Marmite and oozing egg. But whoever it was deserves a CBE for services to their country. Magnificent, and magnificently simple, too.

Fill a large saucepan with water and bring it to just under boiling point. Turn down to a simmer and add the vinegar.

Place the crumpets in a toaster; they should be double-toasted to give them a little crispness.

Crack each egg into a small cup (this makes it easier to poach 4 eggs at the same time). With a slotted spoon, swirl the simmering water around to create a whirlpool in the centre, then gently drop all the eggs into it. Turn the heat back up and, when it starts bubbling again, turn it back down to a low simmer. Poach the eggs for 3–4 minutes – they will rise to the surface when they are done. Remove the eggs from the pan with the slotted spoon and put them on a wad of kitchen paper to soak up the excess water.

Spread the crumpets generously with butter, then spread with Marmite. Divide between 2 plates, top each crumpet with a poached egg and sprinkle with a little ground black pepper.

Serve immediately.

ENSALADA AMAZÓNICA

BY AMAZONICO LONDON

SERVES 4

200g (7oz) good-quality
 tomatoes, peeled, deseeded
 and diced
200g (7oz) ripe avocado flesh,
 diced
200g (7oz) ripe mango flesh,
 diced

Dressing
2 tsp aged sherry vinegar
1 tsp kalamansi vinegar
 (or yuzu vinegar)
1 tbsp light soy sauce
1½ tbsp extra virgin olive oil
2 basil leaves, finely chopped
Pinch of caster sugar
Pinch each of sea salt and
 ground black pepper

A fresh and zingy salad from the luxe and lush Amazonico on Berkeley Square, which serves up sushi and Latin American flavours. This dish is wonderful served on its own for a light and refreshing brunch, with or without sourdough toast. It's also lovely served alongside grilled meat or fish for a more substantial meal.

Add all the ingredients for the dressing to a bowl and whisk vigorously. Set to one side while you assemble your salad.

Add the tomato, avocado and mango to a large bowl and mix together until well combined.

Pour the dressing over the salad and stir gently to coat everything, taking care not to bruise the ingredients.

Serve by itself, or piled onto warm sourdough toast.

FRENCH TOAST WITH TRUFFLED FRIED CHICKEN

BY BALANS

SERVES 1

Established in Soho in 1987, Balans have been serving up good food and good times ever since, with sites now in Kensington, Stratford and Shepherd's Bush. Their brunch menu is enviable, and this recipe is the ultimate indulgence for a lazy weekend. The quantites here serve one, but you can easily increase the ingredients if catering for more people.

Truffle Fried Chicken
2 skin-on chicken thighs
85ml (3fl oz) buttermilk
Vegetable or rapeseed oil,
    for deep-frying
60g (2oz) plain flour
2 tsp rolled oats
Generous couple of pinches
    of salt

Truffle Honey
100g (3½oz) clear honey
35ml (1¼fl oz) truffle oil
2 tsp sherry vinegar
Sea salt and ground black
    pepper

Balans' Famous French Toast
2 eggs
Pinch of ground cinnamon
150g (5½oz) brioche (2 thick
    slices)
125g (4½oz) maple butter
20g (¾oz) butter
2 tsp pecans
1 banana, split lengthways
50g (1¾oz) caster sugar
Icing (confectioners') sugar,
    for dusting

Truffle Fried Chicken

Mix the chicken thighs with the buttermilk, cover and marinate in the fridge for at least 12 hours, ideally overnight.

Half-fill a large saucepan with vegetable oil or rapeseed oil and heat to 175°C (347°F).

Combine the flour, oats and salt in a bowl. Fully coat the marinated chicken with the flour mixture, then deep-fry for 10–12 minutes until golden brown. Drain on kitchen paper.

Truffle Honey

Combine the honey, truffle oil, sherry vinegar and a pinch each of salt and pepper in a bowl, then drizzle over the hot chicken thighs.

Balans' Famous French Toast

Lightly beat the eggs in a shallow bowl and add the cinnamon. Dip the brioche slices into the egg mixture, ensuring they are well soaked.

Melt the maple butter in a frying pan over a medium heat and fry the brioche on both sides until golden and delicious. Remove from the pan.

Melt the butter in a separate frying pan over a medium heat, add the pecans, banana and caster sugar and cook for 4–5 minutes until the banana is caramelised. Glaze the banana with the leftover maple butter from the brioche pan, then remove from the heat.

To Serve

Layer the banana on top of the brioche, drizzle the sauce over the top and dust with icing sugar. Serve with the truffled fried chicken.

CHEESE SU BUREK

BY THE BARBARY NEXT DOOR

SERVES 12

3 eggs, lightly beaten
120ml (4fl oz) oil
25g (1oz) butter, melted
240ml (8fl oz) water
2 x 270g (10oz) packets of filo
  pastry
Sesame seeds, for sprinkling
Sea salt and ground black
  pepper

Cheese Filling
250g (9oz) rosary goat's
  cheese, crumbled
200g (9oz) feta, crumbled
400g (14oz) mozzarella, grated
350g (12¼oz) labneh
250g (9oz) burnt aubergine
  (eggplant), *see* Note
30g (1oz) fresh oregano,
  chopped
Pinch of Aleppo chilli or chilli
  flakes

NOTE — *To make burnt
aubergines, using heatproof
tongs, carefully hold a whole
aubergine over a gas flame,
rotating until the skin is charred
and blackened on all sides.
Alternatively, grill under a high
heat, rotating frequently. Place in
a bowl, cover and leave to cool,
before peeling off and discarding
the charred skin and roughly
chopping the flesh.*

Innovative and clever takes on the fragrant, heady, smoky flavours of
the North African coast (formerly the Barbary Coast) and Moorish Spain
are Daniel Alt's hallmark. The current head chef at Covent Garden's The
Barbary and its laid-back sibling The Barbary Next Door, Daniel grew up in
Israel and trained with acclaimed chefs including Meir Adoni and Yonatan
Roshfeld. He fell in love with London after a short stage at London's
lauded The Ledbury and moved to the city, going on to work at Nobu,
Jamie Oliver's Fifteen and Ottolenghi.

—

'We serve this with a soft-boiled egg, brined cucumber pickle, diced
tomato and a spicy dip.'

Preheat the oven to 200°C (180°C fan/400°F/gas mark 6).

In a large shallow bowl, combine the beaten egg, oil, melted butter and
water. Season with salt and pepper and set aside.

In a separate large bowl, combine the cheese filling ingredients.

Line a 22 x 32cm (8½ x 12½in) baking dish with 4 sheets of filo pastry.
Take another 4 sheets of filo and briefly soak them in the egg and oil
mixture. Scrunch them up and add them to the baking dish, then top with
one-third of the cheese filling. Place 2 more sheets of filo on top of the
filling, then soak another 4 sheets in the egg and oil mixture and scrunch
them over the top. Add another one-third of the cheese filling, then repeat
this process once more. Cover the cheese filling with a final 4 layers of filo,
score into 12 squares by cutting down through the pastry, and pour the
remaining egg and oil mixture over the top. Scatter with sesame seeds.

Transfer the burek to the oven and bake for 30–45 minutes until crisp and
golden. Allow to cool and set before cutting into slices and serving.

ANNA JONES

After earning her stripes in the London restaurant scene and working with Jamie Oliver on his books and TV shows, Anna originally turned to vegetable-centred cooking to reset her tastebuds for a few weeks. This change in her cooking opened up her creativity in the kitchen in a totally different way, and she hasn't looked back. She published her first cookbook, *A Modern Way to Eat*, a decade later. A dedicated vegetarian cookbook that quickly changed the way people thought about plant-based eating and won her legions of devoted fans. Anna's latest book, *Easy Wins*, takes 12 hero ingredients that are guaranteed to make your food sing. It's packed with 100s of super-simple recipes that are bursting with flavour, as well as being kind to the planet. Anna has a soft spot for a vibrant breakfast and brunch, especially at the weekend, when everyone has more time to indulge in what they love.

Anna supports a number of charitable food projects and has always admired OnePlate's ethos of nourishing those most in need, 'which couldn't be more crucial than it is now.'

ANNA JONES' TURMERIC DHAL POACHED EGGS

SERVES 4

1 tbsp olive oil
1 thumb-sized piece of fresh
  ginger, finely chopped
2 garlic cloves, finely chopped
Small bunch of coriander,
  leaves picked, stalks finely
  chopped
1 tsp cumin seeds
1 tsp ground coriander
1 tsp ground turmeric, or
  a small thumb-sized piece
  of fresh root, grated
300g (10½oz) split red lentils
1 litre (35fl oz) boiling water
  from the kettle
200g (7oz) spinach, washed
Juice of 1 lemon
4 eggs
1 green chilli, finely sliced
Sea salt and ground black
  pepper
Yoghurt, to serve

Heat the oil in a large pan that has a lid. Add the ginger and garlic, then the coriander stalks, stirring frequently until the edges of the garlic pick up a little colour.

Add the spices and cook for a minute or so to toast and release the oils. Add the lentils and stir to coat in the oil. Add the boiling water and a good pinch of salt, then stir well. Cook over a low heat for 20–30 minutes, or until the lentils are well cooked and the mixture has thickened. You want it to be thick enough to just about hold its shape when you make a little well for your eggs.

Add the spinach and put the lid on for 2 minutes, or until the leaves have wilted, then stir well.

When you are almost ready to eat, squeeze in the lemon juice and taste the lentils, adding a little more salt if you need to, and some pepper.

Make 4 wells in the lentils, then crack an egg into each well and pop the lid back on until the egg whites are firm and the yolks are still runny – this should take about 5 minutes.

To serve, scatter the eggs with the sliced chilli and coriander leaves, and serve yoghurt on the side for everyone to help themselves.

GREEN EGGS

BY BARE BREW

SERVES 2

1 thick slice of sourdough
  bread
2 tbsp olive oil, plus extra for
  drizzling
100g (3½oz) fresh podded
  peas
100g (3½oz) kale, tough stems
  removed
200g (7oz) Swiss chard,
  trimmed
100g (3½oz) green beans,
  trimmed
100g (3½oz) tenderstem
  broccoli
2 tbsp chilli oil
1 banana shallot, finely
  chopped
60ml (4 tbsp) double cream
50g (1¾oz) hard goat's cheese
⅓ tsp ground nutmeg
4 eggs
1 tsp ground sumac
Sea salt and ground black
  pepper

The coffee is a big deal at this award-winning family-run café in Wanstead, and the brunch dishes on offer are just as good, from Turkish eggs to tiramisu French toast. These greens eggs are the perfect way to set yourself up for a fun-filled weekend.

Preheat the oven to 190°C (170°C fan/375°F/gas mark 5).

Tear the sourdough into chunks and spread out evenly on a small baking tray. Drizzle with a little olive oil, season with salt and pepper, then transfer to the oven and toast for 12–15 minutes until crisp.

In a pot of boiling water, blanch each of the greens separately, allowing 1 minute for the peas, kale and Swiss chard and 3 minutes for the beans and tenderstem broccoli. Immediately plunge the greens into a large bowl of iced water to halt the cooking process. When completely cold drain, dry and roughly chop.

Heat the olive oil and chilli oil in a frying pan over a medium heat for about 2 minutes until it starts to shimmer. Add the shallot and cook for 2 minutes, then add the blanched greens and cook for 4–5 minutes. Pour in the cream, crumble in the goat's cheese, add the nutmeg and stir to combine. Season to taste with salt and pepper.

Meanwhile, poach the eggs (see page 61) in a large wide saucepan of just simmering water.

Divide the greens between 2 bowls and place the poached eggs on top. Sprinkle with a little salt, the sumac and sourdough croûtons.

Serve immediately.

MERGUEZ SAUSAGES WITH BUTTERBEAN RAGOUT & FRIED EGGS

BY CARMEL

SERVES 4

Vegetable oil, for brushing and
  frying
600g (1lb 5oz) merguez
  sausage (individual sausages
  or 1 sausage in a long coil)
4 large eggs
Flaky sea salt and ground black
  pepper

Tomato Dressing
1 tbsp white balsamic vinegar
1½ tsp lemon juice
60ml (4 tbsp) olive oil
1 tomato, finely diced
1 garlic clove, minced

Butterbean Ragout
2 x 400g (14oz) cans of
  butterbeans
2 garlic cloves, minced
1 red chilli, deseeded and
  finely chopped
10g (⅓oz) flat-leaf parsley,
  leaves finely chopped
5g (⅙oz) chives, finely sliced
1 red onion, finely chopped
2 tomatoes, finely diced

To Finish & Serve
1 spring onion, green parts
  only, finely sliced
80g (2¾oz) crème fraîche
80g (2¾oz) best-quality harissa
40ml (1½fl oz) best-quality
  olive oil

Chef and co-owner of Berber & Q Grill House, Shawarma Bar and Carmel restaurant, Josh Katz, grew up in North London and studied marketing in the UK and Australia before his love of great food won out. Switching careers, he trained at Le Cordon Bleu, London, then enjoyed stints at Galvin Bistrot de Luxe and Ottolenghi, creating Levant-inspired, veg-forward, season-led dishes in (and winning accolades for) restaurants across the city, launching Berber & Q Grill House in 2015. His most recent opening, Carmel in Queen's Park, happens to be a brilliant brunch spot.

Tomato Dressing
Whisk the ingredients together in a large bowl and season to taste with salt and pepper. Set aside for at least 1 hour for the flavours to infuse. Mix again just before serving.

Butterbean Ragout
Tip the beans and their liquid into a saucepan and warm over a medium-low heat until simmering. Reduce the heat to very low and keep warm until needed, topping up with a drop of water if necessary to prevent them from catching on the bottom.

Merguez Sausages & Eggs
Preheat a grill to a high heat and grill the sausages, turning occasionally, for 4–6 minutes (or longer for thicker sausages) until cooked through. The sausages can also be cooked on a barbecue over direct heat or in a frying pan.

Meanwhile, heat a little oil in a non-stick frying pan and fry the eggs sunny-side up, basting the top of the eggs with any excess oil to cook the whites on top. Season with salt and pepper.

To Finish & Serve
Drain the beans and mix through the garlic, red chilli, parsley, chives, red onion and tomato. Fold through the dressing and check for seasoning, adding salt and pepper as necessary.

Transfer the beans to individual serving bowls. Add the grilled merguez sausages on top, followed by a fried egg. Garnish each plate with the spring onion strewn over the top, and finish with a dollop of crème fraîche and harissa, and a drizzle of olive oil.

CHICKEN PAILLARD

BY JASON ATHERTON, BERNERS TAVERN

Michelin-starred restaurateur Jason Atherton created Maze for Gordon Ramsay then launched Pollen Street Social, Little Social, Social Eating House and Berners Tavern in London and outposts in the Far East. His Social Company restaurant group has a revered presence, and Jason understands Londoners' love of brunch: the dawn-to-dusk menu at the gloriously glitzy EDITION hotel in Fitzrovia has an expansive offering – think eggs every which way, and modern brasserie fare of the highest order.

SERVES 1

1 boneless, skinless chicken
  breast, butterflied
100ml (3½fl oz) oil infused with
  thyme, rosemary, garlic and
  bay leaf
Salt

Place the chicken in a shallow dish, pour over the oil and massage it into the chicken. Cover and leave to marinate in the fridge overnight.

Wild Garlic Butter
20g (¾oz) wild garlic
125g (4½oz) unsalted butter,
  at room temperature, diced
1 tsp vegetable oil
Lemon juice, to taste

Wild Garlic Butter
Blanch the wild garlic in boiling salted boiling water for 30 seconds, then refresh in iced water. Squeeze it to remove as much water as possible, then finely chop and blitz with the butter in a food processor. Drizzle in the oil and season to taste with lemon juice and salt. Roll the butter into a log, wrap in cling film and chill.

Spiced Mayonnaise
2 small egg yolks
2 tbsp white wine vinegar
2 tsp Dijon mustard
180ml (6fl oz) rose harissa oil
  (or use another chilli oil)

Spiced Mayonnaise
Place the egg yolk, vinegar and mustard in a small food processor. With the motor running, trickle in the rose harissa oil until emulsified. Season with salt. This makes more than you will need – keep in the fridge for up to 3 days.

Classic Dressing
50g (1¾oz) Dijon mustard
100ml (3½fl oz) white wine
  vinegar
300ml (10½fl oz) vegetable oil

Classic Dressing
Combine the mustard and vinegar in a bowl. Slowly whisk in the vegetable oil until the dressing is emulsified. Season to taste with salt.

Mixed Salad
3 white chicory leaves
3 red chicory leaves
3 baby gem leaves
3 radicchio leaves
Snipped chives
Sea salt flakes

Mixed Salad
Combine the leaves in a bowl, season with salt and dress with a little of the classic dressing. Toss to combine and scatter with a few snipped chives.

Chicken
Heat a griddle pan over a high heat. Add the chicken breast and cook for 3 minutes on each side, or until golden and cooked through.

To Serve
Pickled piquillo peppers
Pickled baby onions
Frozen feta

To Serve
Melt 2–3 tablespoons of the wild garlic butter in a saucepan. Place the chicken on a plate and spoon over the melted butter. Top with the salad and add a dollop of harissa mayonnaise. Finish with a few pickled piquillo peppers and baby onions, then finely grate some frozen feta over the top. Serve immediately.

SILK ROAD EGGS

BY BOBO & WILD

A small place with a big heart, Bobo & Wild now have cafés in Shoreditch, Clapham and South Woodford, serving up delicious coffee, brunch, cakes and cocktails. Priding themselves on quality, the vibe is laid back but the food is seriously good.

Pepper & Tomato Sauce
1 tsp cumin seeds
100ml (3½fl oz) olive oil
1 red onion, sliced
4 red and yellow peppers, deseeded and cut into 1cm (½in) strips (or use 400g/14oz jarred roasted peppers)
1 tbsp dark brown sugar
2 bay leaves
6–8 tomatoes, roughly chopped
2 tbsp balsamic vinegar
2 tsp chopped coriander leaves
Pinch of smoked cayenne pepper
Sea salt and ground black pepper

Dukkah Spice Mix
1 tsp cumin seeds
1 tsp coriander seeds
1 tsp fennel seeds
2 tsp sesame seeds
30g (1oz) shelled pistachios

Garlic Labneh
500g (1lb 2oz) labneh or thick yoghurt
2 garlic cloves, mashed
Pinch of sea salt

Hot Chilli Butter
100g (3½oz) butter
1 tsp chilli flakes

To Serve
8 eggs, poached (page 61)
Chopped herbs of your choice
8 slices focaccia, toasted
Olive oil

Pepper & Tomato Sauce
In a very large frying pan, dry-roast the cumin seeds over a high heat for 2 minutes. Add the oil and onion and sauté for 5 minutes, then add the peppers, sugar and herbs and continue cooking for 5–10 minutes to get a nice colour on the peppers (5 minutes will be plenty of time if using jarred roasted peppers).

Add the tomatoes, balsamic vinegar, coriander, smoked cayenne and some salt and pepper, then reduce the heat to low and cook for 15 minutes, adding a little water as the sauce cooks to maintain a pasta sauce consistency. Remove the bay leaves, then taste and adjust the seasoning. Set aside and keep warm.

Dukkah Spice Mix
Preheat the oven to 180°C (160°C fan/350°F/gas mark 4). Combine the ingredients in a small bowl, then spread over a baking tray and cook for 8–10 minutes until the seeds and pistachios are toasted. Transfer to a food processor and pulse a few times, just until the pistachios are chopped.

Garlic Labneh
Whisk the ingredients together in a small bowl.

Hot Chilli Butter
Melt the butter in a frying pan over a low heat and skim off the white solids on the surface. Add the chilli flakes to the clarified butter, then remove from the heat.

To Serve
Spread some garlic labneh on each plate and top with the red pepper and tomato sauce. Add the poached eggs, then sprinkle with the dukkah spice mix, drizzle with the hot chilli butter and garnish with herbs. Serve with the toasted focaccia, drizzled with a little olive oil.

And above all, watch with glittering eyes the whole world around you because the greatest secrets are always hidden in the most unlikely places.

ROALD DAHL

ASPARAGUS WITH MORELS & POACHED EGGS

BY BOURNE & HOLLINGSWORTH

SERVES 4

200g (7oz) fresh morels
50g (1¾oz) unsalted butter
1 garlic clove, finely chopped
50ml (1¾fl oz) Madeira
200ml (7fl oz) strong chicken
  stock
20 asparagus spears, trimmed
4 slices of sourdough bread
4 large eggs
2 tbsp chopped chives
Sea salt and ground black
  pepper

One of the first to bring NYC-style bottomless brunching to the city, Bourne & Hollingsworth nails the breakfast/brunch hybrid. Their Bourne & Hollingsworth Building in Clerkenwell opened in 2014 and is home to a host of working, dancing, eating and drinking spaces, including a restaurant, cocktail bar, cookery school and basement bar and club, but the verdant oasis of the greenhouse room is where you want to make a bee-line for at the weekend (be sure to opt for a never-ending Bellini!).

Gently rinse the morels in water to clean them. Melt half the butter in a large frying pan over a medium heat, add the garlic and morels, season with a little salt and pepper and sauté for 2 minutes. Slosh in the Madeira and let it bubble and reduce by half, then add the chicken stock and bring to the boil. Remove from the heat.

Cook the asparagus in a large pan of boiling water for 3–4 minutes until tender, then drain. Cut in half lengthways if they are very thick.

Toast the sourdough and poach the eggs (see page 61).

Return the mushroom sauce to the boil, whisk in the remaining butter and add the chives.

Place the toast on plates and top with the asparagus. Place an egg on top of each portion of asparagus and finish with the morel sauce.

POTATO CAKE WITH SMOKED TROUT, FENNEL SALAD & SEAWEED BEARNAISE

BY BRAT

SERVES 2–3

2 large waxy potatoes, peeled and coarsely grated
1 small onion, sliced
500ml (17fl oz) boiling water
2 thyme sprigs, leaves picked
50g (1¾oz) butter, melted
2 tbsp rapeseed oil
200g (7oz) smoked trout
Sea salt and ground black pepper

Seaweed Bearnaise
2½ tbsp white wine vinegar
2 tsp lemon juice
20g (¾oz) tarragon leaves, chopped
1 shallot, finely sliced
3 egg yolks
200g (7oz) melted clarified butter (see page 242)
1 tbsp laverbread (seaweed) or finely chopped dried nori sheet

Raw Fennel Salad
1 fennel bulb, shaved (preferably using a mandoline)
2 tbsp roughly chopped dill fronds
2 tbsp extra virgin olive oil
1 tbsp lemon juice
1 tbsp chopped flat-leafed parsley

'Brat' is old English for turbot and the 'king of the sea' is chef and co-owner Tomos Parry's star dish at his Shoreditch restaurant: a whole wood-roasted turbot cooked gently over fire. The grill cooking, inspired by the Basque region's culinary traditions, has won Brat a Michelin star and a devoted fan base. His most recent venture, Mountain, opened recently in Soho and is already a hit on the London food scene.

—

'We've served this dish at Brat x Climpson's Arch a few times, and it works as a delicious brunch or lunch dish. We love the combination of warm potato cake with smoked trout and a vibrant raw fennel salad, all brought together with a seaweed bearnaise. The trout can be substituted with any good-quality smoked fish, such as salmon or kippers.'

To make the seaweed bearnaise, place the vinegar, lemon juice, half the tarragon and the shallot in a saucepan and bring to the boil. Cook until reduced by half, then strain into a heatproof bowl and allow to cool.

Whisk the egg yolks and vinegar reduction together in a clean heatproof bowl, then place over a saucepan of barely simmering water and whisk until the mixture is thick and coats the back of a spoon. Remove the bowl from the heat and very slowly drizzle in the melted clarified butter, whisking constantly, until all the butter is incorporated and the sauce is emulsified. Add the remaining tarragon and stir in the seaweed, then season with salt and pepper. Set aside and keep warm.

Place all the raw fennel salad ingredients in a bowl and toss well. Set aside.

Combine the potato and onion in a large bowl and pour the boiling water over the top. Allow to sit for 2 minutes, then drain. (This softens the potato and removes excess starch.) Squeeze the potato and onion to remove as much water as possible, then return to the bowl, season well and stir in the thyme leaves and melted butter.

Take a large, deep frying pan (or use 2 smaller ones) and heat the oil over a low heat. Drop the potato mixture into the pan and use a spatula to flatten it out. Cook for at least 5 minutes until the edge of the potato cake starts to brown and the potato cake moves around if you shake the pan. When the underside is golden, flip the potato cake over and cook the other side for another 5 minutes or so until golden and crisp on the outside but still fluffy in the middle.

Season the smoked trout with pepper and serve on top of the warm potato cake. Top with the fennel salad and serve the warm seaweed bearnaise in a jug for everyone to add as much as they like.

HASH BROWNS & SPRING ONION MAYO

BY BREAD BY BIKE

MAKES ABOUT 24
(SERVES 8–12)

Hash Browns
2kg (4lb 6oz) chipping or
   roasting potatoes, peeled
250g (9oz) butter, melted
Neutral oil, for deep-frying
Sea salt

Spring Onion Oil
1 litre (35fl oz) rapeseed oil
2 bunches of spring onions,
   finely sliced, plus extra to
   serve
Pinch of salt

Spring Onion Mayo
100g (3½oz) egg yolks
   (from about 5 eggs)
250ml (9fl oz) spring onion oil
   (see above)
Rice vinegar, to taste

A bakery and café just up the road from Camden, Bread By Bike puts ethical and sustainable production at the heart of what they do, churning out incredible flavours that change with the seasons.

Hash Browns

Preheat the oven to 160°C (140°C fan/325°F/gas mark 3). Line a baking tin, about 22 x 32cm (8½ x 12½in), with baking paper.

Grate the potatoes into a large bowl, season with salt, mix and allow to sit for a couple of minutes.

Squeeze as much liquid out of the potato as possible, then return it to the bowl and stir through the melted butter. Transfer the potato to the prepared tin and spread it evenly, then cover with a layer of baking paper and foil (this will prevent the top from burning). Bake for 1 hour or until a knife goes into the potato with little resistance.

Remove the tin from the oven and place something heavy (a couple cans of baked beans or a bag of sugar will do the trick) on top of the potato, then leave to cool to room temperature. Transfer to the fridge, along with the weights, and leave overnight.

Spring Onion Oil

Combine the ingredients in a large saucepan and bring to a simmer over a low heat. Immediately remove the pan from the heat and set aside until cooled to room temperature. Strain the cooled oil through a fine-meshed sieve into a jar and store in the fridge. This makes more than you need for this recipe – the oil will keep for up to 1 week.

Spring Onion Mayo

Place the egg yolks in a blender and on slow/medium speed very gradually pour in the spring onion oil until emulsified into a thick mayonnaise. Season to taste with salt and rice vinegar, then set aside.

To Serve

Portion the chilled potato terrine into whatever shape your heart desires (about 24 pieces).

Half-fill a deep, heavy-based saucepan with neutral oil and heat to 170°C (338°F). Working in batches if necessary, deep-fry the terrine portions until golden brown. Drain on kitchen paper and season immediately with salt.

Divide the hash browns between serving plates, dollop over the spring onion mayo and finish with finely sliced spring onions.

EMILY EZEKIEL & JOSEPH DENISON CAREY

London born and bred, Emily currently works as a food writer, art director and food and prop stylist, based out of her creative space, Narroway Studio, in the heart of Hackney, East London. Her food career, which spans over 15 years, has seen her work with the biggest and most-loved names in the food industry, from high-end kitchens, to remote rural locations.

Born and raised in North London, Joseph undertook his chef training in Italy, before returning to his roots and working at The Water House Project, Pidgin and Caravel. He's since burst onto our screens across British broadcasting channels and runs The Bread + Butter Supper Club.

Having met a couple of years ago, Emily and Joe now work as a regular duo. Their support for OnePlate is evident throughout these pages. Having cooked and styled most of the recipes in this book, the charity holds a very special place in their hearts.

EMILY & JOE'S
PROPER LONDON FRY-UP

SERVES 4

8 bacon rashers
8 sausages
4 eggs
Sea salt and ground black
    pepper

Rosti
800g (1¾lb) maris piper
    potatoes, coarsly grated
1 onion, coarsely grated
150ml (5¼fl oz) olive oil, plus
    extra for frying
8 thyme sprigs, leaves picked

Baked Beans
1 onion, finely chopped
2 garlic cloves, crushed
2 tbsp olive oil
½ tsp smoked paprika
½ tsp chilli flakes
400g (14oz) can tomatoes
1 tbsp brown sugar
Juice of 1 lemon
500g (18oz) jar of cannellini
    beans
1 pickled red chilli, chopped
    (optional)

Golden Mushrooms
4 tbsp olive oil
50g (2oz) unsalted butter
500g (18oz) chestnut
    mushrooms (we use Paris
    brown), sliced
4 garlic cloves, thinly sliced

To serve (optional)
Toast
Ketchup
HP sauce
Hot sauce

There are a few elements to this recipe, but if you are planning a big brunch with your pals you can make the rosti and beans ahead and chill them – simply fry and reheat before you want to enjoy. This recipe serves 4 but is easy to scale up or down.

Start by preparing the rosti. Bundle the grated potato and onion into a clean tea towel and squeeze out all the liquid. Transfer to a mixing bowl and add the oil and thyme leaves, then season with a big pinch of salt and give it a good mix. Leave to stand for 10 minutes.

Next, make your baked beans. Simply add the onion, garlic and olive oil to a heavy-based saucepan and fry over a medium heat for about 5 minutes until translucent, stirring often. Add the spices and fry for 1 minute until fragrant, then add all the remaining ingredients (apart from the cannellini beans), turn up the heat to high and simmer for 5 minutes. Using a stick blender, blend the sauce until smooth (or keep it chunky if you'd prefer), then tip in the jar of cannellini beans, including their liquid. Simmer for 10–15 minutes over a medium heat, then taste and adjust the seasoning to your liking. Stir through the pickled chilli, if using, and keep warm.

Preheat the grill to 220°C (200°C fan/425°F/gas mark 7).

Add a glug of oil to a large frying pan and set over a medium heat. Shape the rosti mixture into 4 equal-sized rounds and fry for 8 minutes on each side or until golden brown and crispy (you may need to do this in batches).

While the rostis fry, arrange the bacon rashers and sausages on a baking tray and cook under the grill, turning often, until cooked.

To make the golden mushrooms, add the olive oil and butter to a large frying pan set over a high heat. Once the butter is foaming, add the mushrooms and fry for 5 minutes. When the mushrooms start to turn golden, add the garlic and continue to fry until the garlic is just starting to colour.

When all your other elements are ready, simply fry the eggs to your liking and plate everything up. We serve our fry-up with the classic condiments of HP sauce and ketchup, but hot sauce works well, too, if you like things spicy. Serve with toast (for those who are extra-hungry) and a cup of tea.

HUEVOS ROTOS

BY BRINDISA KITCHEN BAR

SERVES 4

280g (10oz) potatoes, peeled
  and sliced
Rapeseed oil, for frying
1 small onion, thinly sliced
120g (4¼oz) sobrasada, or
  240g (8½oz) pistou (see
  below)
1½ tsp hot smoked paprika
1½ tsp sweet smoked paprika
8 eggs
Sea salt and ground black
  pepper
Chopped parsley, to serve

Pistou (optional)
100ml (3½fl oz) good-quality
  olive oil
2 garlic cloves, thinly sliced
1 ñora pepper (or 1 tsp sweet
  smoked paprika if you can't
  get ñora)
1 bay leaf
50g (1¾oz) potato, finely diced
50g (1¾oz) red pepper
  (capsicum), finely diced
50g (1¾oz) green pepper
  (capsicum), finely diced
1 onion, finely diced
25g (1oz) aubergine (eggplant),
  finely diced
250g (9oz) good-quality
  tomatoes, blended
2 thyme sprigs, leaves picked

The home of Spanish food in the UK for over 30 years, the Brindisa store in Borough Market is a treasure trove of fragrance and spice. And with one of their many restaurants just around the corner, it's easy to enjoy their delicious tapas with a glass of sherry in hand. Brindisa serve their huevos rotos with either sobrasada, or pistou (for a veggie alternative).

If making the pistou, heat half the olive oil in a frying pan over a low heat. Add the garlic, ñora pepper and bay leaf. Add the potato and cook gently for 5 minutes. Add the peppers and cook for another 1–2 minutes, then add the onion and cook until translucent. Tip in the aubergine and blitzed tomatoes, then bring the sauce to a simmer and cook until the aubergine is soft. Season to taste with salt and add the thyme leaves, then remove from the heat and stir through the remaining olive oil. Remove the ñora and bay leaf before serving.

Shallow-fry the potato rounds in rapeseed oil in a frying pan over a medium heat until golden. Remove from the pan with a slotted spoon and set aside. Drain any excess oil from the frying pan, then add the onion and fry over a medium heat until soft and golden. Add the potatoes back to the pan along with the sobrasada (or pistou) and both paprikas. Season to taste and cook until warmed through.

Fry the eggs separately to your liking, then place them on top of the huevos rotos. Sprinkle with a little parsley and serve.

KIMCHI PANCAKE AND PORK BELLY WITH GOCHUJANG KETCHUP & FRIED EGGS

BY CARAVAN

Founded by three well-travelled Kiwis, this lively and congenial Antipodean restaurant group has seven sites across the city, all of which encourage all-day grazing. The welcoming, eclectic, no-borders menu is the same at all the sites, and good coffee is a given (obsessives can rest easy: Caravan has its own superb roastery). The cavernous hangout on Granary Square Kings Cross was their first site and continues to draw in crowds eager to explore the pick-and-mix menu, with its focus on small plates, salads and grain bowls (alongside sourdough pizza, large plates and puds), and creative iterations of lazy breakfast fare.

SERVES 4

Stock
(makes just over 1 litre/35fl oz)
1.2 litres (40fl oz) water
200ml (7fl oz) soy sauce
1 red chilli
50g (1¾oz) piece of fresh ginger
1 whole garlic bulb, sliced in half horizontally
2 spring onions
4 star anise
20g (¾oz) dried tangerine peel (or use fresh orange peel)
1 cinnamon stick
15 coriander stalks
50g (1¾oz) palm sugar

Gochujang Ketchup
(makes 1 medium jar)
100g (3½oz) gochujang (Korean fermented bean paste)
40ml (1½fl oz) rice wine vinegar
100g (3½oz) tahini
70ml (2¼fl oz) sesame oil
1½ tbsp soy sauce
70g (2½oz) caster sugar
40g (1½oz) confit garlic, mashed with a fork

Pork Belly
800g (1lb 12oz) piece of boneless pork belly
Cold water
Fine sea salt
1 litre (35fl oz) stock (see above)

Stock
Place all the ingredients in a saucepan and bring to the boil. Reduce the heat and simmer for 30 minutes, then remove from the heat and allow to cool. Store in an airtight container in the fridge.

Gochujang Ketchup
Place all the ingredients in a bowl and whisk together to combine. Let stand for 10 minutes to make sure the sugar has dissolved and the garlic has imparted its flavour. The ketchup will keep in a sterilised jar in the fridge for up to 3 weeks.

Slow-cooked Pork Belly
You'll need to start this the day before. Use a very sharp knife to score the skin of the pork at 1cm (½in) intervals. Immerse in a brine made with 100g (3½oz) fine sea salt for every litre (35fl oz) of cold water and leave in the fridge overnight.

Preheat the oven to 170°C (150°C fan/325°F/gas mark 3).

Bring the stock to the boil. Remove the pork from the brine and place in a casserole dish. Pour the hot stock over the pork and cover with baking paper, then seal with foil. Place the pork in the oven and cook for 3½ hours, or until the meat pulls apart easily.

Carefully transfer the pork to a chopping board. Slice off the skin and pull the flesh apart using 2 forks. Put the shredded meat in a dish and spoon over several tablespoons of the stock from the dish. Keep hot.

continued overleaf

Kimchi Pancakes

1½ tbsp tahini
2 tbsp soy sauce
1 egg
130ml (4½fl oz) whole milk
1 tbsp rice wine vinegar
150g (5½oz) plain flour
1 tsp baking powder
260g (9¼oz) kimchi, roughly
   chopped
3 spring onions, finely sliced
Handful of coriander leaves,
   roughly chopped, plus extra
   to garnish
Vegetable oil, for frying

To Serve

8 eggs
Sea salt and black pepper

Kimchi Pancakes

Increase the oven temperature to 180°C (160°C fan/350°F/gas mark 4).

Whisk the tahini, soy sauce, egg, milk and vinegar together in a bowl. Sift in the flour and baking powder and stir until well combined and you have a smooth batter. Add the kimchi, spring onions and coriander, and stir.

Heat a little oil in a 20cm (8in) cast-iron or ovenproof frying pan and pour in half the batter. Cook over a medium heat for a few minutes, then place the pan in the oven for 10 minutes. Remove from the oven, flip the pancake over and return to the oven for a further 5 minutes. Repeat to make a second pancake.

To Serve

When the kimchi pancakes are almost ready, fry the eggs to your liking.

Cut each pancake in half and arrange on plates with the shredded slow-cooked pork and fried eggs. Garnish with coriander leaves and top with a good amount of the gochujang ketchup.

FANCY BACON ROLL

BY DAISY GREEN COLLECTION

SERVES 6

Roti
225g (8oz) self-raising flour,
plus extra for dusting
½ tsp fine sea salt
1 tbsp vegetable oil, plus extra
for brushing and frying
140ml (4¾fl oz) water

Sriracha Hollandaise
250g (9oz) unsalted butter
90ml (3fl oz) egg yolks
(about 4 egg yolks)
1½ tbsp white wine vinegar
and tarragon reduction
(page 260)
Pinch of sea salt
Splash of ice-cold water
80ml (2½fl oz) sriracha

Crispy Shallots
5 banana shallots, thinly sliced
(preferably on a mandolin)
500ml (17fl oz) vegetable oil
Pinch of sea salt

To Assemble & Serve
18 slices of smoked back
bacon
6 very fresh eggs
150g (5½oz) baby spinach
6 roti (see above)
250g (9oz) sriracha hollandaise
(see above)
200g (7oz) crispy shallots
(see above)
Small bunch of spring onions,
finely sliced
3 red chillies, finely sliced
Lemon wedges

Aussie-born Prue Freeman's desire to 'bring relaxed and buzzing Australian food and coffee culture to London' has seen her drop a career in finance to build a food business from scratch that now encompasses over a dozen all-day Antipodean-style cafes and restaurants. Prue (with husband Tom Onions) opened the first Daisy Green café in Marble Arch in 2012 and launched their latest bricks-and-mortar sites in 2023: Johnny Green – named after her father – plus Audrey Green and Larry's Bar at the National Portrait Gallery. With a cross-cultural approach to food and Australia's eclectic culinary landscape, the team's menus are rooted in a commitment to freshness, ethical sourcing and simplicity.

Roti

Sift the flour and salt into a large bowl. Sprinkle over the oil and water, then bring the ingredients together to make a soft dough, adding a little more flour or water if needed. Transfer to a work surface and knead gently until smooth. Cover and leave to rest for about 30 minutes.

On a floured work surface, divide the dough into 6 equal pieces and roll each one into a thin circle about 2mm (⅟₁₆in) thick.

Brush the bottom third of one of the roti with oil and dust with a little extra flour, then fold the oiled third towards the middle. Repeat with the top third and fold inwards again. Give the roti a quarter turn (90 degrees) and repeat the folding process – you should end up with a rough square. Leave to rest while you repeat with the remaining rotis.

Heat a little oil in a heavy-based frying pan over a medium heat. Roll out one of the roti thinly into a circle, then fry on one side until it puffs up and is speckled brown on the underside. Turn it over and fry on the other side for a few minutes until it too is puffed and speckled brown. Remove from the pan, allowing the roti to cool for a few seconds, then fold into quarters. Wrap in a clean tea towel placed in a colander until ready to eat. Repeat until all the roti are cooked. Keep warm.

continued overleaf

Sriracha Hollandaise

Melt the butter in a saucepan and skim off and discard any white solids from the surface. Keep the butter warm.

Put the egg yolks, vinegar reduction, salt and ice-cold water in a heatproof glass bowl that will fit over a small saucepan and whisk for a few minutes until foamy. Half-fill the saucepan with water and bring to a bare simmer. Place the bowl over the pan and whisk constantly for 3–5 minutes until you have a pale and thick sauce.

Remove the bowl from the heat and slowly whisk in the melted butter, bit by bit, until incorporated and you have a creamy hollandaise (if it gets too thick, add a splash of water). Whisk in the sriracha until the hollandaise is a deep orange colour. Keep warm.

Crispy Shallots

Place the shallots and oil in a saucepan over a high heat and cook for 5–6 minutes, until the oil starts to bubble. Reduce the heat to low and cook for 8–10 minutes until the shallots start to turn a light golden brown (pay close attention as they are quick to burn). Using a slotted spoon, transfer the crispy shallots to a plate lined with kitchen paper to drain, and sprinkle with the salt. Any crispy shallots you don't use will keep in an airtight container for a couple of weeks.

To Assemble & Serve

Cook the bacon to your liking (under the grill, in the oven or a frying pan) and poach the eggs (see page 60).

Grab some plates and pile some baby spinach and bacon onto each roti. Place a poached egg on top then spoon the sriracha hollandaise over.

Sprinkle with the crispy shallots, spring onion and chilli, and serve with a lemon wedge for squeezing.

CHILAQUILES

BY CAVITA

SERVES 6

1 litre (35fl oz) rapeseed oil
30 corn tortillas, cut into
   triangles
250g (9oz) sour cream
300g (10½oz) fresh cheese or
   feta (or use Parmesan for a
   stronger flavour), crumbled
½ red onion, finely sliced
1 avocado, diced
15g (½oz) coriander leaves

Tomato Sauce
20–25g dried morita chillies,
   deseeded and ribs removed
1kg (2lb 3oz) ripe tomatoes
2 medium white onions, peeled
   and halved
6 garlic cloves, peeled
150ml (5fl oz) olive oil
500ml (17fl oz) chicken or
   vegetable stock
Sea salt

TIP — *Top the chilaquiles with
fried, scrambled or poached
eggs for a bigger breakfast.
Sliced chorizo or grilled chicken
also work well.*

Mexican food is designated by UNESCO as a cuisine of Intangible Cultural Heritage of Humanity – showcasing and celebrating its complex history is at the heart of chef Adriana Cavita's first London venture. While studying gastronomy in Mexico, she won a cooking competition, the prize for which was a chance to train at the iconic El Bulli in Spain. A stint at celebrated Pujol in Mexico City followed, then a move to London. Her invigorating iterations of Mexico's vibrant, diverse food culture – tacos, tostadas, raw seafood and wood-fired dishes – have placed her at the forefront of London's Mexican food scene.

For the tomato sauce, soak the dried chillies in a bowl of warm water for 10 minutes until softened, then drain.

Meanwhile, heat a large frying pan over a high heat. Add the tomatoes, onions and garlic and roast, turning frequently, until blistered and brown in spots. Transfer to a blender, along with the drained chillies, and blend until smooth. Strain the mixture into a bowl.

Heat the olive oil in a large saucepan over a medium heat. Add the strained tomato mixture and cook for 10 minutes, or until slightly reduced, then add the stock and bring the mixture to the boil. Season to taste and cook for 10 minutes, ensuring the sauce remains quite liquidy (this will prevent the chilaquiles from drying out).

Heat the rapeseed oil in a large, heavy-based saucepan to 170°C (338°F). Working in batches, deep-fry the tortillas until golden and crisp, then drain on kitchen paper to absorb the excess oil.

Add the totopos (fried tortilla chips) to the bubbling tomato sauce and stir together very well.

Immediately transfer the chilaquiles to a serving plate and top them with sour cream, crumbled cheese, red onion, avocado and coriander leaves.

Look at everything as
though you are seeing
it for the first time, with
the eyes of a child, fresh
with wonder.

JOSEPH CORNELL

POACHED TROUT
NIÇOISE SALAD

BY JORGE MARTINEZ, CHARLOTTE STREET HOTEL

SERVES 4

A super-tasty salad, full of flavour, for sunny days. The delicate poached trout adds an extra layer of texture. Niçoise salad is easy to assemble and looks impressive.

100ml (3½fl oz) red wine
    vinegar
100g (3½oz) sugar
400ml (14fl oz) water
400g (14oz) skinless trout
    (we use ChalkStream), cut
    into 3cm (1¼in) squares
    (or use sea trout or salmon
    if unavailable)
300g (10½oz) new potatoes
100g (3½oz) green beans
4 eggs, at room temperature
100g (3½oz) mixed salad
    leaves or gem lettuce
200g (7oz) good-quality cherry
    tomatoes, halved (we use
    Datterini)
10 anchovy fillets in oil
50g (1¾oz) large pitted green
    olives (we use Nocellara)
Good pinch of dried oregano
Sea salt and ground black
    pepper

French Dressing
2 tbsp Dijon mustard
2 tbsp white wine vinegar
150ml (5fl oz) extra virgin olive
    oil

To poach the trout, combine the vinegar, sugar and water in a saucepan and bring to the boil for 1 minute, then remove from the heat. Place the trout in a small non-reactive heatproof container and pour the hot liquor over the top, ensuring that the trout is submerged. Allow to cool. Once cool, remove the trout from the poaching liquor.

To make the French dressing, in a small bowl, whisk together the mustard and white wine vinegar. Slowly whisk in the olive oil until emulsified, then season to taste with salt and pepper.

Place the potatoes in a saucepan of salted water, bring to a simmer and cook for 15 minutes. Add the green beans and cook for a further 5 minutes, or until the vegetables are tender. Drain the vegetables and plunge into ice-cold water. Once cool, drain and set aside. Cut the potatoes in half.

Bring a saucepan of water to the boil and lower in the eggs. Boil for 7 minutes, then plunge into a bowl of ice-cold water to cool. Carefully peel the eggs and cut them in half. Season with salt and black pepper.

In a large mixing bowl, combine the potato and green beans with a good drizzle of the French dressing. Add the salad leaves and gently toss to combine, then tip onto a large serving dish. Place the tomatoes, trout, eggs, anchovies and olives over the salad and finish with another drizzle of the dressing and a sprinkling of dried oregano.

JAMIE OLIVER

MBE

Jamie Oliver is a global phenomenon in food and campaigning. During a 24-year television and publishing career he has sold nearly 50 million books, and his TV series are watched by millions around the world. As a result, Jamie has inspired a generation to cook fresh, delicious food from scratch. His mission to create a happier, healthier world through the joy of food is at the heart of everything he does.

He also likes a good brunch! Jamie says, 'Anything goes at brunch. It's a time to be big, bold and confident. Gather your favourite people together, be hospitable, be generous and above all, be happy.'

And he loves supporting OnePlate: 'It's been a privilege to support this brilliant cause that helps children in developing countries. The joyful, amazing thing about food is that it brings people together and is the best way to share the love.'

JAMIE OLIVER'S AVOCADO & JALAPEÑO HASH BROWN WITH POACHED EGGS

SERVES 4

250g (9oz) ripe cherry
  tomatoes on the vine
2 tbsp olive oil
800g (1lb 12oz) Maris Piper
  potatoes
4 spring onions
2 fresh jalapeños
1 ripe avocado
20g (¾oz) Parmesan
4 large eggs
4 coriander sprigs
1 lime
Sea salt and ground black
  pepper

TIP — *Cooked avocado is utterly delicious; however, it does divide people. If you're not a fan, simply leave it out of the hash brown and serve it fresh on top.*

Preheat the oven to 190°C (170°C fan/375°F/gas mark 5).

Place the tomatoes on a baking tray, drizzle with 1 tablespoon of olive oil, season with salt and pepper, then roast for 30 minutes.

Meanwhile, scrub and coarsely grate the potatoes, then squeeze dry in a clean tea towel. Roughly slice the spring onions and jalapeños (deseeded, if you like), then finely slice the avocado.

Place a large non-stick ovenproof frying pan over a medium heat. Add the potatoes, spring onions, jalapeños, avocado and remaining tablespoon of oil, mix together and cook for 5 minutes, stirring occasionally. Finely grate in half the Parmesan and season with salt and pepper, then pat and flatten everything down into an even layer. Cook for 10 minutes, or until golden and crisp on the bottom, then transfer to the oven for a final 10 minutes.

Meanwhile, poach the eggs to your liking (see page 60). Turn the hash brown out onto a board (it should be the perfect combo of soft and crispy), then grate over the remaining Parmesan. Slice and divide the hash brown between plates, top with the tomatoes and poached eggs, then tear over the coriander leaves. Slice the lime into wedges and serve alongside for squeezing over.

KEJRIWAL

BY DISHOOM

SERVES 1–2

80g (2¾oz) mature Cheddar, grated
1 or 2 thick slices of white bloomer, sourdough or brioche (depending on size and level of hunger)
2 spring onions, chopped
1 green chilli, very finely chopped
1 tsp vegetable oil (optional)
1 or 2 large eggs (1 per slice of toast)
Coarsely ground black pepper
Tomato ketchup, to serve

TIP — *The most convenient way of finishing the eggs here is to use a frying pan that can go in the oven. If you don't have one, fry the eggs until cooked in the pan, then top with the cheese, spring onion, chilli and pepper. The cheese won't melt quite as much, but it will still be delicious. If your frying pan is reliably non-stick you should need little or no oil.*

Styled after the Irani cafés that were once part of the fabric of life in old Bombay, Dishoom has struck gold with an all-day dining formula, launching a proliferation of sites in London and beyond. The trademark sub-continental faded art-deco interior and relaxed approach attracts queues of eager tourists and locals. The fun, vibrant iterations of Bombay fare include the 'Big Bombay full English', their cult bacon naan, Indian-spiced porridge, sharing plates, snacks and grills, which you might pair with an aromatic chai, cooling lassi or something a little stronger.

—

'Fried eggs atop chilli cheese on toast is a favourite of the well-to-do Willingdon Club, the first such Bombay institution to admit Indians. It is reputedly named after the member (not to be confused with the Indian politician Arvind Kejriwal) who, not allowed by his wife to eat eggs at home, kept asking for the dish in his club.'

Let the grated cheese come to room temperature; it needs to be quite soft and workable.

Preheat the oven to 240°C (220°C fan/475°F/gas mark 9). Place a baking tray inside to warm up.

Toast the bread until very lightly browned on both sides. Set aside to cool slightly while you prepare the topping.

Put a small handful of the grated cheese, roughly 1 tablespoon of chopped spring onion and a pinch of green chilli to one side, to be used when you fry the eggs.

Place the remaining cheese, spring onion and green chilli in a bowl, add plenty of black pepper and mix well. Using the back of a spoon (or your fingers), work the cheese mixture into a paste by pressing it firmly into the side of the bowl. Spread this mixture evenly over the toast and press it in, using the back of the spoon, to create a firm, even layer that goes all the way to the edges. Place on the warm tray in the oven and cook for 6–8 minutes until deep golden and bubbling.

Crack the eggs into cups, being careful to keep the yolks intact.

While the chilli cheese toast is cooking, warm an ovenproof frying pan over high heat and, if using, add the oil. Gently tip the eggs into the hot pan and add some black pepper. Top with the reserved cheese, spring onion and green chilli. Place the frying pan in the oven for 2 minutes, or until the cheese is melted and the eggs are cooked but the yolks are still runny.

Carefully slide the eggs onto the chilli cheese toast and serve right away, with plenty of tomato ketchup.

FRIED CHICKEN WITH WAFFLES & HOT HONEY

BY ROB MITCHELL, DRAKE & MORGAN

SERVES 4

4 skinless, boneless chicken
  breasts
200g (7oz) plain flour
1½ tsp paprika
200ml (7fl oz) buttermilk
2 tbsp honey
1 jalapeño, finely sliced
100ml (3½fl oz) olive oil
4 store-bought sweet waffles
2 large avocados, diced
Juice of 1 lemon
60g (2¼oz) crème fraîche
Sea salt and ground black
  pepper

TIP — *If you have time, place the
unfloured butterflied chicken in
a large bowl with the buttermilk,
then cover and chill overnight
in the fridge. The buttermilk will
tenderise the chicken.*

Serving up dishes from the land and sea, Drake & Morgan caters to Londoners across the city. It's easy to get distracted by the incredible cocktail menu here, but don't overlook their weekend brunch offerings.

Preheat the oven to 180°C (160°C fan/350°F/gas mark 4).

Butterfly each chicken breast, then lay each piece between 2 pieces of cling film and bruise with a rolling pin to flatten slightly.

In a shallow bowl, combine the flour, paprika and a pinch each of salt and pepper. Pour the buttermilk into a separate, large bowl.

Dip each chicken piece into the flour mixture, turning to coat lightly, then dip in the buttermilk bowl, again turning to coat. Repeat these steps twice, then place the chicken on a tray and repeat with the remaining chicken pieces.

Combine the honey and a pinch of the jalapeño in a small bowl and set aside to infuse.

Heat the olive oil in a large frying pan over a medium heat. Add one of the coated chicken pieces and fry for 3–4 minutes until the base is a rich golden brown. Turn the chicken over and continue to fry for 2–3 minutes until golden and cooked through. Transfer to a plate lined with kitchen paper to drain, then place the fried chicken on a baking tray in the oven to keep warm while you fry the remaining chicken. If you're not confident that the chicken is cooked all the way through, cook in the oven until the centre of the chicken reaches 75°C (167°F) on a temperature probe or the juices run clear when pierced with a knife.

Spread the sweet waffles out on a separate baking tray and place in the oven to warm through.

Meanwhile, combine the avocado, remaining jalapeño and the lemon juice in a small bowl and season to taste.

Divide the waffles between plates and top with the avocado and fried chicken. Add a spoonful of crème fraîche to each plate and finish with a drizzle of the hot honey.

ONEPLATE: THE AVOCADO PROJECT

KENYA

It would be hard to find a modern brunch menu that doesn't include avocado! One of the most versatile and healthy fruits on the planet, the avocado is also perfect produce to grow in Kenya's warm, tropical climate, and a wonderful addition to the diets of the disadvantaged children that we serve.

Due to numerous challenges of farming traditional crops like maize, and cash crops like coffee and tea, fruit tree farming is now a popular trend in Kenya and with the right environment produces exceptional results.

OnePlate's Avocado Project in Kenya has focused on establishing beautiful Hass-avocados on three acres of land. After preparation, including soil testing and adding nutrients, more than 300 quality certified avocado seedlings were purchased and planted.

A water-drip irrigation system, water tank and stand were installed and OnePlate also invested in additional costs for maintaining the farm.

It is especially exciting that the need for maintenance of orchard facilities, such as fencing, landscaping and walk paths, along with ongoing soil maintenance – adding manure, weeding and pruning – has created numerous jobs for the local community.

The farm is a fantastic training facility to learn about farming and managing produce, and as such has the possibility to make an exceptional long-term impact for children, families and communities.

As the trees burst into stunning bloom, they also provide pollen and nectar for our nearby Bee Project (pages 34 and 407). With hives bustling with busy bees, the flowers are fulfilling a dual purpose; producing fruit and helping bees do their important work.

Similar to the Bee Project, the Avocado Project gives OnePlate the opportunity to change lives in multiple ways, by improving diet and nutrition, livelihoods, income, educational opportunities and building positive futures for hundreds of children and community members.

The orchard is now part of an ongoing food security solution in Kenya. Once the orchard has been successfully fruiting for 10 years, we expect a harvest of more than 1,750 fruit per year, providing food and an income source. What a wonderful bounty to feed our children and communities for many years to come.

BRAISED BEANS, CHICKPEAS, GOAT'S CHEESE & MINT

BY DUCKSOUP

SERVES 4

150ml (5fl oz) extra virgin olive oil, plus extra for drizzling

2 onions, sliced

4 garlic cloves, sliced

2 bay leaves

Pared zest of 1 lemon, plus a good squeeze of juice

100ml (3½fl oz) white wine

500g (1lb 2oz) trimmed fine green beans

50ml (2fl oz) water

250g (9oz) good-quality cooked chickpeas, rinsed

Handful of mint leaves, torn

150g (5½oz) good-quality soft goat's cheese or curd

Sea salt and ground black pepper

The small but mighty Ducksoup restaurant and natural wine bar was opened Clare Lattin and Tom Hill in 2011. The food here is led strictly by the seasons, exploring a diverse range of eating cultures, with a clever cross-continental approach resulting in an exciting menu of small plates that change weekly. This recipe, by Head Chef Tom Lake, is a perfect example of their celebration of quality ingredients. Head to the Little Duck Picklery in Dalston to explore their fermenting endeavours.

Warm the olive oil in a large, heavy-based frying pan over a medium heat, then add the onions, garlic, bay leaves, lemon zest and a good pinch of salt. Sweat down for 15 minutes, or until the onion is tender. Add the wine and boil off the alcohol until reduced slightly.

Add the green beans and water to the pan and stir well, then cook for 10–15 minutes until the beans are just tender. Check the seasoning and add salt to taste and a few twists of black pepper. Transfer the mixture to a large bowl and allow to cool to room temperature.

When ready to serve, combine the bean mixture with the chickpeas, lemon juice and half the torn mint. Taste and adjust the seasoning, if needed. Add a spoonful of the beans and chickpeas to each plate and top with a few blobs of the goat's cheese. Repeat with the remaining beans and chickpeas, and goat's cheese. Finish with the remaining torn mint, a good drizzle of olive oil and some twists of black pepper.

EGGS, CHILLI & CHEESE

BY DUSTY KNUCKLE

SERVES 1–2

3 tbsp Moscatel vinegar (or
    another white wine vinegar
    with 2 tsp sugar added)
1 green chilli, finely sliced
1 spring onion, finely sliced
2 pieces of focaccia, halved
    horizontally
Oil, for frying
2 eggs
2 generous handfuls of grated
    Lincolnshire Poacher or
    mature Cheddar
Handful of coriander leaves
    and tender stalks
Sea salt and ground black
    pepper

Obsessive bakers and childhood friends, Rebecca Oliver and Max Tobias, founded their bakery and social enterprise in 2014 with Daisy Terry, selling bread from a freight container in a Hackney car park. The café and bakery quickly gained a cult following and they upgraded to a larger premises on the same site, now their HQ (they have a second café in Haringey). The fully loaded sandwiches and knockout 'house sour' loaves have acquired legendary status. They continue to run a youth training and mentorship programme and have extended their all-day menu to include woodfired pizzas on selected evenings.

—

'We made this dish the first weekend we opened our container hatch to the public. We now sell up to 180 most Saturdays, which is no easy feat from a small kitchen with just one plancha grill. I'm fairly sure the idea grew from a cheese on toast spin-off, using green chillies, inspired by Meera Sodha's book *Fresh India*. So, thanks, Meera!'

Combine the vinegar (and sugar if using) and a pinch of salt and stir until dissolved. Add the chilli and spring onion and mix well, then set aside for 5 minutes to pickle.

Heat a frying pan over a medium heat and toast the focaccia halves, cut-side down, until lightly browned. Remove to a plate.

Add a drizzle of oil to the pan and fry your eggs (we are not going to tell you how!). When just about ready, season the yolks with salt and pepper and sprinkle the cheese on top. Leave for 20 seconds, then flip so that the cheese touches the pan and starts to melt. Immediately remove with a spatula and place the cheesy eggs on the toasted focaccia halves.

Using a slotted spoon, pile on the pickled spring onion and chilli, dousing your fingertips in the liquid and then flicking it onto the egg. Finish with a generous load of coriander. Season with salt and pepper and eat!

SOURDOUGH FLATBREADS

BY E5 BAKEHOUSE

MAKES 12

Sourdough Leaven
50g (1¾oz) rye starter
100ml (3½fl oz) room-
   temperature water
50g (1¾oz) dark rye flour

Flatbreads
120g (4oz) active sourdough
   leaven (see above)
240ml (8fl oz) whole milk
120ml (4fl oz) hot water (about
   40°C/104°F)
35ml (2 tbsp plus 1 tsp) olive oil
300g (10½oz) strong white
   flour, plus extra for dusting
300g (10½oz) stoneground
   00 flour, sifted
2 tsp salt
2 tsp sugar

TIP — *To keep the flatbreads for longer, place them in a plastic bag while still warm and seal the bag. Store in the fridge for up to 5 days.*

These breads are the perfect introduction to working with sourdough as you get all the flavour and nutritional benefits of sourdough without the pressure of having to make the bread rise... because they're flat! With practice, you will learn how to maintain a sourdough starter and how to read its signals, such as when it's 'healthy' and when it is 'underactive' – both essential skills to becoming an accomplished sourdough baker. The added bonus of sourdough flatbreads vs regular yeasted ones is that they really do last longer.

Feed your starter by mixing it with the water and rye flour, then leave in a warm spot to ferment for at least 3–4 hours until it looks bubbly and active and 'alive'. You can then use it straight away, or put it back into the fridge and use it within 24 hours. Just note that the longer you leave the leaven, the more acidic it will become and this will affect the flavour of your flatbreads.

In a large bowl, combine the rye leaven, milk, hot water and olive oil, then add the flours, salt and sugar. Mix by hand until it comes together into a dough and there are no lumps left. Don't worry about kneading the dough as we are going to use the 'stretch and fold' technique.

Scrape down the edge of the bowl with a spatula or dough scraper, then cover with a damp tea towel and let the dough rest for 3 hours. During that time, stretch and fold the dough every hour, pulling up one side of the dough and folding it over the opposite side, working your way around the bowl.

Once the dough has rested, cut it into 95g (3¼oz) pieces and roll into balls, dusting your hands with a little flour as you go. Cover with a damp tea towel and let the dough rest for another hour.

Preheat the oven to its maximum temperature. Place a pizza stone or the lid of a cast-iron frying pan in the oven to heat up.

Using a rolling pin and a little flour on your worktop, flatten and shape the flatbreads into rounds.

Prepare a container to put the breads in by lining it with a tea towel, top and bottom, to prevent them from drying out.

Working with one flatbread at a time, carefully place it on the pizza stone or cast-iron lid and bake for about 1 minute, until the bread puffs up into a ball (this indicates that the bread has steamed inside). Remove the flatbread as soon as it has just a bit of a colour on the base and no more; otherwise it won't remain soft. Place between the tea towels and repeat with the remaining flatbreads. Enjoy while still warm, or simply reheat in a toaster until they become supple again.

SUMMER PEA & MINT SALAD WITH HOT-SMOKED SALMON AND QUAIL EGGS

BY FAIRMONT WINDSOR PARK

SERVES 3

---

6 quail eggs (we use Burford Brown)
3 slices of sourdough bread
Olive oil, for drizzling
Sea salt

Oven-dried Tomatoes
100ml (3½fl oz) extra virgin olive oil
100g (3½oz) cherry tomatoes, sliced
2 garlic cloves, chopped
1 tsp flaky sea salt
1 thyme sprig

Pea & Mint Salad
100g (3½oz) fresh garden peas
Small handful of mint leaves, chopped
20ml (1½ tbsp) olive oil
Zest and juice of 1 lemon
Pinch of ground sumac
30g (1oz) fennel, shredded

To Serve
Seeds of 1 pomegranate
Small handful of pea shoots
Edible violet flowers
Bunch of radishes, shaved
200g (7oz) hot-smoked salmon, flaked
2–3 tbsp crème fraîche

This is a favourite dish here at Fairmont Windsor Park. We love picking summer vegetables in our Walled Garden and using them to create new recipes. There's nothing better than a light, fresh brunch with juice and tea, and this dish really gets the day going in the right way.

Preheat the oven to 60°C (150°F/lowest gas mark).

Combine the ingredients for the oven-dried tomatoes in a bowl, then spread out on a baking tray. Transfer to the oven for about 4 hours until dehydrated. If you have any leftovers, the tomatoes will keep in a sterilised jar in the fridge for a few weeks.

Boil the quail eggs for 2½ minutes, then refresh in iced water. Peel, cut in half and dust with sea salt.

Combine the pea and mint salad ingredients in a large bowl, then set aside while you toast the bread.

Drizzle the sourdough with olive oil and season with salt. Heat a chargrill pan or frying pan over a high heat, add the sourdough and toast on both sides.

To serve, arrange the pea and mint salad on plates and top with the eggs, pomegranate seeds, pea shoots, flowers, radishes, smoked salmon and crème fraîche. Serve the toasted sourdough on the side.

YOTAM OTTOLENGHI

Credited with enlivening the nation's store-cupboards and expanding Western palates with the likes of sumac and pomegranate molasses, Israeli-born Ottolenghi's impact on the modern culinary landscape has been remarkable. His pioneering approach puts vegetables at the centre of the plate, and the trademark alchemic plates of food at his deli-cafés and restaurants are a riot of colours and textures. The chef, restaurateur and cookery writer's passion for food didn't become his profession until he moved to London from Tel Aviv. He teamed up with Palestinian chef Sami Tamimi and they opened their first London deli in 2002, and the rest – as they say – is history. An Ottolenghi breakfast or brunch is a seductive proposition, with flavours heading to the Middle East one moment, to Asia the next – 'shakshuka is my ideal brunch fare' he tells us.

'I didn't hesitate for a second to donate a recipe for *Brunch in London*. Food brings sustenance and joy to many lives, just like the OnePlate team, which tirelessly works to nourish and empower communities through sustainable farming.'

YOTAM OTTOLENGHI'S FRIED BOILED EGGS IN CHILLI SAUCE

8 large eggs, at room
  temperature
100ml (3½fl oz) vegetable oil
1½ tbsp cornflour
2 onions, finely sliced
1 tsp caraway seeds, toasted
  and lightly crushed
¾ tsp cumin seeds, toasted
  and lightly crushed
1 tbsp tomato paste
2 garlic cloves, crushed
1 dried ancho chilli, torn into
  5–6 pieces, stalks discarded,
  deseeded and soaked in
  250ml (9fl oz) boiling water
  for 20 minutes
1½ tsp pul biber (Turkish chilli
  flakes), or half that amount
  of regular chilli flakes
1 spring onion, finely sliced on
  an angle
Small handful of coriander
  leaves, roughly chopped
Sea salt
Pickled green chillies, to serve

This was a bit of an experiment, but I'm rather pleased with the result; it looks glorious, too. Serve on fresh or grilled bread for a rich, spicy breakfast, or as part of a meze spread, in which case it will feed about eight alongside all the other dishes.

Half-fill a large saucepan with water and bring to the boil, then turn down the heat to medium-high, so the water is boiling gently. Lower in the eggs and cook for 6 minutes. Drain, and leave the eggs under cold running water for a few minutes to stop them cooking any more, then peel.

Heat the oil in a large frying pan over a medium-high heat. Mix the cornflour in a small bowl with a pinch of salt, then toss the peeled eggs in the mix. Once the oil is very hot, carefully lay the eggs in the pan and fry for 3 minutes, turning them a few times until light golden brown all over (there's a chance the eggs may break and spit a bit, so keep a safe distance from the pan and don't worry if they look a bit misshapen). Remove with a slotted spoon and transfer to a plate lined with kitchen paper.

Fry the onions in the same pan for 7 minutes, stirring frequently, until golden brown, then add the caraway, cumin, tomato paste, garlic and teaspoon of salt. Cook for 2 minutes, stirring from time to time, until aromatic. Stir in the ancho chilli and its soaking liquid and the pul biber, cook for about 90 seconds until the sauce thickens and turns a rich, deep red, then return the eggs to the pan to warm through for 30 seconds. Sprinkle over the spring onion and coriander, and serve hot with pickled chillies.

SOBA NOODLES & SHIITAKE WITH SOY & SAKE BROTH

BY GREENBERRY CAFÉ

SERVES 3–4

25g (1oz) kombu dashi powder
240ml (8fl oz) sake
70ml (2¼fl oz) light soy sauce
2 litres (70fl oz) water
250g (9oz) shiitake
  mushrooms, sliced
20g (¾oz) dried wakame
250g (9oz) soba noodles
100g (3½oz) bean sprouts
100g (3½oz) firm tofu, diced
Juice of 2 limes
Bunch of spring onions, finely
  sliced on an angle

This soba noodle dish has been a staple on the menu for some time. It's a great vegan alternative to other noodle broths that are often made with pork and chicken stock. You can pick up all of these ingredients in most supermarkets. If not, pop to your local Asian food store and support your local independent businesses. The shiitake mushrooms and seaweed help to add flavour to the broth, but you can then add any other ingredients you like, such as pak choi.

Place the dashi powder, sake, soy sauce and water in a large saucepan and bring to the boil, then reduce the heat to very low and simmer gently for 20 minutes.

Add the shiitake mushrooms and wakame and return the stock to the boil. Cook for 1–2 minutes, then add the soba noodles and cook according to the packet instructions, which should be about 4 minutes. Now add the bean sprouts, tofu and lime juice and stir well.

Using tongs, divide the noodles, vegetables and tofu between serving bowls, then pour the broth over the top. Garnish with the sliced spring onion and serve.

ONEPLATE: THE MUSHROOM FARM
CAMBODIA

Simple to seed, cultivate and sell, and packed with nutrition and immunity building benefits, mushrooms are 'powerhouse produce'. OnePlate's Mushroom Farm Enterprise has been transformational for communities in Cambodia.

Countless children and communities along the Cambodia-Thailand border are in a perpetual struggle with social and economic difficulties. Children are left alone while their parents go off to find work, and are often abandoned and exploited. Without work and skills, entire communities must resort to begging and looking for food in rubbish dumps to survive.

OnePlate's Mushroom Farm Enterprise has a dual purpose; to produce nutritious food to sustain these at-risk children and create employment and income for families on the Cambodia-Thailand border. The key to success was knowledge, resources and commitment, and with ample encouragement and support, families have embraced the chance to turn their lives around and provide good, healthy food for their children.

To begin this innovative social enterprise opportunity, OnePlate sourced and funded the technical expertise and facilities required to establish a mushroom spawn production facility, developing mushroom packets for growth by the community.

Mushroom packets were distributed to as many families as possible, along with training and materials needed to equip families to grow the mushrooms. Because mushrooms do not need much light, they can be grown inside houses wherever there is space – perfect in a community where many people live in small huts and shacks.

Dany is raising two children on her own because their parents left them behind to work in Thailand. She was given mushroom kits, materials and training and is excited to farm mushrooms for additional income to support the household. Dany says the mushrooms are easy to plant and grow even inside the house, and she can sell them at a higher price than other vegetables. Now she wants to order 1,000 more packets of mushroom spawn to collect more yield every day, to feed themselves, and also to sell to buy school supplies for the children.

For families like Dany's, the Mushroom Farm Enterprise is an empowering way to support themselves independently for years to come.

POSH CRUMPETS

BY GROUCHO CLUB

SERVES 4

2 tbsp rapeseed oil
160–180g (5¾–6¼oz) wild
    mushrooms, cleaned and cut
    into even-sized pieces
1 tbsp chopped parsley
4 duck eggs
4 crumpets (see page 320 for
    homemade), toasted
Softened butter, for spreading
Sea salt and ground black
    pepper

For the dressing
1½ tsp HP (brown) sauce
1 tbsp rapeseed oil
1 tsp cider vinegar

Created as an 'antidote to stuffy gentlemen's clubs' and refuge for creative luminaries in the 1980s, this Soho members club has a fabled history. And now one of the city's favourite chefs and restaurateurs Mark Hix MBE (himself a decades-long member of the club, much-adored for his modern British cooking and art-filled dining rooms), has been brought on board to oversee the epicurean offerings.

—

'We serve this dish at the Groucho Club and I often enjoy it at home for breakfast or a snack, if I've been out on a forage. The curiosity of crumpets on the breakfast menu always draws people in, as I think most people will admit to enjoying a crumpet. They make the perfect brunch base for eggs and, in this case, some seasonal wild mushrooms.'

Heat half the rapeseed oil in a frying pan over a medium heat, add the mushrooms and season. Cook for 2–3 minutes, then remove from the heat and stir through the parsley.

Meanwhile, lightly fry the duck eggs in the remaining oil to your liking, lightly seasoning them as they are cooking.

To make the dressing, whisk the HP sauce, oil and vinegar together, along with a splash of water.

Butter the toasted crumpets, top each with a duck egg and transfer to warmed serving plates. Spoon the mushrooms around the crumpets and drizzle with a little of the dressing. Serve immediately.

POLLO 'NDUJA

BY HARRY'S DOLCE VITA

125g (4½oz) heritage tomatoes
1 garlic bulb
2 tsp rapeseed oil
1 skinless, boneless chicken
  breast, lightly bashed
1 thick-cut slice rye sourdough
  bread
2 slices of Parma ham
90g (3oz) 'nduja cream
  (see below)
Basil leaves, to serve

'Nduja Cream
1 garlic bulb
100ml (3½fl oz) double cream
50g (1¾oz) mascarpone
25g (1oz) crème fraîche
1 tsp sea salt flakes
100g (3½oz) n'duja, at room
  temperature
2 tbsp water

TIP — *This will make more
'nduja cream than you need.
Store in the fridge for up to
3 days.*

In the heart of Knightsbridge sits Harry's Dolce Vita, a polished restaurant inspired by 1950s Italy serving up seasonal dishes cooked with care and plated with passion. It's a stone's throw from Harrods, so the perfect place to indulge after a spot of shopping.

Preheat the oven to 120°C (110°C fan/250°F/gas mark ½). Place the tomatoes in an oven dish and slow-roast for about 1 hour, until collapsed.

Increase the oven temperature to 200°C (180°C fan/400°F/gas mark 6).

Slice the garlic bulb in half horizontally, wrap in foil then roast in the oven for 1 hour until soft. Squeeze out the flesh and measure out 25g (1oz) for the 'nduja cream and set aside. Store any remaining garlic in the fridge for a few days (it's great spread on toast).

To make the 'nduja cream, combine the cream, mascarpone, crème fraîche and salt in a bowl and set aside.

Heat a frying pan over a medium heat, add the 'nduja and all of its oil and the roasted garlic and cook, stirring constantly, for 5–6 minutes until the 'nduja is cooked through and starting to crisp. Add the water and mix well, then pour the 'nduja into the cream mixture, whisking to combine. Keep warm.

Heat the rapeseed oil in a heavy-based frying pan over medium-high heat, add the chicken and cook for 7–8 minutes on each side until cooked through and golden brown. Remove from the pan and cut the chicken into 3 even-sized pieces.

Toast the bread and generously top with some of the 'nduja cream. Add half the chicken, then the Parma ham. Spoon over another layer of 'nduja cream, then add the remaining chicken, some slow-roasted tomatoes and a few basil leaves before serving.

What counts in life is not
the mere fact that we have
lived. It is what difference
we have made to the
lives of others that will
determine the significance
of the life we lead.

NELSON MANDELA

SOCCA

BY HELMA

SERVES 8

Fermented Runner Beans
250g (9oz) runner beans, cut
 into bite-sized pieces
1 litre (35fl oz) water
50g (1¾oz) Himalayan sea salt
Pinch of black peppercorns
Pinch of coriander seeds
1 garlic clove
1 thyme sprig

Socca
300g (10½oz) gram flour
600ml (20fl oz) water
Pinch of sea salt
Pinch of ground turmeric
1 tbsp oil per crêpe, for frying

Slaw
1 red cabbage, finely sliced
200g (7oz) curly kale, torn
Handful of picked dill fronds
Handful of parsley leaves
½ bunch of spring onions,
 finely sliced
Zest and juice of 1 lemon
2–3 tbsp olive oil
Pinch of Aleppo chilli
Sea salt and ground black
 pepper

The duo behind Helma café and wine shop in East London, Swedish Therese (Tess) Gustafsson and Georgian Kosta Chkadua, met while working at London's Zetter Restaurant in 2006. Helma is a conflation of their children's names, Henry and Alma, and their café is a convivial set-up, serving predominantly plant-based food and natural wines (expect plenty of delicious bottles from Kosta's home country). Nourishing dishes from the all-day menu feature an abundance of homemade preserves and ferments, from kimchi to kombucha and cultured butter, and their signature Helma wrap is brunch heaven.

—

'We think this is a great dish, as it's easily adaptable according to the season and what you have in your pantry or fridge. You can use kraut or any lacto-fermented vegetable, but we love these fermented runner beans.'

Fermented Runner Beans

Place the runner beans in a large sterilised glass jar.

Combine the water and salt in a jug and stir until the salt is dissolved, then pour the brine over the beans in the jar, making sure the beans are completely submerged. Add the peppercorns, coriander seeds, garlic and thyme sprig, then seal with the lid and gently shake the jar. Allow the beans to ferment for 1 week.

Socca

Whisk together the gram flour, water, salt and turmeric in a large bowl, then leave to rest in the fridge overnight.

The next day, heat a frying pan over a medium heat with a generous amount of oil. Let it get nicely hot, then add a small ladleful of batter and cook for 1–2 minutes on each side until golden, turning once. Repeat to make 8 socca.

Slaw

Combine the ingredients in a bowl and season to taste.

continued overleaf

Tempeh & Carrot

200g (7oz) tempeh, torn into chunks
1 garlic clove, grated
Pinch of ground turmeric
Pinch of sea salt
2 tbsp olive oil
2 roasted carrots, cut into sticks
2 tsp apricot harissa

Green Tahini

150g (5½oz) spinach, leaves washed
¼ bunch of basil
¼ bunch of dill
½ bunch of chives
½ bunch of parsley
Good squeeze of maple syrup
60ml (4 tbsp) lemon juice
½ roasted garlic bulb (see page 156)
125ml (4¼fl oz) olive oil
Good pinch of sea salt
250g (9oz) tahini

To Serve

150g (5½oz) dukkah, ideally hazelnut-based
Coriander cress (optional)
Kale and spring onion salad (optional)

TIP — You can use any of your favourite soft herbs in the green tahini, or whatever you have in the garden and/or fridge.

Tempeh & Carrot

Toss together the tempeh, garlic, turmeric and salt in a bowl. Heat the oil in a frying pan over a medium heat, add the tempeh mixture and fry for 3 minutes until nice and golden. Transfer to a bowl, add the roasted carrot and apricot harissa and toss to combine.

Green Tahini

Place all the ingredients except the tahini in a high-speed blender and blend until smooth. Add the tahini and blitz again, adding a little water, if necessary, to loosen.

To Assemble

Divide the socca between plates and spread with a generous spoon of green tahini. Top with the slaw, tempeh and carrot, fermented beans and dukkah, garnish with coriander cress and serve with a kale and spring onion salad, if you like.

FLATBREADS WITH FERMENTED HOT HONEY BUTTER

BY KURO EATERY

MAKES 5

Fermented Honey
200g (7oz) good-quality honey
6 garlic cloves, crushed

Hot Honey Butter
50g (1¾oz) butter
75g (2½oz) fermented honey
(see above)
1–2 tbsp chilli flakes,
depending on how much heat
you like

Flatbreads
200ml (7fl oz) lukewarm water
12g (½oz) fresh yeast
1 tbsp good-quality olive oil
15g (½oz) caster sugar
300g (10½oz) strong white
flour, plus extra for dusting
15g (½oz) fine sea salt

To Serve
Good-quality goat's cheese,
Gorgonzola, Barkham Blue
or other funky cheese
Snipped chives

TIP — *You can use regular
honey to make the hot honey
butter, but only cook the mixture
for 3 minutes.*

*Try adding fermented honey to
fried chicken, salad dressings,
or simply drizzle it over cheese.*

With its elegant, minimalist aesthetic and thoughtfully composed menu, it's little wonder that Kuro is one of the most sought-after tables in west London. The menus are designed for sharing and their goat's cheese flatbread is the talk of the town. A delicious slab of salty cheese atop pillowy dough, drizzled in sticky-sweet fermented honey and chilli flakes.

Can't get a table? Make sure to check out their bakery and coffee shop on the same little corner of Notting Hill Gate. (Kuro Coffee's iced matcha lattes and the Bakery's sākuro pastries are veritable Instagram sensations.)

Fermented Honey

Combine the honey and garlic in a sterilised glass jar and leave to ferment in a warm spot for 1 week. Stir the mixture daily and ensure that the garlic remains submerged in the honey. The honey is ready when it becomes thinner and has a slightly acidic taste. Store, covered in the fridge for up to 1 month.

Hot Honey Butter

Melt the butter in a small saucepan. Add the fermented honey and chilli flakes and simmer for 5 minutes, stirring constantly. Remove from the heat and allow the honey to cool to room temperature. Store in a jar in the fridge for up to 1 week.

Flatbreads

Combine the water, yeast, olive oil and sugar in the bowl of a stand mixer until everything is dissolved. Combine the flour and salt in a separate bowl, then add this to the yeast mixture. With the dough hook attached, knead on low speed for 10 minutes, making sure the dough doesn't overheat.

Tip the dough onto a floured work surface and form into a ball by tucking the sides underneath the dough. Transfer to a greased bowl and prove in the fridge for at least 2 hours but ideally overnight.

Divide the dough equally into 5 pieces and shape into balls. Place on a floured tray until ready to use. (The dough can be prepared in advance and kept in the fridge for up to 2 days.)

continued overleaf

To Assemble & Serve

Preheat the oven to 200°C (180°C fan/400°F/gas mark 6).

Heat a cast-iron frying pan that has a lid over a high heat until scorching hot. Roll out one of the dough balls on a floured surface into a 15cm (6in) disc. Drop the flatbread into the hot pan and cover with the lid. Cook on each side for 2 minutes, then top the bread with a generous slice of cheese. Transfer the pan to the oven, uncovered, and cook for 2 minutes, or until the cheese warms up and starts to melt.

Remove the pan from the oven and blast the cheese with a blowtorch, if you have one (or serve it as it is). Drizzle with a good quantity of the hot honey butter and a pinch of snipped chives. Repeat with the remaining dough balls.

The flatbreads are best served warm, so wait for a couple of minutes before digging in to the scorching-hot cheese.

CROQUE MADAME WITH BLACK TRUFFLE

BY HIDEAWAY LONDON

SERVES 4

---

8 slices of sourdough bread,
  1cm (½in) thick
1 tbsp Dijon mustard
200g (7oz) Gruyère, coarsely
  grated
8 slices of sandwich ham,
  such as Wiltshire
1 black truffle

Garlic Butter
100g (3½oz) salted butter,
  softened
1 small garlic clove, minced

Béchamel
500ml (17fl oz) whole milk
1 clove
Pinch of ground mace
Pinch of freshly grated nutmeg
50g (1¾oz) unsalted butter
40g (1½oz) plain flour
Pinch of sea salt
150g (5½oz) Gruyère, grated
15g (½oz) Dijon mustard
4 egg yolks

To Serve
4 eggs (we use Cacklebean)
Salted butter, for frying the
  eggs
Flaky sea salt (we use Maldon)
Ground black pepper

A boutique café in Mayfair and the little sister of Ollie Dabbous' Michelin-starred restaurant HIDE, Hideaway creates stunningly playful patisserie, sandwiches and waffles that see visitors travel from far and wide.

To make the garlic butter, combine the ingredients in a bowl and keep at room temperature.

To make the béchamel, pour the milk into a saucepan and bring to the boil, then remove from the heat, add the spices, cover and allow to infuse for 30 minutes. Strain the milk into a jug.

Melt the butter in a saucepan over a low heat and add the flour, whisking to combine, until a roux forms. Add the milk gradually, whisking constantly until smooth, then bring to the boil, whisking constantly, and cook until thickened. Remove from the heat and whisk in the salt, Gruyère and mustard. Finally, whisk in the egg yolks and check the seasoning.

Preheat the oven to 180°C (160°C fan/400°F/gas mark 4) and the grill until medium-hot.

Spread both sides of the bread slices generously with the garlic butter and grill until golden on one side. Make sure you use pieces next to each other as pairs for the sandwich; they must match perfectly.

Lay the bread, toasted-side down, on a tray and spread half the slices (these will be the bases) lightly with the Dijon mustard, then top generously with some of the Gruyère, 2 slices of the ham, some truffle shavings, followed by the remaining Gruyère. Top with the other matching slices of bread, toasted-side up. Push down to compact and secure the sandwich.

Spread the top of the croque with the béchamel neatly and generously, then glaze under the grill until golden. Transfer to the oven for a further 5 minutes to ensure the filling is warmed through and the cheese has melted.

Meanwhile, fry the eggs gently in salted butter and season lightly with flaky sea salt and black pepper once they are cooked.

Divide the croque Madames between plates and top with the fried eggs. Finish with extra shavings of truffle.

ONEPLATE: THE BAKERY PROJECT

KENYA

Every day, talented baker, Timothy, awakes at 3am, proudly puts on his spotless white baker's uniform, dons his sky high hat and sets off to work in his newly refurbished bakery kitchen in north-west Kenya. As he fires up his commercial ovens for another day of work, his wide smile of delight shows how much he loves his work, helping feed the children we serve.

Watching Timothy quickly and effortlessly knead and hand shape hundreds of mouth-watering buns and loaves, it's hard to believe he has not been baking his whole life. It is his joy and passion to create bread products for the children and for local retail sale, and to know he is helping to feed the community.

OnePlate's Bakery Project has contributed to transforming the lives of hundreds of local children, and providing important variety in their diet. Originally created as a self-sustaining fundraising model to help care for 100 children, this pilot program quickly succeeded in its three main objectives: to provide bread for the children in the home and school, to teach them how to bake, and sell the bread locally.

Transitioning from pilot program to a full commercial enterprise, the bakery was moved to new premises and had floor tiling, plumbing, new benchtop fixtures and a full fit-out of commercial equipment, including industrial ovens, a bread mixer and slicer, proof boxes, trays and a weighing scale. This is a first for this region in Kenya. As a result, the bakery is expanding from producing 300 loaves per day, to more than 1,000 loaves.

The bakery not only feeds the children, but serves as a business in south-west Kenya, producing and selling high-end baked goods to retail and wholesale customers. This is also a good income stream to support educational costs for the children.

To further improve opportunities for social enterprise in the community, the bakery business offers additional training classes, in the hope of encouraging local people into a baking career.

OMELETTE CURRY

BY KARAN GOKANI, HOPPERS LONDON

SERVES 2

2 tbsp oil
¼ tsp fenugreek seeds
   (optional)
100g (3½oz) finely chopped
   red onion (about 1 small)
2 tsp minced garlic
1 tsp minced ginger
½ tsp ground turmeric
1½ tsp unroasted curry powder
¾ tsp chilli powder
300g (10½oz) ripe tomatoes
   (about 2 large), finely sliced
8–10 curry leaves
1 green chilli, cut lengthways
200ml (7fl oz) coconut milk
1½ tsp salt
Handful of coriander leaves,
   to garnish
Crispy fried onions, to garnish

Omelette
1 tbsp unsalted butter
80g (2¾oz) finely chopped red
   onion
4 large eggs, beaten
100g (3½oz) finely chopped
   ripe tomatoes
2 green chillies, finely chopped
2 tbsp finely chopped
   coriander
6–8 curry leaves, finely
   chopped
½ tsp salt
½ tsp freshly ground black
   pepper

Karan Gokani, the co-founder of the well-loved Hoppers restaurant group, grew up in Mumbai and moved to London in 2005. It wasn't long before his passion for food led him to a career in hospitality, and this passion was well-placed, with Hoppers receiving a Michelin Bib Gourmand in its first year. This warming brunch dish is a perfect example of the Sri Lankan and South Indian dishes they are so well known for.

Heat the oil in a heavy-based frying pan over a medium heat. Add the fenugreek seeds, if using, and swirl for 15 seconds, then add the onion and fry until light brown, about 4–5 minutes. Add the garlic and ginger, followed by the turmeric, curry powder and chilli powder. Cook for a minute, then add the tomatoes, curry leaves and chilli. Cook for 10–12 minutes until the tomato is jammy and there are bubbles of oil on the surface – keep stirring the mixture to ensure it doesn't catch on the base of the pan.

Meanwhile, to make the omelette, melt the butter in a non-stick frying pan over a medium heat until it begins to foam. Add the onion and sauté until soft and light brown. In a bowl, whisk the remaining ingredients together until frothy, then pour the mixture over the onion. Swirl around the pan for a few seconds until the egg just begins to set. Using a spatula, carefully fold the egg into a half-moon shape, then reduce the heat and move the omelette to one side of the pan. Cook for 2–3 minutes, then flip over and cook for another 1–2 minutes. Slide the omelette onto a plate.

Add the coconut milk and enough water to the curry to achieve your preferred consistency; I like it quite thick and creamy. Reduce the heat to low and simmer for 3–4 minutes, then season to taste with the salt.

Gently slip the omelette into the curry and simmer for a couple of minutes, to heat through. Garnish with coriander leaves and crispy fried onions and serve.

BLACK TRUFFLE & IBÉRICO HAM WELSH RAREBIT

BY ALEX DILLING, ALEX DILLING AT HOTEL CAFÉ ROYAL

SERVES 2

240ml (8fl oz) Guinness
100g (3½oz) Comté, roughly chopped
75g (2½oz) mature Cheddar, roughly chopped
15g (½oz) plain flour
10g (⅓oz) fresh breadcrumbs
1 tbsp Dijon mustard
1 tsp Worcestershire sauce
40ml (2½ tbsp) whole milk
1 egg, plus 1 egg yolk
1 tsp sea salt
15g (½oz) chopped black truffle
2 thick slices of brown bread, such as granary or sourdough
4 slices of Ibérico ham

To serve
Handful of rocket leaves (or green leaves of your choice)
Lemon juice, to taste
Olive oil, to taste
Pinch of sea salt

London-born Alex Dilling worked with culinary luminaries including Alain Ducasse in New York and Hélène Darroze at The Connaught, before taking the helm at the acclaimed The Greenhouse in London where he won a multitude of plaudits for his flawless, elegant modern French cooking and reworking of classic Gallic dishes such as pâté de campagne. Less than a year after opening his first self-titled restaurant at Hotel Café Royal in Mayfair, it was awarded 2 Michelin stars – an astounding feat. Expect napery and book well ahead: this is the pinnacle of destination dining.

Reduce the Guinness in a saucepan over a medium heat until sticky – this will take a few minutes. Transfer to a food processor, add the Comté, Cheddar, flour, breadcrumbs, mustard and Worcestershire sauce and blitz to combine.

Bring the milk to the boil in a small saucepan, then pour into the food processor and blitz until the mixture is quite smooth. Leave the mixture to cool for 10–15 minutes, then stir through the whole egg, egg yolk, salt and truffle.

Put the bread in the toaster, and only lightly toast. Preheat the grill to high.

Lightly dress the rocket leaves with lemon juice, salt and olive oil, to taste, then place on one side of a serving plate.

Generously spread the cheese mixture onto the toast, then grill until golden – this won't take long, so watch it carefully. Plate the Welsh rarebit next to the salad, dress with the Ibérico ham and serve.

CLARA'S PASTA ESTIVA

BY IDA

SERVES 4

400–500g (14–18oz) short
   ridged pasta, such as rigatoni,
   paccheri or penne
4 handfuls of the reddest,
   juiciest vine cherry tomatoes
   you can find (unless you
   are lucky enough to grow
   the pleated cuore di bue, or
   oxheart, variety which Clara
   uses)
3 tbsp extra virgin olive oil
1 garlic clove, peeled
¼ small red onion, peeled
About 100g (3½oz) Parmesan
   or pecorino, grated, plus extra
   to serve
½ red chilli, deseeded
Handful of basil leaves, to
   serve
Sea salt

With roots respectively in Tuscany and Le Marche, Simonetta Wenkert and her husband, Avi Reichenbach, opened Ida in north-west London's Queens Park in 2007. It became a badly kept secret that their cosy dining room was home to some of the best home-style Italian food in London, inspired by Avi's mother Ida and the recipes she taught her son, and they have won a multitude of awards for their fresh, handmade pasta and gnocchi, and their famous ragù.

—

Simonetta says: 'My sister-in-law, Clara's holiday cooking is simple food at its best. And nothing, to me at least, encapsulates this philosophy as much as her pasta estiva. It's also the perfect brunch dish, because it doesn't involve slaving over a hot stove, and is light enough to be enjoyed by those who don't feel especially hungry in the mornings. The 'sauce' is more of a blitzed smoothie, emulsified with plenty of garlic and oil, and is shockingly tasty when used to dress freshly cooked pasta. And, of course, it can be prepared in advance, but I wouldn't recommend keeping it longer than half a day in the fridge, as the tomatoes will start to oxidise, and it will lose its almost pressé taste.

Pasta is my life – declared our middle daughter, Fiammetta, extravagantly, when she took her first forkful of this dish. And it was hard to disagree.'

Fill your largest saucepan with water and bring to the boil. Once it boils, add enough salt so that it tastes like seawater, or even saltier, and drop the pasta in.

Place the remaining ingredients (except the basil leaves) and a pinch of salt, in a blender or similar, and whizz until you have a shiny, smoothie-like sauce, the colour of watermelon flesh.

When the pasta is the right side of al dente, drain it and tip it into a large salad bowl.

Quickly stir the sauce through the pasta, and serve immediately with torn basil on top and extra Parmesan on the table.

DIANA HENRY

Diana Henry grew up with three siblings in the Northern Irish countryside, in a home where good food was always on the table, and she developed an adventurous palate. Travel to distant shores, however, was something she could only dream about, until at the age of 15 she travelled to France as an exchange student – a formative experience which kicked off a love for travel. Training as a journalist after studying English at Oxford, she went on to work in TV, before swapping studios for a food writing career when she became a mother. Henry is now widely considered one of the UK's finest food writers, having penned 12 cookbooks and a longstanding weekly column for the *Telegrap*h. Sustenance, abundance and comfort are synonymous for Henry, and her cookbooks are the antithesis of fancy, trend-driven food.

In her trademark evocative style, she communicates her innate understanding and appreciation of the simple pleasures of eating well, sharing OnePlate's passion for passing on this appreciation to everyone: 'access to good food should be a right, not a privilege'.

DIANA HENRY'S ASPARAGUS, RICOTTA & 'NDUJA ON TOAST

SERVES 4

2 tbsp extra virgin olive oil, plus a little extra for drizzling
80g (2¾oz) 'nduja
1 small garlic clove, grated to a purée
200g (7oz) asparagus spears, trimmed
4 slices of sourdough bread
100g (3½oz) ricotta
Sea salt and ground black pepper

Blissfully simple. You can use purple sprouting broccoli instead of asparagus when it's in season.

Heat the oil in a frying pan over a low heat and add the 'nduja, using the back of a wooden spoon to gently break it down – it's really important that you don't burn it, but rather allow it to melt slowly (there will still be some meaty lumps in it). Stir in the garlic purée. Turn off the heat.

Steam or microwave the asparagus until only just tender, checking for doneness with the point of a knife. Put the asparagus in a warm tea towel – this keeps it warm and also absorbs the moisture – and toast the bread.

Spread the ricotta thickly on each slice of toast, put the asparagus on top (cut the asparagus in half if they're very large) and season. Gently reheat the 'nduja and spoon it over each toast. Serve immediately.

VEGETABLE SHAWARMA TACOS WITH PILPELCHUMA

BY KAPARA

Pilpelchuma Paste
10 garlic cloves
100g (3½oz) paprika
1 tbsp cumin seeds
1½ tsp caraway seeds
10g (2 tsp) salt
600ml (20fl oz) vegetable oil

Vegetable Shawarma
2 sweetheart cabbages, leaves separated
1 celeriac, sliced 1cm (½in) thick
500ml (17fl oz) pilpelchuma paste (see above)
200g (7oz) portobello mushrooms

To Serve
Corn or flour tortillas, warmed
Tahini, for drizzling
Chilli pickle (or any pickle you like)

Bringing the laid-back vibes of Tel-Aviv to Soho, Kapara is a place where the soundtrack is debaucherous and the food is a spectrum of Middle Eastern flavours.

Pilpelchuma Paste
Place all the ingredients except the oil in a food processor and blitz to a fine paste. With the motor running, slowly drizzle in the oil until you have a loose paste. Store any leftover pilpelchuma in a jar in the fridge and use as a base for stews, marinades and sauces.

Vegetable Shawarma
Bring a large saucepan of heavily salted water to the boil. Add the cabbage leaves and cook for a minute or two until al dente, then remove with a slotted spoon and place in a large bowl. Add the celeriac to the boiling water and cook for about 10 minutes until al dente, then drain and add to the cabbage. When the vegetables are cool enough to handle, add the pilpelchuma paste and mushrooms and massage the paste into the veg. Set aside to marinate for 2 hours.

Preheat a barbecue or turn on your grill to high.

Push the marinated vegetables onto long metal skewers to form a doner-kebab-like shape. Start with a cabbage leaf, followed by a mushroom, then a slice of celeriac and repeat, packing the vegetables very tightly and brushing with the leftover marinade in the bowl as you go. You should have 4–6 skewers.

Cook the kebabs over direct heat on the barbecue, or under the grill, turning frequently, until the outside is coloured and starting to char.

To Serve
Divide the shawarma between tortillas, drizzle with tahini and top with your choice of pickle.

OX HEART LAAP

BY KILN

200g (7oz) ox heart (see Note)
20ml (1½ tbsp) vegetable oil
100ml (3½fl oz) chicken stock
1½ tbsp fish sauce
20g (¾oz) coriander leaves
20g (¾oz) Thai shallot (or
  banana shallot), finely sliced
10g (¾oz) lemongrass, finely
  chopped

Laap spice
2 tsp coriander seeds
1 star anise
20g (¾oz) large dried red
  chillies
1 tsp Sichuan peppercorns
1 tsp cumin seeds
1 tsp Thai cardamom pods
  (or green cardamom pods)
1 tsp black peppercorns

To serve
Steamed rice
Sliced red chilli

NOTE — *The dish is pretty
versatile – feel free to swap the
ox heart for beef or venison.*

A synthesis of British ingredients and northern regional Thai flavours cooked over fire and embers is the order of service at Kiln in Soho. Aromatic, fragrant, spicy, pungent and deeply savoury small plates... there's enough sensorial stimulation to make your head spin. Try the aged lamb and cumin skewers, then go for a curry, or opt for claypot baked glass noodles with pork, or maybe raw prik laap at lunch.

Start by removing any sinew from the heart, then use a cleaver to finely chop. Set aside.

To make the laap spice, dry-roast the spices in a frying pan over a medium heat until fragrant, then remove from the pan and allow to cool. Using a mortar and pestle, pound the spices to a powder.

Heat a wok or heavy-based frying pan over a high heat, add the oil and when it starts to smoke, add the ox heart and stir-fry for a couple of minutes until almost completely cooked. Add 2 tablespoons of the laap spice and quickly stir it through – if it catches on the base of the wok or pan, it will render it bitter. Add the chicken stock and allow to simmer for about 3 minutes, or until the ox heart is cooked through.

Season with the fish sauce, then transfer to a serving bowl and add the coriander, shallot and lemongrass. Serve with steamed rice and chopped chilli.

The greatest gift
someone can give to
another is the gift of
unconditional love.

MAMA CONOSLER

COURGETTE & PECORINO SARDO FRITTERS WITH POACHED EGGS

BY HEAD CHEF ALESSANDRO GRANO, LA FROMAGERIE

SERVES 2

250g (9oz) green courgette (zucchini)
2 pinches of table salt
120g (4¼oz) plain flour
150ml (5fl oz) water
2 medium eggs
50g (1¾oz) pecorino sardo, finely grated
50g (1¾oz) Parmigiano Reggiano, finely grated
½ tsp baking powder
1 tbsp finely chopped parsley leaves
1 tbsp finely chopped mint leaves
2 spring onions, finely sliced, plus extra to serve
2 tbsp vegetable oil
Sea salt and ground black pepper

To Serve
2 poached eggs (see page 61)
Handful of parsley leaves
50g (1¾oz) pecorino sardo, finely grated

Founder of La Fromagerie, Patricia Michelson, first started trading cheese from her garden shed, after she mistakenly ordered an entire 35kg wheel of Beaufort Chalet d'Alpage in the alpine resort of Meribel and drove it back to London. A stall at Camden Market soon followed, and she opened her first artisan cheese shop in Highbury in 1991. La Fromagerie Marylebone followed in 2002 with a cheese and wine bar, café and food shop. In 2017 La Fromagerie Bloomsbury opened on Lambs Conduit Street with a restaurant and food shop. All of them have their signature walk-in cheeserooms. Head to Marylebone or Bloomsbury for brunch – the croque monsieur and madame are superlative.

Coarsely grate the courgette using a large grater, then place in a bowl, mix through the table salt and set aside for 15–20 minutes.

Empty the courgette into a clean tea towel and squeeze out all the excess moisture.

In a large mixing bowl, stir together the flour and water until well combined. Add the eggs, grated cheeses, baking powder, herbs and spring onions, and mix well. Add the courgette, season with salt and pepper and gently mix to combine.

Heat the vegetable oil in a large non-stick frying pan over a medium heat. Scoop a tablespoon of the batter into the pan, then repeat, leaving 2–3cm (¾–1¼in) between scoops as they spread to form small fritters (the batter should yield 6 fritters). Cook for 2–3 minutes on each side until golden and cooked all the way through.

Serve the fritters topped with poached eggs, then scatter with parsley leaves, spring onions and the grated pecorino.

SCRAMBLED TOFU ON SOURDOUGH TOAST

BY LINNÆAN

SERVES 2

125g (4½oz) firm tofu, drained
12g (½oz) nutritional yeast
Small pinch of ground turmeric
Small pinch of fine sea salt
1 tsp vegan butter
Pinch of kala namak (black salt)
Sourdough bread, toasted, to
  serve

To Serve (optional)
Cherry tomatoes
Sliced avocado
Sautéed spinach
Shelled hemp seeds
Chilli flakes

A café, restaurant, spa and apothecary combined, Linnæan is a place for eating well and feeling well. A plant-rich menu set within their stunning dining room will ensure you feel nourished for the rest of the day.

Crumble the tofu into a bowl or use a fork to roughly mash it. Add the nutritional yeast, turmeric and salt, and mix to combine.

Melt the vegan butter in a saucepan over a medium heat and add the tofu mixture. Cook, stirring constantly, for 5 minutes, or until the water from the tofu has nearly evaporated and the mixture resembles scrambled eggs. Turn off the heat and season with the kala namak, to taste.

Divide the scrambled tofu between slices of toasted sourdough and top with your choice of tomatoes, avocado, spinach, hemp seeds and chilli flakes.

RED-BRAISED PORK BELLY RICE BOWL

BY LUCKY & JOY

SERVES 4

Red-braised Pork Belly
2 tbsp neutral oil
500g (1lb 2oz) skinless pork belly,
  cut into 2cm (¾in) chunks
4 tbsp sugar
4 knobs of fresh ginger, sliced
4 garlic cloves, sliced
3 spring onions, cut into batons
150ml (5fl oz) Shaoxing wine
75ml (2½fl oz) light soy sauce
1½ tbsp dark soy sauce
1 cinnamon stick
2 star anise
2 bay leaves
200ml (7fl oz) water

Pickled Cucumber
1 cucumber
1 tsp salt
Knob of fresh ginger, grated
1 garlic clove, grated
50ml (2fl oz) rice vinegar
10ml (2 tsp) toasted sesame oil
2 tbsp golden syrup

Pickled Carrot
2 carrots, julienned
2 tbsp golden syrup
1 tsp salt
4 tbsp rice vinegar
knob of fresh ginger, grated

To Serve
4 eggs
200g (7oz) steamed sushi rice
50g (1¾oz) crispy shallots
1 red chilli, sliced
Handful of coriander leaves
2 tbsp toasted sesame seeds
Splash of rice vinegar

Bristol-born Ellen, chef and founder of Lucky & Joy, spent years working in the kitchen at Moro, the much-loved Moorish-influenced restaurant in East London, before setting up the Art of Dining supper club and developing a passion for Chinese food. Exploring the US and China with her best friend Pete Kelly (now business partner) led to her developing a style altogether her own, a joyful conflation of influences and a celebration of the diversity of Chinese regional cuisine. Initially a pop-up, Lucky & Joy now has a permanent (and gloriously kitsch) bricks-and-mortar site in Hackney.

Red-braised Pork Belly
Heat the oil in a wok or large non-stick frying pan over a medium heat. Add the pork belly and cook until evenly browned all over. Add the sugar and stir well, then cook for a few minutes until the pork becomes sticky and golden. Add the remaining ingredients, reduce the heat to low and cook for about 1 hour until the pork is tender and glossy.

Pickled Cucumber
Cut the cucumber in half lengthways and scrape out the seeds using a teaspoon. Slice the cucumber into half-moons, place in a bowl and sprinkle with the salt, then leave to stand for 15 minutes to help draw out the moisture. Add the remaining cucumber pickle ingredients and check the seasoning. Set aside to pickle until ready to serve.

Pickled Carrot
Mix everything together and leave for 10 minutes. Check the seasoning.

To Serve
Cook the eggs in a saucepan of simmering water for 6½ minutes until soft-boiled, then plunge them into iced water. Peel the eggs and cut them in half. You can also poach or fry the eggs.

To assemble, divide the rice between bowls. Top with the pork belly, pickled cucumber and carrot, egg, crispy shallots, sliced chilli, a few coriander leaves and toasted sesame seeds. Finish with a splash of rice vinegar and serve.

SPRING SLAW WITH HORSERADISH, APPLE & HAZELNUTS

BY LULU'S

SERVES 4

---

1 large or 2 medium beetroots, julienned

½ celeriac, julienned

1 kohlrabi, julienned

½ hispi cabbage, finely sliced

75ml (5 tbsp) lemon juice

250ml (9fl oz) good-quality extra virgin olive oil

2 tsp Dijon mustard

1 tbsp finely chopped dill fronds

Pinch of sugar

100g (3½oz) watercress, tough stalks removed

1 sweet and juicy apple, such as Pink Lady or Fuji, cored and julienned

3 tbsp toasted, crushed hazelnuts

5cm (2in) piece of fresh horseradish

Sea salt and ground black pepper

A deli-meets-wine bar, the unassuming yet wonderfully delicious Lulu's is tucked into a quiet corner of London's Herne Hill. Their older sister, Llewelyn's, just around the corner, is a delightful spot for those in the know – in warmer months grab a table outside on a Saturday to people watch and immerse yourself in the thrum of the market.

Combine the beetroot, celeriac, kohlrabi and cabbage in a large bowl and season generously with salt and pepper.

Make a dressing by whisking together the lemon juice, olive oil, mustard and dill, and season with the sugar and salt and pepper to taste (the sugar helps to brighten the lemon flavour).

Pour the dressing over the vegetables and add the watercress, apple and hazelnuts. Toss to combine, then grate the fresh horseradish over the top.

Serve as part of a larger brunch feast.

STEAK FRITES

BY MIKE REID, M RESTAURANTS

SERVES 2

250g (9oz) skirt steak
4 large Maris Piper potatoes,
    peeled and cut into chips
    6mm (¼in) thick
Rapeseed oil, for brushing
200ml (7fl oz) Parisian sauce
    (see below)
1 romaine lettuce, separated
    into leaves
Flaky sea salt

Blood Orange Vinaigrette
1 rich egg yolk
15g (½oz) Dijon mustard
30ml (2 tbsp) blood orange
    vinegar
Juice of 1 lemon
150ml (5fl oz) early harvest
    olive oil

Parisian Sauce
50g (1¾oz) banana shallots,
    finely sliced
250g (9oz) unsalted butter
2 chervil sprigs
50g (1¾oz) flat-leaf parsley,
    stalks and leaves
20g (¾oz) confit garlic
40g (1½oz) good quality
    anchovy fillets in oil
2 eggs
1 tsp Dijon mustard

With over 20 years' experience working at top restaurants in the UK and Australia, Mike Reid is no stranger to creating ground-breaking gastronomic playgrounds. Often appearing on our screens, Mike is also the Culinary Director of Rare Restaurants – the boutique hospitality group encompassing Gaucho, the renowned modern Argentinian steak restaurants – and M Restaurants.

Remove the steak from the fridge at least 30 minutes before cooking. Prepare a charcoal barbecue and leave the coals until they are glowing and grey.

Meanwhile, bring the potatoes to the boil in a large saucepan of salted water and cook until a knife slips through the outer portion, but there is still a little resistance in the middle. Drain and gently ruffle them in a colander (this enables you to get a crisper chip).

Transfer the potatoes to an air-fryer and cook on a high heat for 15 minutes or until crispy.

Meanwhile, to make the vinaigrette, in a metal bowl, whisk together the egg yolk, mustard, vinegar and lemon juice. Add the olive oil and whisk to combine. Season to taste with salt.

To make the Parisian sauce, place the shallots and 70g (2½oz) of the butter in a saucepan and melt over a medium heat. Add the remaining butter and let it melt, then add the herbs, confit garlic and anchovies and heat until fragrant. Transfer the mixture to a blender and blend until smooth, then pour back into the pan.

Add the eggs to the blender, along with the mustard, and blend until smooth. With the blender running, very slowly add the butter mixture back to the blender until you achieve an emulsified sauce.

When the coals are ready, brush one side of the steak with a little rapeseed oil and place, brushed side down, on the grill. Season generously with salt and grill for 3 minutes. Flip the steak over, add another light sprinkling of salt and continue grilling for a further 2 minutes.

Remove the steak from the grill and rest somewhere warm for 4 minutes, before cutting into slices.

Place the steak on serving plates, along with the chips, and spoon the Parisian sauce over the steak. Toss the blood orange vinaigrette through the romaine lettuce and serve alongside.

CLAIRE PTAK

Claire Ptak named her renowned Hackney bakery after the vivid wild violets that entranced her as a child growing up in balmy California, where her mother and paternal grandmother encouraged a love of cooking. Working in local bakeries from a young age, there was a brief film-studies interlude before she committed to a culinary career, landing a job at Alice Waters' legendary Berkeley restaurant Chez Panisse. Moving to London in 2005 for food styling and stints at some of the city's top restaurants, then selling cakes from a market stall, her Californian sensibility and fiercely seasonal approach to baking captivated Londoners. A bricks-and-mortar site swiftly followed, as did a sequence of celebrated cookbooks: *Love is a Pink Cake* – her fifth book – includes recipes for every time of day, including breakfast and brunch. Being asked to bake Harry and Meghan's wedding cake sent her reputation truly stratospheric.

Ptak identifies as a 'total cake-for-breakfast person', so 'saying yes when OnePlate asked me to contribute to this book was a no-brainer, especially as the charity funds sustainable and vital food projects in developing countries'.

CLAIRE PTAK'S EGGS, POTATOES & AIOLI

SERVES 6

12 small waxy potatoes,
  unpeeled and washed
6 eggs
Bunch of radishes
1 cauliflower
6 carrots
1 can of good-quality anchovy
  fillets
Olives, to serve

Aioli
1 garlic clove, peeled
Pinch of sea salt
3 egg yolks
300ml (10½fl oz) olive oil, plus
  extra for drizzling
1 tsp lemon juice

For the aioli, I prefer to use a mortar and pestle but it does take a long time and you need a nice large one. If you don't have one you can use a balloon whisk or an electric mixer. Crush the garlic clove into a smooth paste with the salt. If not using a mortar, use a garlic crusher or the back of a fork. Whisk in the egg yolks. Now start to add your oil, 1 teaspoon at a time, down the inside of your mortar or bowl. After each addition it is imperative to emulsify the mixture. Keep going until all the oil is added. A good aioli should be very thick. Add the lemon juice at the end and whisk well. Chill until ready to use.

Bring a large saucepan of salted water to the boil over a high heat. Add the potatoes and cook until a knife slips through easily, then drain and return to the pan. Cover with the lid and leave to steam for about 10 minutes. Remove the lid and, when cool enough to handle, use a paring knife or your fingers to peel the papery skins off. Set aside.

Place the eggs in a saucepan large enough to hold them in one layer. Cover with water and place over a high heat. As soon as the pan comes to the boil (keep a close eye on it), turn the heat down slightly to a rolling boil rather than a rapid one. Set a timer for 6 minutes. As soon as the timer goes, drain the water and refresh the eggs in cold water. Leave to cool while you prepare the vegetables.

Trim the radishes and cauliflower and cut into bite-sized pieces. Peel the carrots and leave them whole, or halve lengthways if thick. Arrange the vegetables and potatoes on plates or a platter on your table. Place the aioli in a small serving bowl, and peel and halve the eggs and place on a pretty plate.

Drain any oil from the anchovies and place the anchovies on a small plate. Drizzle with good-quality olive oil and add this to the table, alongside a bowl of olives.

CRAB KEDGEREE
BY THE MARKSMAN

SERVES 6

300g (10½oz) basmati rice,
  soaked in cold water for
  30 minutes
150g (5½oz) butter
100g (3½oz) finely sliced white
  onion
Large pinch of sugar
Large pinch of sea salt
100g (3½oz) brown crabmeat
100g (3½oz) white crabmeat
350ml (12fl oz) fish stock
Pinch of saffron threads,
  soaked in a little warm water
2 cardamom pods
1½ tbsp lemon juice
6 eggs
Chopped parsley leaves, to
  serve
Chopped watercress, to serve

Curry Paste
¼ tsp ground turmeric
½ tsp chilli powder
¼ tsp ground fenugreek
  powder
¼ tsp ground cumin
2 tsp garlic paste
2 tsp ginger paste
½ tsp fine sea salt
1½ tbsp olive oil

Renowned chefs Tom Harris and Jon Rotheram met in London and worked together at the iconic nose-to-tail restaurant St. JOHN before teaming up in 2015 to jointly run this historic East London pub. The Marksman declares itself a 'proper boozer' and serves some of the best no-frills British food in the city. Both chefs are dedicated to celebrating food that evokes the culinary story of London: their hearty beef and barley bun with horseradish cream is a cult dish for those in the know, as is the brown butter and honey tart, and the Sunday lunch is legendary.

To make the curry paste, toast the dry ingredients in a dry frying pan over a medium heat for a moment until fragrant. Transfer to a bowl, add the remaining ingredients and gently mix until combined. You can also use a food processor to do this.

Drain and rinse the rice, then set aside. Melt the butter in a large saucepan over a medium heat. Add the onion and cook, stirring occasionally, until soft. Add the curry paste, sugar and salt, increase the heat slightly and cook until the mixture starts to caramelise. Add the brown crabmeat and stir to combine, then add the rice and stir to coat the grains in the buttery mixture. Add the fish stock, along with the soaked saffron and cardamom pods, and bring to the boil. Reduce the heat to a simmer and cook until the water has reduced to the top of the rice. Reduce the heat to the lowest possible setting, cover with a lid and cook for 15 minutes.

Remove the pan from the heat and stir through the white crabmeat and lemon juice. Leave to rest while you boil the eggs.

Cook the eggs in a saucepan of boiling water for 7 minutes. Drain and rinse under cold water, then peel and halve.

Serve the kedgeree on a large platter, topped with the eggs, chopped parsley and watercress.

SAVOURY

HENRIETTA
STREET WC2
CITY OF WESTMINSTER

EGGS BENEDICT WITH HAM HOCK, SPINACH & PICKLED DAIKON

BY MILK BEACH

SERVES 4

Pickled Daikon
2 daikon, julienned
600ml (20fl oz) water
400ml (14fl oz) white wine
 vinegar
200g (7oz) caster sugar
20g (¾oz) table salt

Ham Hock
2 smoked ham hocks
½ brown onion, roughly
 chopped
1 carrot, roughly chopped
2 celery sticks, roughly
 chopped
2 garlic cloves, peeled
¼ bunch of thyme
2 bay leaves

Hollandaise
80g (2¾oz) egg yolks
 (from 4–5 eggs)
10ml (2 tsp) white wine vinegar
250ml (9fl oz) melted clarified
 butter (see page 242)
Tabasco sauce, to taste
Salt

To Serve
200g (7oz) spinach, wilted
4 slices of toast, buttered
4 poached eggs

TIP — *This will make more
pickled daikon and ham hock
than you need for this recipe.
Store leftovers in the fridge.*

This Aussie-style all-day restaurant-café covers all bases, from breakfast (go for house-made lamingtons with morello cherry jam or banana bread with espresso cream cheese) and brunch to sharing plates in the evening, serving Antipodean fusion food at its best. With two locations in the city, in Queen's Park and in Soho, Milk Beach also specialises in natural wines and they are serious about coffee, so expect a superior brew – the founder is champion coffee roaster and creator of Album Coffee Roasters.

—

'This classic brunch staple has been given the Milk Beach overhaul. This is quite a substantial dish – the richness of the poached eggs and luxurious hollandaise are counterbalanced by the pickled daikon.'

Pickled Daikon
Place the daikon in sterilised Kilner jars or similar. Combine the remaining ingredients in a small saucepan and bring to the boil. Once boiling, pour the pickle liquid over the daikon and leave to pickle for at least 1 hour.

Ham Hock
Preheat the oven to 120°C (110°C fan/250°F/gas mark ½). Place the ham hocks in a stockpot. Cover with cold water and bring to the boil. Reduce the heat to a simmer and cook for 5 minutes. Drain the ham hocks and wash thoroughly to remove excess scum.

Place the vegetables, garlic and herbs in a large deep oven tray or casserole dish. Add the ham hocks and fully cover with cold water. Seal the tray with cling film and foil, or add the lid to the dish, then transfer to the oven and leave to steam overnight. When cool enough to handle, pull apart the meat.

Hollandaise
Place the egg yolks, vinegar and a few tablespoons of warm water in a large heatproof bowl set over a saucepan of barely simmering water. Whisk the mixture for 4–5 minutes until it thickens. Continuing to whisk, then slowly drizzle in the clarified butter, making sure each addition of butter is fully emulsified before adding any more. Once all the butter is added, season to taste with salt and Tabasco, then remove from the heat.

To Serve
Place some wilted spinach on a slices of buttered toast followed by some ham hock. Top with a poached egg, a large spoonful of hollandaise and some pickled daikon.

CROQUE MONSIEUR

BY MINNOW

MAKES 1

2 slices of white sourdough
  bread
10g (⅓oz) butter, melted
½ tsp Dijon mustard
50g (1¾oz) mature Cheddar,
  grated
2 slices of Parma ham

Béchamel
150ml (5fl oz) whole milk
½ garlic clove, crushed
½ small onion, roughly
  chopped
1 bay leaf
10g (⅓oz) butter
10g (⅓oz) plain flour
1 tsp Dijon mustard
Pinch of ground nutmeg
Dash of Worcestershire sauce
Sea salt and ground black
  pepper

A park-side spot in Clapham, Minnow is the perfect place to enjoy a laid-back cup of coffee and a restorative breakfast. The romantic interiors and extensive terrace make catching up with friends a dream.

To make the béchamel, place the milk, garlic, onion and bay leaf in a small saucepan over a medium heat until the liquid starts to simmer, then take off the heat and leave for 10 minutes to infuse. Pass the infused milk through a sieve and discard the bay leaf and onion.

Place the butter for the béchamel in a saucepan over a medium heat. When the butter has melted and starts to foam, add the flour and cook for 1 minute, stirring constantly. Gradually whisk in the infused milk and bring to a gentle simmer, stirring constantly, until starting to thicken. Stir through the mustard, nutmeg and Worcestershire sauce, and season with salt and pepper to taste. The béchamel should be thick and creamy. Remove from the heat.

Preheat the grill.

Brush one side of each bread slice with the melted butter. Place the slices on a baking tray, buttered-side up, and toast under the grill until golden. Remove from the grill and preheat the oven to 220°C (200°C fan/425°F/gas mark 7).

Spread the untoasted sides of the bread with the mustard, then divide two-thirds of the béchamel and grated Cheddar between the slices and top with the Parma ham. Press the slices into a sandwich with the contents on the inside, then spread the remaining béchamel over the top and sprinkle with the remaining Cheddar. Transfer to a baking tray and bake in the oven for 10 minutes or until golden.

PEA & BROAD BEAN SHAKSHUKA

BY FRANCO FUBINI, NATOORA

SERVES 4–6

1 small onion (ideally Roscoff or Tropea), finely chopped
Good-quality olive oil
Pinch of ground cumin
Pinch of ground coriander
1 garlic clove, finely chopped
400g (14oz) can good-quality chopped tomatoes
120ml (4fl oz) water
Sugar, to taste (optional)
500g (1lb 2oz) broad beans, podded
500g (1lb 2oz) fresh peas, podded
Splash of good-quality red wine vinegar
4 eggs
250g (9oz) ricotta (we use Sardinian sheep's ricotta)
Bunch of chives, finely snipped
Bunch of parsley, leaves roughly chopped (or left whole)
Sea salt and ground black pepper
Good-quality bread of your choice, to serve

Founded by Franco Fubini in 2004, the high-end grocer Natoora has been supplying London with the finest produce ever since. Following the sun around Europe, they're able to deliver chef-quality fruits and vegetables to both restaurants and home cooks. With the aim of fixing the food system, Natoora wants to bring back the joy of food through nutritionally dense and flavour-first groceries. Take a browse through one of their grocers and you'll feel as through you're in a luxury store rather than a veg shop.

Place the onion in a frying pan with a heavy glug of olive oil, a little salt and the cumin and coriander. Cook over a medium heat for 5–7 minutes until the onion is soft and the edges begin to colour, then add the garlic and cook for another minute. Add the tomatoes, a little more salt, some black pepper and the water. Cook, uncovered, for about 30 minutes. Taste and adjust the seasoning towards the end of cooking, adding a little sugar if you feel the sauce needs it.

While the sauce is cooking, bring a saucepan of water to the boil and prepare a bowl of iced water. Blanch the podded broad beans for mere seconds before plunging straight into the iced water. Once cold, remove their outside skins; the blanching will have loosened them, making this easier. Set aside and add the podded peas to the same bowl.

When the sauce is ready, add the vinegar, peas and broad beans, mixing everything together. Finally, crack the eggs into the sauce and cook, uncovered, for about 5 minutes (or covered if you prefer the tops of the eggs to cook a little more). Serve immediately with dollops of ricotta and the herbs scattered over the top. Enjoy with thick slices of bread.

NOT AVOCADO ON TOAST

BY TOM CENCI, NESSA

SERVES 1–2

250g (9oz) fresh broad
  beans in pods (frozen are
  also great; you'll need
  150–200g/5½–7oz)
50ml (2fl oz) olive oil, plus
  extra for drizzling
Zest and juice 1 lemon
Pinch of fennel seeds
Pinch of cumin seeds
Pinch of caraway seeds
Pinch of chilli flakes
2 slices of sourdough bread
Sea salt and ground black
  pepper
Mixed herbs, such as dill,
  parsley, mint and tarragon,
  chopped, to serve

TIP — *Serve with poached eggs
for an extra brunch treat.*

Tom's immersion into the world of hospitality started young: as a schoolboy he worked weekends at the Michelin-starred Cliveden Hotel in Buckinghamshire, going on to study for a diploma in the Academy of Culinary Arts. Following stints and stages at some of Europe's most celebrated restaurants, including Restaurant Laurent in Paris and Noble Rot in London, he joined Nessa bistro in Soho as Executive Chef in 2023. His playful and inventive modern food, served from breakfast through to dinner, underpinned by seasonality and judicious sourcing, has proved an unmitigated hit.

Pod the broad beans, then blanch them in boiling water for 30 seconds. Drain and plunge into ice-cold water before peeling (this makes peeling the skins easier, but it isn't compulsory).

Pulse the peeled beans in a food processor with the olive oil, lemon zest and juice and salt and pepper to taste, until chunky. Check the seasoning and set aside.

Toast the spices in a dry frying pan over a medium heat until their aroma starts to fill the kitchen, then tip into a bowl and allow to cool.

Toast the sourdough, then spread the broad bean mixture over the top. Sprinkle with the toasted seeds and finish with soft herbs and an extra drizzle of olive oil.

Appreciation is yeast,
lifting ordinary to
extraordinary.

MARY ANN PETRO

SALMON & SCRAMBLED EGG DONBURI

BY NOBU LONDON

SERVES 1

80g (2¾oz) skin-on salmon
  fillet
Pinch of flaky sea salt, ideally
  Maldon
1 tsp extra virgin olive oil
2 large eggs, beaten
2 tsp tomato juice
10g (⅓oz) finely chopped
  jalapeño
10g (⅓oz) finely chopped red
  onion

To Serve
60g (2¼oz) steamed Japanese
  rice
1 tsp light soy sauce
Shredded nori
Toasted white sesame seeds
Salmon ikura (roe)
Finely chopped chives

Nobu Matsuhisa opened his first LA restaurant, Matsuhisa, over 30 years ago. His high-end synthesis of Japanese and Peruvian cuisine was an instant hit, and Nobu has gone on to become a leviathan, a prestige global brand encompassing dozens of hotels and restaurants that is ever-expanding. The menus at its three London restaurants (two of which are also hotels) boast the familiar yellowtail sashimi and Nikkei-style sushi, hot dishes (Nobu signature black cod miso is also ever present), set menus and omakase for an 'I'll leave it up to you' experience.

Preheat the oven to 140°C (120°C fan/280°F/gas mark 1).

Season the salmon with the salt and olive oil, then pan-fry in an ovenproof frying pan, skin-side down, over a medium heat for 4–5 minutes until lightly seared but not over-coloured. Transfer to the oven and roast for 6–8 minutes until just cooked through. Remove from the oven and allow the salmon to rest for the same amount of time it was cooked, then gently flake into large pieces and set aside.

Meanwhile, combine the eggs with the tomato juice, jalapeño and onion. Cook the egg mixture in a saucepan over a medium heat, stirring constantly, until the egg is lightly scrambled and soft.

Place the steamed rice in a shallow bowl and drizzle the soy sauce over the top. Scatter a little shredded nori around the rice and sprinkle with a few toasted sesame seeds. Place the flaked salmon on top of the rice, leaving a space in the middle for the scrambled egg. Spoon the scrambled egg into the centre, garnish with ikura and a few chives, and serve.

MELISSA HEMSLEY

Melissa Hemsley is a food writer, chef and sustainability champion who is passionate about the power of feel-good food. Her relaxed, comforting, minimal waste approach to home cooking has been influenced by her Filipino mum (who never wasted a grain of rice), years of cooking nourishing meals for private clients such as Take That, and the juggle of now being a new mum herself. She has written five cookbooks, including her latest book *Feel Good,* with a focus on fuss-free recipes that bring a bit of comfort and joy into our kitchens and beyond.

She loves brunch best when it's 'big pans or trays of food straight down on the table and everyone squeezed around, dogs all around our ankles – a bit chaotic, a bit messy, a bit DIY – everyone passing around food, serving each other and making their brunch exactly how they like it.'

'I'm a big fan of OnePlate and the work they do – every child deserves to be safe, fed and cared for.'

MELISSA HEMSLEY'S SMOKY BEAN TACOS WITH AVOCADO & FRIED EGGS

SERVES 2

Chickpea Wraps
250g (9oz) chickpea flour
350ml (12fl oz) warm water
1½ tbsp coconut oil or ghee
2 tbsp za'atar
Extra virgin olive oil, for
  drizzling (optional)
Sea salt and ground black
  pepper

Jalapeño Salsa
2 garlic cloves, finely chopped
1–2 fresh jalapeños, deseeded
  and finely chopped (or to
  taste)
Large handful of coriander,
  finely chopped
Zest and juice of 1 lime
Extra virgin olive oil
Raw honey or maple syrup
  (optional)

Filling
1 tbsp butter or ghee
1 tsp smoked paprika
1 tbsp tomato paste
400g (14oz) can of chickpeas
  (or any bean of your choice),
  drained and rinsed
1 avocado, thinly sliced
4 eggs
½ x quantity jalapeno salsa
  (see above)

To Serve
Small handful of coriander
  leaves, roughly torn
1 red chilli, deseeded and
  sliced

Fried eggs go perfectly here, but if you're making this for more than two people, scrambled eggs are best as they are much quicker and easier to do for a group. The chickpea wraps are super-fast to make, so start with these and enjoy the leftover wraps for packed lunches during the week.

Chickpea Wraps
Whisk together the chickpea flour, water, 1 teaspoon of salt and ½ teaspoon of black pepper and leave to sit for 10 minutes.

Melt 1 teaspoon of the coconut oil or ghee in a medium frying pan over a high heat. Add 3 tablespoons of the batter, swirling it around to cover the base of the pan, and cook for 1½ minutes, sprinkling over the za'atar, then flip over and cook on the other side for another 30 seconds.

Tip the wrap onto a plate, making sure you remove any excess bits from the pan or they'll burn when you cook the next wrap, and repeat – adding a little more of the oil or ghee each time – until you have used all the batter.

Jalapeño Salsa
Mix together all the ingredients, seasoning to taste with salt and pepper.

Filling
Heat a wide frying pan to high, add half the butter or ghee, the smoked paprika and tomato paste, and fry over a medium heat for 1 minute before stirring in the chickpeas. Heat through for 2–3 minutes, then season with salt and pepper to taste and divide between the chickpea wraps. Lay the sliced avocado on top.

Wipe the pan clean with kitchen paper and melt the remaining butter. When the butter has melted, crack in the eggs and cook over a medium-high heat for 3–4 minutes until the whites are becoming crisp around the edges but the yolks are still runny. Season with salt and pepper to taste, then add an egg to each of the wraps and drizzle over the salsa. Serve sprinkled with the fresh coriander and chilli.

PEPPERS STUFFED WITH BEEF & RICE IN TOMATO SAUCE

BY OREN

SERVES 4

---

4 red peppers (capsicums)

Rich Tomato Sauce
1½ tbsp olive oil
3 garlic cloves, chopped
2 mild red chillies, sliced
50g (1¾oz) tomato paste
500g (1lb 2oz) canned
    chopped tomatoes
Sea salt and ground black
    pepper

Stuffing
250g (9oz) basmati rice
250g (9oz) minced beef
75g (2½oz) coriander, finely
    chopped
75g (2½oz) parsley, finely
    chopped
150g (5½oz) onions, chopped
2 tsp chopped garlic
1 tsp ground cumin
1 tsp sweet paprika
½ tsp ground cinnamon
1 tsp fine sea salt
½ tsp ground black pepper

Israel-born Oded Oren trained and worked in Tel Aviv kitchens before moving to London in 2011 and cooking for pop-ups and as a guest chef across the city. He opened Oren in Dalston, East London, in 2019, and a deli nearby in 2023. His trademark bold, pared-back, small plates – the dishes smouldering from the grill are ludicrously good – celebrate the rich culinary heritage of the Middle East and the Mediterranean coast where he grew up.

To make the tomato sauce, heat the oil in a frying pan over a medium-low heat, add the garlic and chilli and sauté gently for 2–3 minutes until softened. Stir through the tomato paste for 2 minutes, then add the canned tomatoes, season with salt and pepper and gently simmer for 30 minutes over a low heat.

Meanwhile, wash the rice in cold water until the water runs clear, then drain.

Place the rice and the remaining stuffing ingredients in a large bowl and mix well until completely combined.

Cut the tops off the peppers and set aside. Use a spoon to scoop out the seeds and white membranes, then stuff the rice and beef mixture into the peppers until they are three-quarters full. Place the tops back on the peppers.

Preheat the oven to 180°C (160°C fan/350°F/gas mark 4).

Place the stuffed peppers in a roasting tin high enough to hold them standing upright. Pour the tomato sauce around the peppers and cover with a lid or foil. Roast for about an hour, or until the peppers are tender and the sauce has thickened.

Serve with a green salad.

SRI LANKAN DHAL

BY PAVILION BAKERY

SERVES 4

This is a unique dhal flavoured with coconut milk, curry leaves and spices. It's also vegan, gluten-free and high in protein. Dhal or 'parippu' is a staple in Sri Lankan cuisine. It's such a simple dish, quick and easy to make, but packed with flavour. It can be eaten with rice and other curries, roti, naan or with string hoppers.

Ancho-gochujang Red Pepper Chilli Jam

100g (3½oz) dried ancho chillies
4 tbsp olive oil
1 red onion, chopped
200g (7oz) galangal, grated
100g (3½oz) fresh ginger, grated
3–4 garlic cloves, chopped
200g (7oz) gochujang red pepper paste
Pinch of salt
Olive oil, to cover

Coconut Sambal

6 small dried red or green chillies
½ fresh coconut, grated (about 250g/9oz flesh), or use frozen grated coconut
½ tsp salt
6 small Bombay onions or 1 red onion, finely diced
Bunch of coriander, leaves finely chopped
10g (⅓oz) fried curry leaves
Juice of 1 lime

Sri Lankan Pol Roti (coconut roti)

440g (15½oz) plain flour, plus extra for dusting
125g (4½oz) desiccated shredded coconut
1 red onion, finely chopped
3 long green chillies, finely chopped
Pinch of fine sea salt
240ml (8fl oz) water

Ancho-gochujang Red Pepper Chilli Jam

Place the ancho chillies in a large heatproof bowl and cover with boiling water. Cover and let sit for about 20 minutes to soften. Drain, remove the stems from the chillies, then slice the chillies open and remove the seeds. Drop the chillies into a food processor.

Heat the oil in a small frying pan over a medium heat, add the onion, galangal and ginger and cook for 10–15 minutes until softened. Add the garlic and cook, stirring, for another minute, then remove from the heat and transfer the mixture to the food processor. Add the salt and process to a paste, then stir in the gochujang to form a thick paste. Transfer to an airtight container and top with a layer of olive oil. Refrigerate for up to 2 weeks.

Coconut Sambal

Grind the chillies and onion using a mortar and pestle into a fine paste with no visible seeds. Add the coconut and grind into the paste until it absorbs the colour of the chillies. Add the salt, onions, coriander, fried curry leaves and lime juice and mix well. Transfer to a serving bowl and set aside until ready to serve.

Sri Lankan Pol Roti

To make the roti, place the flour, coconut, onion, chilli and salt in a large bowl. Mix to combine well.

Add the water to the flour mixture, a little at a time, while stirring the flour with your fingertips (or a fork). After adding about half the liquid, there will likely be some clumps and dry spots of flour. Drizzle more liquid over the dry parts of the flour, while mixing, to form a dough. Add 1–2 more tablespoons of water only if needed. The dough should come together, but still have dry spots on the surface. (If you add too much water, sprinkle in a little extra flour and lightly knead it into the dough; but don't over-knead!) Shape the dough into a rough ball and set aside to rest, covered, for 1–2 hours until very soft. If it's still very sticky after resting, flour the dough and your work surface to prevent it from sticking.

continued overleaf

Dhal

1 cup red lentils
600ml (20fl oz) water
1 small red onion chopped
3 garlic cloves, sliced
1 green chilli, halved
  lengthways
2 curry leaf sprigs
1 tsp ground turmeric
1 tsp sea salt
125ml (4fl oz) full-fat coconut
  milk
Coriander leaves, to serve

Tempering

1 tbsp oil
1 tsp mustard seeds
½ tsp cumin seeds
1 curry leaf sprig
1 dried red chilli, broken into
  pieces
4 cardamom pots

Cut the dough into 8 wedges and lightly roll each portion into a rough ball. Working with one ball at a time, sprinkle the top with flour, then flatten it into a disc and roll out into a circle about 5mm (¼in) thick and 15cm (6in) in diameter. Cover with a clean tea towel or cling film while you roll out the remaining dough.

Heat a cast-iron or non-stick skillet over a medium-high heat. Add a roti to the pan and cook for 2–3 minutes until the base starts to develop brown spots. Flip the roti over and cook the other side another 2–3 minutes until you get brown spots on that side too. Transfer to a wire rack to cool while you repeat with the remaining roti.

Dhal

Rinse the red lentils until the water runs clear. Add to a saucepan along with 360ml (12fl oz) of the water, the onion, garlic, chilli, curry leaves, turmeric and salt. Bring to the boil, then reduce the heat to medium, cover and cook for about 15 minutes until the water is absorbed and the lentils are cooked through. Add the coconut milk and remaining water and stir to combine. Cover and simmer for 5 minutes, then check the seasoning, adding more salt if necessary.

Tempering

Heat the oil in a non-stick frying pan over a medium heat, then add the remaining ingredients and cook until the mustard seeds start to splutter.

To Serve

Pour the tempering over the dhal, sprinkle over the coriander leaves and serve with the chilli jam, sambal and roti.

HERITAGE TOMATOES AL FORNO WITH GARDEN HERBS

BY PETERSHAM NURSERIES

SERVES 8–10 AS A SIDE DISH

3.5kg (7½lb) mixed heritage
   tomatoes
6 garlic cloves, sliced
Small bunch of thyme
Handful of sage leaves
2 large rosemary sprigs
1 green chilli, chopped
1 litre (35fl oz) olive oil
Sea salt and ground black
   pepper

Petersham Nurseries in Richmond is a little a trek from central London, but the bucolic greenhouse setting more than makes up for the journey. Sitting beneath a headily fragrant canopy of flowers, it's all too easy to let go of city cynicism. The Italian-led menu and organic, slow-food ethos is central at all sites: the Boglione family who own Petersham also operate The Petersham restaurant in Covent Garden, a dine-in and takeaway deli, and casual aperitivo and cicchetti bar, La Goccia.

—

'We make vats of these roasted tomatoes in oil, blitzing them in a food processor to create a smooth sauce for pasta or a dressing, or simply spooning out the tomatoes and aromatic oil as a side dish, or to eat with beef or chicken. Enjoy with a glass of Langhe Chardonnay from Poderi Roccanera.'

Preheat the oven to 190°C (170°C fan/375°F/gas mark 5).

Place all the ingredients, with salt and pepper to taste, in a large casserole dish and bake for 50–60 minutes until the skins of the tomatoes are starting to split. Allow to cool and use as desired.

The Restaurant is Straight on

The Teahouse is around to the right and down past glasshouse

Dwell on the
beauty of life.

MARCUS AURELIUS

BURNT ONION SOUP
BY PERILLA

SERVES 6

10 white onions, finely sliced
2 tbsp oil
250g (9oz) unsalted butter
1 litre (35fl oz) chicken stock
150g (5½oz) pata negra fat
200g (7oz) crème fraîche
Lemon juice, to taste
Sea salt and ground black
  pepper

Burnt Onion Powder
2 white onions, thinly sliced

Ben Marks, chef and co-owner of Stoke Newington's Perilla, opened the laid-back restaurant with business partner and old school friend Matt Emmerson after a series of celebrated pop-ups. He started young, moving to Sweden when he was 15 to work at Stockholm Michelin-starred Operakällaren then returning to study at London's Academy of Culinary Arts alongside an apprenticeship at Claridge's before heading back to Europe for a stint at Noma. A year later he was back, working at The Square with chef Phil Howard, a strong influence on his style of seasonal, modern-European cooking.

Preheat the oven to 250°C (230°C fan/480°F/gas mark 10).

To make the burnt onion powder, place the 2 sliced onions on a baking tray in a single layer and roast for 15 minutes until completely burnt. Allow to cool, then transfer to a food processor and blitz to a powder. Set aside.

Lower the oven temperature to 120°C (100°C fan/250°F/gas mark ½).

In a large saucepan over a medium heat, slowly sweat the 10 sliced onions in the oil and a touch of salt until translucent. Add the butter and continue to cook slowly for about 10 minutes until the onion is completely soft, ensuring it doesn't caramelise or colour. Add the stock and bring to the boil, then reduce the heat to a gentle simmer and cook for 1 hour.

Meanwhile, place the pata negra fat in a small baking tin and transfer to the oven to gently render for 45 minutes.

Remove the soup from the heat and stir through the crème fraîche. Use a stick blender to blend the soup, slowly adding the rendered fat to help it emulsify, until smooth. Finish the soup with a dash of lemon juice, salt and pepper to taste. Sprinkle over a little of the burnt onion powder to serve.

MORTADELLA, RICOTTA, PEPPER & AUBERGINE SANDWICH

BY POPHAMS

MAKES 2

4 slices of sourdough bread
90g (3¼oz) mortadella
50g (1¾oz) rocket
Sea salt and ground black
  pepper

Oregano Ricotta
500g (1lb 2oz) ricotta
25g (1oz) oregano leaves
Zest and juice of 1 orange
1 garlic clove, finely grated

Tomato Jam
500g (1lb 2oz) tomatoes,
  roughly chopped
75g (2½oz) caster sugar
30ml (2 tbsp) Moscatel vinegar
  or red wine vinegar

Roasted Vegetables
1 large or 2 small aubergines
  (eggplants), sliced
  lengthways into long strips
1 tsp fine salt
2 yellow peppers (capsicums),
  deseeded and thickly sliced
30ml (2 tbsp) extra virgin olive
  oil, plus extra for drizzling
10ml (2 tsp) red wine vinegar

The classic maple-bacon croissant at Pophams bakery is rightfully a cult favourite. A site of pilgrimage for coffee and pastry fiends, Pophams has three all-day cafés in town – Islington, London Fields and Victoria Park – with their London Fields site open at night for seductive Italian-British pasta dishes (the filled and hand-rolled pasta is crafted on-site). Renowned for their inventive artisan pastries – like Welsh rarebit Danish or apple tart croissant (the roster is constantly changing) – this innovative approach sees some stellar sandwich offerings too: the beef ragu toastie is the stuff of dreams.

Oregano Ricotta
Blend the ingredients together in a food processor until completely smooth. Season to taste with salt and pepper.

Tomato Jam
Blend the tomatoes in a food processor until smooth. Transfer to a saucepan with the sugar and vinegar and simmer over a medium heat for 45–60 minutes until it has reduced to a spreadable jam. Taste and season with salt as needed. Keep the leftovers in a jar in the fridge and spread over sandwiches or pair with cheese.

Roasted Vegetables
Preheat the oven to 200°C (180°C fan/400°F/gas mark 6).

Place the aubergine in a colander and toss through the salt. Leave for 15–30 minutes for the salt to draw out some of the moisture from the aubergine.

Drizzle a little oil over the pepper and salted aubergine, then spread out on a baking tray and roast in the oven for 20–25 minutes until soft and golden. Allow to cool completely.

Make a quick dressing by combining the olive oil and vinegar with a little salt and pepper and a pinch of sugar. Once the roasted vegetables have cooled, mix them with the dressing.

To Assemble
Spread some tomato jam on two slices of bread and some oregano ricotta on the other two. Lay the pepper, aubergine and mortadella over the ricotta, finishing with the rocket and the other slices of bread. You will have ricotta and jam left over, but these both store well in the fridge.

MASALA POTATOES WITH FRIED EGGS & GREEN CHUTNEY

BY SALT THE RADISH

SERVES 2–3

½ red onion, finely sliced
100ml (3½fl oz) white wine
  vinegar
2–3 tbsp oil
500g (1lb 2oz) large potatoes,
  peeled and cut into chunks
4 tbsp masala spice mix
  (store-bought is fine)
250g (9oz) chestnut
  mushrooms, quartered
1½ bunches of mint, leaves
  roughly torn
Bunch of coriander, leaves
  roughly torn
80g (2¾oz) baby watercress
  (or regular watercress)
Salad dressing of your choice
2 eggs per person
Sea salt and ground black
  pepper

Green Chutney
20g (¾oz) mint leaves
20g (¾oz) parsley leaves
40g (1½oz) coriander leaves
½ tsp cumin seeds, toasted
10g (2 tsp) caster sugar
8g (¼oz) green chilli, deseeded
50ml (1¾fl oz) lime juice
50ml (1¾fl oz) water

Mint Yoghurt
½ bunch of mint, leaves only,
  chopped
500g (1lb oz) thick Greek
  yoghurt

After travelling and cooking her way across Asia for a year, Kat Halliday opened her veg-focused Finsbury Park café in 2017. Serving breakfast, brunch and lunch, and superb coffee, her welcoming neighbourhood spot offers porridges, soups and 'winter warmer' stews in colder months and iced drinks, gussied-up eggs on toast and salads and herby frittatas when it hots up, with pastry specials all year round. Her regular communal supper clubs sell out quickly.

Combine the red onion and vinegar in a small bowl. Cover with cold water and chill in the fridge for 1 hour.

Meanwhile, to make the green chutney, place the ingredients in a blender and blend until smooth. Season with salt to taste and transfer to a serving bowl.

Preheat the oven to 180°C (160°C fan/350°F/gas mark 4). Add the oil to a roasting tin and place in the oven to heat up.

Place the potatoes in a pan of salted water and bring to the boil. Cook for 5 minutes, then drain, return to the pan and leave to steam dry for a few minutes. Carefully tip the potatoes into the roasting tin and turn to coat in the hot oil. Sprinkle over the masala spice mix and a little salt, then roast for 30 minutes or until golden and crispy. Add the mushrooms to the roasted potatoes, mix well and roast for another 5–10 minutes.

To make the mint yoghurt, combine the mint and yoghurt in a bowl. Season to taste with salt and pepper.

Make a quick salad by combining the torn herb leaves, watercress and quick-pickled red onion in a bowl. Dress the salad however you like: it can be simply lemon, oil and salt or we sometimes make a Dijon mustard vinaigrette.

Fry 2 eggs per person – crispy edges and sunny side up is best!

Scoop a generous amount of mint yoghurt onto each plate and top with the masala potatoes and mushrooms. Drizzle with the green chutney, then finish with the eggs and salad. Enjoy!

SALMON ROYALE HASH

BY SEABIRD

SERVES 4–5

Oil, for frying
4–5 eggs
120g (4¼oz) smoked salmon
Sea salt and cracked black
  pepper
Dill and chives, finely chopped,
  to serve

Lime Hollandaise
300g (10½oz) butter
2 egg yolks
10ml (2 tsp) lemon juice
10ml (2 tsp) lime juice
Dash of Tabasco (optional)

Hash Browns
1kg (2lb 3oz) Maris Piper
  potatoes, peeled and grated
15g (½oz) salt
125ml (4½fl oz) melted butter
90g (3¼oz) plain flour

Fourteen floors up, on the rooftop of The Hoxton Hotel in Southwark, this Mediterranean restaurant and bar boasts London's longest oyster list and gorgeous city views. The 'sea-to-table' Med-inspired menu, served at terrace tables or the raw seafood bar, features a plethora of small plates and luxurious mains. Spanish and Portuguese influences writ large, with iberico jamon croquetas, whole lobster rice; or there's Oyster Happy Hour with cold Martinis.

To make the hollandaise, first clarify the butter. Melt the butter in a saucepan over a low heat and simmer until the milk solids separate from the butter fat – don't be tempted to stir! Skim the solids from the fat with a slotted spoon and discard. Reserve the clear clarified butter.

Set up a bain marie by placing a heatproof bowl over a saucepan of just simmering water. Add the egg yolks, lemon juice and a pinch of salt to the bowl and whisk until the eggs reach 80°C (176°F) on a kitchen thermometer and just start to thicken.

Remove the bowl from the bain marie and very slowly add the clarified butter, whisking constantly (if you add the butter too quickly the egg will split). The mixture will thicken into a luscious golden hollandaise. Once all the butter is incorporated, add the lime juice and adjust the salt to taste. Add a good crack of black pepper and a dash of Tabasco, if you're feeling spicy.

Preheat the oven to 160°C (140°C fan/325°F/gas mark 3).

To make the hash browns, rinse the grated potato until the water runs clear (this removes the starch). Dry the potato, place in a bowl with the salt and mix thoroughly. Allow the potato to stand for 10 minutes to soften and release more water.

Squeeze the excess water away and dry the potato again. Return the potato to the bowl and stir through the melted butter, followed by the flour and some black pepper. Pile 200g (7oz) portions of the hash brown mixture into 10cm (4in) ring moulds and place on a baking tray, pressing down on the potato to compress it (you should get 4–5 portions). Transfer to the oven and bake for 30 minutes.

Heat a little oil in a frying pan over a high heat. Add the hash browns and fry for 1½ minutes on each side until crispy and golden. Poach the eggs (see page 61).

Divide the hash browns between serving plates and top with the smoked salmon. Place a poached egg in the middle and spoon over a generous amount of lime hollandaise. Garnish with a generous amount of dill and chives and serve.

DRUNKEN NOODLES

BY SMOKING GOAT

600g (1lb 5oz) ho fun (fresh flat
noodles)
200g (7oz) smoked pork jowl
(or use your favourite cut of
beef or chicken), sliced
4 tbsp vegetable oil
50g (1¾oz) fresh green
peppercorns
2 long red chillies, sliced, plus
extra to serve
200g (7oz) celery, stalks sliced
on an angle, leaves reserved
120g (4¼oz) spring onions, cut
into 2.5cm (1in) lengths
20g (¾oz) Thai basil
20g (¾oz) pickled garlic,
roughly chopped (plus a little
of the pickle liquid)
40g (1½oz) pickled chillies
1 tsp ground white pepper

**Drunken Noodle Sauce
(makes 300ml/10½fl oz)**
80ml (2½fl oz) oyster sauce
80ml (2½fl oz) soy sauce
180ml (6fl oz) filtered water
2 tsp Mekhong Thai Spirit
(35%) (or use golden rum)
20g (¾oz) white sugar

This quirky spot in Shoreditch will take you to the streets of Bangkok
with punchy flavours in a lively setting. Try these noodles for a delicious
change from your usual eggs on toast.

To make the drunken noodle sauce, combine the ingredients in a bowl and
stir until the sugar has dissolved. Set aside.

In a hot, dry wok or deep frying pan set over a high heat, add the fresh
noodles and leave to char slightly. Add the pork jowl and vegetable oil and
cook until the noodles start to soften, then add the green peppercorns, red
chilli and celery stalks and toss well.

Once the noodles have softened completely and gained small areas of
crust, add the spring onions, Thai basil, celery leaves and the drunken
noodle sauce. Toss well, using either a good wrist action or a wok spoon.
Finally, add the pickled garlic and liquid, pickled chillies and ground white
pepper. Give everything a final stir, then divide between plates and serve
topped with extra chopped chilli.

BREAKFAST S+DWICH

BY SONS & DAUGHTERS

MAKES 4

4 hash browns
8–16 slices of streaky bacon
4 ciabatta baps
Sea salt and ground black
  pepper

Omelette
3 large eggs
45g (1½oz) mature Cheddar,
  grated
A little butter, for greasing

Spicy Ketchup
100g (3½oz) tomato ketchup
  (we use Heinz)
Horseradish sauce, to taste
Tabasco sauce, to taste
Worcestershire sauce, to taste

James Ramsden, founder of the acclaimed Hackney restaurant Pidgin, launched this sandwich spot in 2019. Stop by their flagship site in Kings Cross for some tasty sustenance before doing some window shopping in Coal Drops Yard.

Preheat the oven to 200°C (180°C fan/400°F/gas mark 6).

Cook the hash browns according to the packet instructions and the bacon to your preference (we bake it along with the hash browns until crispy).

To make the omelette, whisk together the eggs and cheese and season with salt and pepper. Grease 4 holes of a muffin tin and divide the egg mixture evenly between the holes. Transfer to the oven and bake for 5 minutes.

Mix the ketchup with the remaining spicy ketchup ingredients to your taste – we like it punchy!

When you're ready for breakfast, halve and toast your baps. Liberally spread with the spicy ketchup and top with a hash brown, bacon and an omelette. Eat in a hurry.

ANGELA HARTNETT

OBE

Chef, restaurateur and author, Angela Hartnett's passion for great food could be said to be predestined: as a young girl growing up in Kent, her Italian grandmother and mother would show her how to make bread and pasta from scratch. After studying history, she got straight into the kitchen, first at hotels, then joining Gordon Ramsay's brigade at Aubergine in London. Ramsay was her mentor for many years, which included working under Marcus Wareing at Pétrus, ascending the ranks from sous to head chef in a matter of months and helping it win its first Michelin star. A celebrated female figurehead on the male-dominated dining scene, she went on to launch the now Michelin-starred Murano, before expanding to Hartnett Holder & Co. and Café Murano, where her modern-European dishes have a distinct Italian influence woven through them and exude her trademark warmth and down-to-earth approach to food.

An advocate for numerous charities, for Angela food isn't just about what you put on the plate: it's about the pleasure of sharing a meal with others – something that is central to OnePlate's ethos.

ANGELA HARTNETT'S EGGS FRIED IN SAGE AND CHILLI BUTTER

SERVES 1

1 slice of sourdough bread
1 garlic clove
Glug of olive oil
Knob of butter
Small handful of sage leaves
Pinch of chilli flakes, to taste
  (I use pepperoncini)
2 eggs
Sea salt and ground black
  pepper

An easy and delicious way to elevate the humble fried egg. Adding a mound of sautéd spinach to sit under the eggs is lovely too.

Toast the sourdough then rub one side with the garlic clove.

In a frying pan set over a medium heat, add the olive oil and butter. When the butter is foaming, add the sage and chilli and fry for a couple of minutes.

Crack the eggs into the pan and fry until the edges are crispy but the yolks are still soft.

Transfer the eggs to the sourdough and pour any excess sage butter on top. Season well and serve.

MANOUCHE GRILLED CHEESE

BY JOHN GREGORY-SMITH

SERVES 1

2 slices of sourdough bread
30g (1oz) butter
2 tsp olive oil
1 tbsp za'atar
60g (2¼oz) mozzarella, grated
50g (1¾oz) Monterey Jack
  Cheddar, grated
Sea salt

John Gregory-Smith is a TV chef, content creator and author who specialises in Middle Eastern and North African cuisine. You have most likely seen one of his mouth watering videos on your instagram feed or watched him cook up a storm on TV where he is a regular face on BBC1's *Morning Live*, Channel 4's *Sunday Brunch* and ITV's *This Morning*.

'Given everything that's been going on in the world over the last few years, it's more important than ever to look after each other. Giving is so simple and every little helps. I'm thrilled to be a part of this extraordinary project that provides the tools for communities to build a brighter future for generations to come.'

—

'Breakfast on the go in Lebanon is a fabulous affair. You buy a flatbread from one of the many bakeries, called a manouche. It's a round bread, baked to perfection, crispy and chewy and covered in a za'atar, oil and cheese. It's rolled up and then wrapped in paper so you can scoff it on the way to work. Sadly, living in London, I don't have a local baker who can make this for me so I have adapted it into a lush grilled cheese sarnie. It's by no means the same thing but the flavours are just divine.'

Spread one side of the sourdough slices with 20g (¾oz) of the butter and place, buttered-side down, on a chopping board.

Rub the oil over the unbuttered side of a sourdough and sprinkle with the za'atar and a little salt. Arrange the grated cheese over the za'atar and top with the remaining slice of sourdough, buttered-side up.

Melt the remaining butter in a frying pan over a medium heat. Add the grilled cheese and cook for 2–3 minutes on each side until golden. Take off the heat and cover the pan for 30–60 seconds to get the cheese uber oozy. Slice and serve.

DUCK LEGS & CARROTS

BY ST. JOHN

SERVES 6

---

1 tbsp duck fat or butter
6 duck legs
1 white onion, sliced
2 leeks, sliced
8 garlic cloves, peeled
14 medium carrots, peeled and
 chopped into rounds about
 7mm (¼in) thick
Bundle of parsley and 4
 rosemary sprigs (you have to
 be very careful with rosemary;
 as delicious as it is, it can take
 over)
2 bay leaves
1 red chilli, left whole (this just
 emits a slight warmth to the
 dish, rather than if the chilli
 was chopped)
About 1.5 litres (50fl oz)
 chicken stock
Sea salt and ground black
 pepper

To Serve
Sourdough bread, toasted if
 you like
Simple green salad

Fergus Henderson's approach to cooking has sparked myriad imitations since he opened the seminal (and Michelin-starred) St. JOHN with Trevor Gulliver in Clerkenwell in 1994. Their celebration of nose, tail and everything in between has revolutionised British cooking, which you can now enjoy at three restaurants across the city, in Smithfield, Marylebone and Spitalfields. There are bakeries, a winery and online shop too. The food's artful simplicity epitomises 'what you see is what you get' and is fiercely seasonal. Head to Marylebone for coffee and pastries for a 'light breakfast' (if doughnuts count as light...) then wait until lunch service for their famous Welsh rarebit.

Preheat the oven to 170°C (150°C fan/325°F/gas mark 3).

Melt the duck fat or butter in a large frying pan over a medium heat. Wait until it is sizzling, then add the duck legs and brown on both sides. Remove from the pan and set aside. In the same pan, cook the onion, leeks and garlic for 10 minutes. Mix in the carrots and cook for 3 minutes, then decant all the vegetables into a deep oven dish.

Nestle in the herb bundle, bay leaves and chilli. Press the duck legs into the carrot bed, skin-side up, then season the dish and pour the stock over until the duck legs look like alligators in a swamp. Transfer to the oven and cook for 1½ hours, keeping an eye on it to ensure it doesn't burn – if it threatens to, cover the dish with foil. Check the legs with a knife; you want them to be thoroughly giving.

When cooked, the carrot will have drawn up the duck fat, the stock will have reduced to a rich juice and the duck skin should be brown and crispy.

Serve with bread or toast, and follow with a green salad.

VEGAN FALAFEL & BEETROOT SALAD BOWL

BY SUNDAY

SERVES 2

Chefs Alan Turner and Terrence Williamson love brunch so much they wrote a book about it, and their restaurant of the same name, Sunday, serves up modern British dishes to a host of dedicated customers in Islington.

Hummus
400g (14oz) can chickpeas, drained and rinsed
1½ tbsp water
4 tbsp olive oil
2 garlic cloves, crushed
Juice of 1 lemon
3 tbsp tahini
1 tsp ground cumin

Hummus
Place the chickpeas in a food processor with the water and blitz until smooth. Add the remaining ingredients and blitz for 2–3 minutes until smooth again. Season to taste, transfer to a bowl, cover and refrigerate.

Falafel
400g (14oz) can chickpeas, drained and rinsed
½ bunch of coriander, chopped
½ bunch of parsley, chopped
2 garlic cloves, roughly sliced
1 tsp ground cumin
½ tsp baking powder
1 tsp ground coriander
½ red chilli, finely chopped
2 spring onions, finely chopped
3 tbsp rapeseed oil
Sea salt and ground black pepper

Falafel
Add all of the falafel ingredients to a food processor, except the oil, and with salt and pepper to taste. Pulse until you have a fairly smooth mixture – some chunks are fine. Using clean, wet hands, divide the mixture into 4 equal portions. Shape each piece into a round patty about 1.5cm (⅔in) thick.

Add the rapeseed oil to a heavy-based frying pan over a medium heat. When hot, add the falafel and fry for 4–5 minutes on each side until golden and crisp. Remove the falafel from the pan and keep warm in a low oven while you prepare the salad.

Dressing
Pinch of sumac
1 garlic clove, crushed
1 tsp sea salt
1 tsp sweet smoked paprika
4 tbsp extra virgin olive oil
2 tbsp lemon juice

Dressing
Whisk together the ingredients in a bowl. Set to one side until needed.

Toasted Quinoa
30g (1oz) quinoa
1 tbsp olive oil

Toasted Quinoa
Rinse the quinoa two or three times in cold water, then transfer to a pan of salted water. Bring to a rolling boil, then reduce the heat and simmer for 8 minutes or until the quinoa has puffed and doubled in size. Drain.

Heat the olive oil in the pan you cooked the falafel in over a medium heat and add the cooked quinoa. Using a wooden spoon, start moving the quinoa around the pan; as it gets hot and the excess water evaporates, it will start to pop and turn brown, and release a delicious nutty aroma. Once you get to this stage, remove from the heat, transfer the quinoa to a bowl and allow to cool.

To Serve
150g (5½oz) baby spinach
1 avocado, sliced
1 uncooked beetroot, peeled and cut into fine matchsticks
Pomegranate seeds

To Serve
In a bowl, toss together the spinach, avocado and beetroot with the sumac dressing.

Spread 2 tablespoons of the hummus in the bottom of two serving bowls. Divide the salad between them, top with the crispy quinoa and falafel, sprinkle with the pomegranate seeds and serve.

To give and not expect
anything in return, that is
what lies at the heart of love.

SALT BEEF HASH WITH DUCK EGGS & SPICED TOMATO

BY BEN BOEYNAEMS, THE BEAUMONT HOTEL

SERVES 2

Sea salt (we use Maldon) and ground black pepper
1 spring onion, julienned
2 tbsp finely chopped chives

Hollandaise
150ml (5fl oz) white wine
50ml (1¾fl oz) white wine vinegar
1 small shallot, finely sliced
1 tsp black peppercorns
1 tarragon sprig
1 egg yolk
250g (9oz) melted clarified butter, cooled slightly (see page 242)
Lemon juice, to taste

Spiced Tomato
200g (7oz) peeled tomatoes
¼ small red chilli, diced
100g (3½oz) shallots, finely chopped
2 tbsp tomato paste
1 garlic clove
Caster sugar, to taste

Hash
50g (1¾oz) butter
100g (3½oz) onion, diced
1 garlic clove, chopped
2 thyme sprigs
4 cold roast potatoes, diced
100g (3½oz) cooked salt beef, diced

Duck Eggs
2 duck eggs
Clarified butter, for frying (see page 242)

A stunning hotel in the heart of London's West End, The Beaumont's old-school aesthetic was brought to life by the same architects who designed Fortnum & Mason. Now in charge of the food here, Ben Boeynaems began his career working for the likes of Gordon Ramsay and Eric Chavot in some of London's most renowned kitchens.

Hollandaise
To make a white wine vinegar reduction, combine 50ml (1¾fl oz) of the white wine, the vinegar, shallot, peppercorns and tarragon in a small pan. Bring to a simmer over a low heat and reduce by half. Set aside to cool completely then strain into a clean container. You will need 50g (1¾oz).

Whisk the egg yolk with the vinegar reduction and remaining white wine in a heatproof bowl set over a pan of just simmering water, until the mixture stops looking frothy and starts to thicken (about 70°C/158°F on a kitchen thermometer). Once it has thickened, whisk in the melted clarified butter slowly and steadily (ensure it is not too hot or the hollandaise will split), then season with salt and lemon juice. Remove from the heat and set aside.

Spiced Tomato
Gently cook the ingredients with a splash of vegetable oil in a saucepan over a medium heat, breaking the tomatoes down with the back of a spoon as they cook, until reduced and very thick. Adjust the seasoning with salt and sugar, set aside and keep warm.

Hash
Melt half the butter in a frying pan over a medium heat, add the onion, garlic and thyme and cook until translucent but not coloured. Meanwhile, in a separate frying pan, gently fry the roast potatoes in the remaining butter over a medium heat for 10 minutes until golden and crisp, then add the salt beef and warm through. Remove the thyme and garlic from the onion and add the beef and potato mixture. Add a tablespoon of the hollandaise sauce to the hash and season with black pepper.

Duck Eggs
Gently fry the duck eggs in a little clarified butter until cooked to your liking.

To Serve
Divide the hollandaise between two plates and gently spread with the back of a spoon. Add the hash, duck egg and a spoonful of the spiced tomato, and finish with a sprinkling of spring onion and chives.

SMOKED SCOTTISH SALMON WITH HOMEMADE ENGLISH MUFFINS

BY SHAUN WHATLING, THE BERKELEY

SERVES 2 (with plenty of leftover muffins)

4 eggs (we use Burford Browns)
80ml (5 tbsp) double cream
30g (1oz) unsalted butter, plus extra for spreading
160g (5½oz) Scottish smoked salmon, half chopped
Sea salt and ground black pepper
Snipped chives, to serve
Lemon wedges, to serve (optional)

English Muffins
(makes 18 – they freeze well)
250ml (9fl oz) whole milk
250ml (9fl oz) warm water (45°C/113°F)
7g (¼oz) active dried yeast
750g (1lb 10½oz) plain flour, plus extra for dusting
60g (2¼oz) melted butter or margarine
1 tsp salt
2 tbsp cornmeal polenta

Once a humble coffee house, in the 300 years since, The Berkeley has transformed into the luxury hotel we know today, rich with heritage and delights. Overseen by Executive Chef Shaun Whatling, The Collins Rooms boasts a light-filled dining room perfect for early morning working breakfasts, laid-back lunches and dark intimate dinners.

To make the English muffins, heat the milk in a small saucepan until it bubbles, then remove from the heat and let it cool until lukewarm.

Mix together the warm water and yeast in a small bowl. Let it stand for 10 minutes, or until creamy.

Combine the milk, yeast mixture, half the flour and the melted butter in a large bowl and beat until smooth. Mix in the salt and the remaining flour, and knead until a soft dough forms. Place the dough in a greased bowl and cover, then leave to rise in a warm place until it has doubled in volume, about 1 hour.

Punch down the dough, then roll it out on a lightly floured surface to a 1.5cm (½in) thickness. Cut out rounds using a cutter or a drinking glass. Dust some cornmeal on a sheet of waxed paper and place the dough rounds on top. Sprinkle the rounds with a little more cornmeal, cover and allow to rise for 30 minutes.

Heat a greased griddle pan over a medium heat. Cook the muffins on the griddle for about 10 minutes each side until lightly browned.

Crack the eggs into a large jug or mixing bowl. Add the cream and a little seasoning, then whisk until pale yellow.

Cut two of the muffins in half and toast until desired, then spread generously with butter (store the leftover muffins in an airtight container).

Melt the butter in a frying pan over a medium heat. Turn up the heat slightly and add the beaten egg. Leave it to cook for 20 seconds, then gently mix with a spatula or wooden spoon. Cook for another 20 seconds, then stir in half the salmon that you've chopped. Mix until just cooked through.

To serve, place the remaining smoked salmon on a serving plate. Place the scrambled eggs on the buttered toasted muffin halves and sprinkle with a few chopped chives. Serve with the lemon wedges on the side, if you like.

PORK FAT & SCOTCH BONNET TOAST WITH PICKLED PEPPERS

BY THE CAMBERWELL ARMS

SERVES 4

---

4 slices of bread

Pork Fat
5 Scotch bonnet chillies (or as many as you can handle)
500g (1lb 2oz) minced pork fat (this will naturally include some minced pork)
1 tbsp sweet smoked paprika
Sea salt and ground black pepper

Pickled Peppers
200ml (7fl oz) caster sugar
200ml (7fl oz) red wine vinegar
200ml (7fl oz) water
500g (1lb 2oz) red peppers (capsicums), deseeded and cut into large squares or strips

Chef-director at The Camberwell Arms pub and restaurant since 2014 (he opened the pub at the tender age of 25), London-born Mike Davies, trained on the job, grafting in some of the city's finest gastropubs from the offset, including the award-winning Anchor and Hope in Waterloo and The Canton Arms. He opened Frank's Café and rooftop bar in a multi-storey car park in Peckham in 2008, a hot-spot which opens every summer (and does a mean weekend brunch) and his pub excels at modern British fare, with plenty of sunny Med charm and inventive touches.

—

'This dish has been on our menu since day one. Inspired by owner and head chef Mike after watching a lot of *The Sopranos* around the time of opening, it felt like a bit of a throwaway, but people have loved it ever since.'

To make the pork fat, wearing kitchen gloves, slice open the Scotch bonnet chillies and carefully remove the stems, but leave the seeds intact.

Put the pork fat in a saucepan over a low heat and add the Scotch bonnets and paprika. Cook gently until the fat has melted out of the mince and the remaining pieces have started to turn a light golden brown and crisp up a bit. Season with salt and pepper to taste, then transfer to a heatproof container and allow to cool. This makes more than you need for this recipe, but it will keep in an airtight container in the fridge for months.

For the pickled peppers, combine the sugar, vinegar and water in a small saucepan and simmer over a low heat for 5 minutes. Remove from the heat and allow to cool completely.

Lightly char the peppers by either roasting in very hot oven for a few minutes, grilling on a preheated barbecue flat plate or cooking in a dry frying pan over high heat until starting to blacken. Set aside to cool completely.

Place the peppers in a non-reactive bowl or container, pour over the pickle liquid and gently stir. Leave to sit in the liquor until cool. The pickled peppers will keep in the fridge for a few weeks.

When you're ready to serve, toast your bread, then spread it thickly with spicy pork fat, making sure to include some of the crispy bits. Place under a preheated grill for a couple of minutes, just to take the chill off the pork fat if it's coming from the fridge. Top liberally with the pickled peppers and serve immediately.

ONEPLATE: UGANDAN FARM
UGANDA

The skill to grow food from seed, to savour fresh, organic produce and regularly enjoy the comfort of a full stomach... at OnePlate this is something we want every child, no matter where they live in the world, to experience.

Set over 10 acres in Uganda, the OnePlate farm has been established as a source of nutritious food, skills training opportunities and income sources through various social enterprises, all of which aim to support the children we serve.

This is a wonderful project that offers a safe home and education to vulnerable and abandoned children, who are the major beneficiaries of the produce. Up to 150 children, previously malnourished and unable to escape a cycle of poverty, now receive a range of wholesome, healthy produce from the farm, including dairy, poultry, fruit and vegetables. In time, the goal of the farm is to generate three meals a day and 164,000 meals per year for the children.

Our aim is that the diversified farm will allow for a series of social enterprise opportunities, bringing year-round income sources. Education is a crucial by-product of the farm, with a skills training centre now established on site to upskill local farmers.

The entire team were delighted with the addition of a tractor to the farm, which is of significant benefit. The farm manager also rents the tractor out to other farmers, generating further income to go back into the maintenance of the farm. The tractor is both a tool and an enterprise, all in one.

The children who benefit from the bounty of produce have the opportunity to spend time enjoying the beautiful open spaces of the farm, learning how to care for the animals and crops. Children who choose not to go on to secondary school will have the opportunity to take advantage of agricultural training and employment opportunities for the longer term, joining the farm as team members.

ARNOLD BENNETT OMELETTE

BY MARTYN NAIL, THE DORCHESTER

MAKES 1

3 eggs
20g (¾oz) salted butter
Sea salt and ground black
  pepper

Mornay Sauce
250ml (9fl oz) whole milk
1 onion, peeled and quartered
1 bay leaf
2 cloves
30g (1oz) salted butter
30g (1oz) plain flour
100g (3½oz) mature Cheddar,
  grated
1 tsp English mustard
1 egg yolk
100ml (3½fl oz) whipping
  cream, whipped until it holds
  soft peaks

Smoked Fish
250ml (9fl oz) whole milk
100g (3½oz) smoked haddock,
  cubed

Previously the executive chef of Claridge's for 36 years, Martyn Nail joined the team as Culinary Director of The Dorchester, overseeing all aspects of culinary operations and the development and management of an entire brigade. From winning numerous awards himself, Martyn has been instrumental in building teams of excellence for three decades, who, over the years, have continued to win coveted accolades ensuring consistency, growth and an undivided spirit of camaraderie.

—

'This recipe makes one omelette but enough Mornay sauce to glaze four omelettes. For breakfast for four, you'll need 12 eggs and 400g (14oz) of fish, but you only need to increase the milk for poaching the fish to 500ml (17fl oz). Mornay sauce should always be made fresh, and never frozen, but it will keep in the fridge for 3–5 days.'

Begin by making the Mornay sauce. In a small saucepan over a medium heat, combine the milk, onion, bay leaf and cloves, then bring to the boil. Immediately reduce the heat to low and simmer for 5 minutes.

Meanwhile, in a separate saucepan, melt the butter over a medium heat, then stir in the flour with a wooden spoon or spatula until you have a smooth paste. Reduce the heat to low. Pass the milk through a sieve (discarding the onion, bay leaf and cloves) into the flour and butter paste. Whisk well to remove any lumps and cook over very low heat for 2–3 minutes until thickened.

Remove the pan from the heat and stir in the grated cheese until melted and smooth. Stir in the mustard and season to taste with salt and pepper, then beat in the egg yolk until completely incorporated. Cover the sauce and keep warm. (If you're making the Mornay sauce in advance, transfer to an airtight container, laying some cling film directly on the surface of the sauce to prevent a skin forming.) At this point, the sauce should have a velvety consistency but still be spoonable. When you're getting ready to glaze the omelette, loosen the Mornay sauce with a splash of the fish poaching liquid, as required, before folding in the whipped cream.

To poach the fish, bring the milk to the boil in a heavy-based saucepan, then carefully add the haddock. Reduce the heat to low and poach for 5 minutes. You will know the haddock is ready when you pierce it with a sharp knife and encounter no resistance. Remove from the heat.

continued overleaf

While the fish is poaching, make the omelette. Preheat the oven to 200°C (180°C fan/400°F/gas mark 6) or turn on your grill.

Crack the eggs into a mixing bowl and, using a fork, whisk until they are nice and foamy. Add pepper. You can add salt, too, but keep in mind the smoked fish will be salty and the Mornay sauce was made with salted butter.

In a non-stick frying pan, melt the butter over a medium-high heat, then add the egg. Let the egg sit, untouched, for 15–20 seconds then, as it begins to set, use a fork or spatula to continuously move the edge of the egg, folding it towards the centre – to prevent any scorching – while also, every so often, shaking the pan back and forth over the heat, which will ensure your egg remains spread out across the pan and your omelette sets evenly (to an untrained eye, it might look like you're scrambling the eggs). About 3 minutes into this, stop fiddling with it and let the omelette finish setting in the pan for a few moments. The omelette will continue to cook after it comes off the heat, so undercook it slightly.

Using a spatula, fold the omelette into a half-moon, then carefully slide it onto an ovenproof dish or plate. Gently unfold it back to its full-moon shape. (If you're making more than 1 omelette, make the remaining omelettes now.)

Using a slotted spoon, remove the haddock from the milk. Place it on the omelette and gently flake into smaller pieces. Carefully spoon about one-quarter of the Mornay sauce over the haddock to cover it completely. Transfer the dish or plate to the oven or grill and cook for 2–3 minutes until the Mornay sauce is golden and browned in spots.

KILLER SCOTCH EGG

BY THE BULL & LAST

MAKES 6

Light rapeseed oil, for deep-
  frying, plus 2 tsp for frying
1 small onion, finely diced
1 large garlic clove, finely
  chopped
6–8 sage leaves, chopped
6 eggs, at room temperature
300g (10½oz) pork mince
150g (5½oz) pork sausage
  meat
Sea salt and ground black
  pepper
English mustard, to serve

Coating
100g (3½oz) plain flour
200ml (7fl oz) whole milk
2 eggs
120g (4¼oz) panko
  breadcrumbs

TIP — *A deep-fat fryer is helpful
here, but not essential.*

This restored 300-year-old pub and coaching inn in Highgate, North London, is just a few steps from the verdant splendour of Hampstead Heath. A haven for everyone, from locals with their beloved dogs to the landlord's collection of taxidermy, it's your quintessential British pub taken up a few notches. Chef Ollie Pudney's menu is creative, seasonal and gutsy. Start with bar snacks – their killer Scotch egg is rightly famous – then consider roast beef sandwich with pickles, horseradish, frîtes and aioli, or ricotta and wild herb gnudi.

—

'A British classic, best eaten in a pub, and we're famous for ours. We've made a fair few of them over the years, so we know what we're doing!'

Heat the 2 teaspoons of oil in a frying pan over a medium-low heat, add the onion and garlic and sweat until soft but not coloured. Remove from the heat, add the chopped sage, season with salt and pepper and allow to cool.

Bring a medium saucepan of water to the boil. Place all 6 eggs in the water quickly and carefully and cook for exactly 5 minutes and 45 seconds (a digital timer is useful here). While they are cooking, fill a mixing bowl with a handful of ice cubes and add some cold water. When the eggs are cooked, carefully lift them out of the water with a slotted spoon and put them straight in the bowl of iced water to stop them cooking.

Put the pork mince, sausage meat and cooled onion and garlic mixture in a mixing bowl. Season with salt and pepper and mix everything together very well before weighing out into 6 balls (each ball should weigh roughly 75g/2½oz).

Now remove the eggs from the water and gently peel off the shells.

Spread a piece of cling film about 60cm (23½in) long out on the worktop, then fold it over lengthways to make it double the thickness. Pat a ball of pork meat in the centre of the cling film and flatten to create a round shape about 10–12cm (4–5in) in diameter. Put an egg on top and use the cling film to help roll the meat around the egg. Use your hands to press it gently to shape it and hold it together (remembering there is a soft egg in the middle). Remove from the cling film and set aside, then repeat with the remaining balls and eggs. Place in the fridge for at least 20 minutes.

Heat enough rapeseed oil for deep-frying in a deep-fat fryer (or fill a heavy-based, deep saucepan no more than two-thirds full) until it reaches 165°C (329°F). If you don't have a thermometer, test the oil by dropping in a cube of bread – it should brown in 30 seconds.

continued overleaf

Place the flour in a wide, shallow bowl and season it with salt and pepper. Whisk the milk and eggs together in a second bowl until smooth. Place the panko breadcrumbs in a third bowl. Now you are going to coat the Scotch eggs – have a slotted spoon ready. Place a cooling rack inside a baking tray, ready for draining the fried eggs.

Lightly dust a chilled egg with flour all over, then submerge it completely in the milk and egg mixture. Remove with the slotted spoon so it is only lightly coated then place it in the breadcrumbs, moving it quickly to coat completely. Use your hands to press the crumbs onto the egg evenly if you need to. Return the Scotch egg to the milk and egg mixture for a second coating, then back into the breadcrumbs for a final coating. Repeat this process for all 6 eggs.

Depending on the size of the fryer (or your pan), you may need to fry the eggs in batches. Cook the eggs for 5 minutes and 15 seconds, then lift them from the oil with a slotted spoon and transfer them to the cooling rack and tray to drain. Season with salt and pepper and allow to rest for 10–12 minutes.

To serve, cut each egg in half, season with salt and pepper and serve with a generous blob of mustard.

LOBSTER OMELETTE
BY THE GORING

SERVES 4

12 eggs
240g (8½oz) fresh cooked
  lobster meat (see *Note* below)
Sea salt and ground black
  pepper
Finely chopped chives, to serve

Thermidor Glaze
35g (1¼oz) butter
35g (1¼oz) plain flour
2 egg yolks
120ml (4fl oz) good-quality
  shellfish stock
½ tsp Dijon mustard
15g (½oz) Parmesan, grated
150ml (5fl oz) double cream
115ml (3¾fl oz) whole milk
Juice of 1 lemon

NOTE — *Ask your fishmonger
for par-cooked lobster and ask
them to remove the meat for
you. One lobster is enough for
4 people. You can substitute the
lobster meat for fresh picked
white crabmeat if you prefer,
or if it's more readily available.*

Long associated with royalty – it's the closest hotel to Buckingham Palace and Kate Middleton stayed here the night before marrying Prince William – The Goring hotel in Belgravia has a stately reputation. Executive chef Graham Squire oversees a menu of sumptuous dishes in the Michelin-starred Dining Room, classic at heart yet not fussily so. For breakfast or brunch in the Dining Room there's Full English or Continental and in The Bar and Lounge there's the signature lobster omelette, classic club sandwich and the Goring Caesar salad.

To make the thermidor glaze, melt the butter in a heavy-based saucepan over a low heat, add the flour and mix with a spatula until a smooth paste forms that comes away from the sides of the pan. Continue to cook for about 3 minutes, constantly stirring with the spatula.

Once the flour has cooked out, remove the pan from the heat and add the egg yolks, shellfish stock, mustard and Parmesan, and mix until smooth. Now add the milk, cream and lemon juice, with salt and pepper to taste. Mix well to incorporate and set aside (this will keep in the fridge for up to 3 days).

Preheat the oven to 220°C (200°C fan/425°F/gas mark 7) on the grill setting.

Use 3 eggs per omelette. Lightly beat the eggs in a bowl and season with salt and pepper.

Heat a 24cm (9½in) non-stick frying pan over a medium heat. Add the beaten egg and gently cook, folding constantly, until an omelette begins to form but is still runny on top. Slide the omelette into a 24cm (9½in) ovenproof dish, runny-side up. Repeat with the remaining eggs to make 3 more omelettes, placing each in its own individual ovenproof dish (if you only have one dish, cook one at a time).

Place some lobster meat on top of each omelette (reserving some for serving) and add a generous spoonful of the thermidor glaze, spreading it to create a smooth layer on top.

Place the omelettes in the oven and grill for about 3 minutes, or until golden brown. Fold them over into three, then transfer each omelette to a warmed plate. Serve immediately, with the reserved lobster meat and remaining glaze and a few chives sprinkled on top.

SHEPHERD'S PIE
BY THE IVY

A little sunflower oil
200g (7oz) lean minced beef
200g (7oz) lean minced lamb
2 shallots, finely chopped
100g (3½oz) button
  mushrooms, brushed clean
  and finely chopped
1 medium carrot (about
  100g/3½oz), finely chopped
3 thyme sprigs, leaves picked
1 tbsp tomato paste
200g (7oz) chopped canned
  tomatoes
100ml (3½fl oz) red wine
1 tbsp plain flour
2 tbsp Worcestershire sauce,
  plus extra to taste
300ml (10½fl oz) veal stock
  (available from good-quality
  supermarkets – if you can't
  find it, use beef or chicken
  stock)
3 oregano sprigs, leaves
  chopped
Sea salt and ground black
  pepper

Mashed Potato Topping
1kg (2lb 3oz) potatoes, peeled
  and chopped into even-sized
  chunks
50g (1¾oz) unsalted butter
Ground white pepper

The original, iconic West End restaurant, famous for being 'the place to be seen', started life as an Italian café in 1917. Fast forward a few decades and The Ivy brand has expanded, with a series of casual dining locations opening their doors across the UK. Its ethos of timeless elegance has endured and seasonal, classic comfort food with a touch of luxury is at the core of what they offer – their shepherd's pie is ambrosial. Classy weekend brunch specials include lobster and prawn benedict, eggs royale, and truffled egg Florentine.

Lightly oil the minced beef and lamb. Heat a large frying pan over a high heat until smoking, add the minced meats and cook, stirring constantly, for about 5 minutes until light brown. Pour off the excess liquid and transfer the meat to a dish.

In the same pan, heat a little oil over a medium heat and gently sweat the shallots, mushrooms, carrot and thyme for about 8 minutes until soft. Return the mince to the pan, stir in the tomato paste and cook for about 5 minutes, then add the chopped tomatoes and red wine and reduce for about 10 minutes. Add the flour and mix thoroughly, then add the Worcestershire sauce and stock. Bring to the boil and simmer for 30 minutes. Season with salt and pepper, then add more Worcestershire sauce to taste, if required, followed by the oregano. Remove the pan from the heat.

Preheat the oven to 180°C (160°C fan/350°F/gas mark 4).

Cook the potatoes in salted boiling water for about 15 minutes until soft, then drain and return the potatoes to the pan over gentle heat to remove excess moisture. Using a masher or ricer, thoroughly mash the potato, then stir through the butter and season to taste with salt and white pepper.

Spoon the mince mixture into an ovenproof dish. Top with the mashed potato (you can pipe it if you have the time), transfer to the oven and bake for about 30 minutes until golden.

AVOCADO WITH TOMATO SALSA & YUZU DRESSING

BY THE IVY ASIA

SERVES 2

Taking you on journey through the senses, The Ivy Asia is a vibrant and playful destination for high-class food and theatrical cocktails. Try this dish instead of your usual avocado on toast.

Pickled Red Onion
45g (1½oz) caster sugar
1 tsp table salt
3 tbsp rice vinegar
100g (3½oz) red onion, finely sliced

Tomato & Coriander Salsa
100g (3½oz) tomato,
100g (3½oz) red onion
10g (⅓oz) coriander
10g (⅓oz) green chilli
20ml (1½ tbsp) lemon juice
Large pinch of sea salt flakes

Yuzu Dressing
25g (1oz) aji amarillo pepper paste
1½ tbsp rice vinegar
2 tsp soy sauce
1 tsp lemon juice
1 tsp yuzu juice
2 tsp vegetable oil

To Assemble & Serve
1 avocado, halved and sliced at an angle 1cm (½in) thick
3 tbsp yuzu dressing (see above)
30g (1oz) tomato and coriander salsa (see above)
10g (⅓oz) pickled red onion (see above)
8 slices of deseeded green chilli
Finely sliced spring onion
Micro herbs (optional)
10g (⅓oz) masago arare (popped rice crackers) (optional)

Pickled Red Onion
Dissolve the sugar and salt in the rice vinegar. Place the onion in a non-reactive container and pour the pickling vinegar over the top. Refrigerate for 48 hours before use.

Tomato & Coriander Salsa
Very finely chop the tomato, onion, coriander and chilli together, then transfer to a bowl. Add the lemon juice and salt, then mix well. Transfer to the fridge, covered, and leave for several hours, but preferably overnight, for the flavours to meld together.

Yuzu Dressing
Whisk all the ingredients except the vegetable oil in a metal bowl until combined. Whisking constantly, slowly pour in the vegetable oil until you have an emulsified dressing.

To Assemble & Serve
To serve, place the sliced avocado on a plate and dress with the yuzu dressing. Sprinkle over the salsa, pickled red onion, chilli, spring onion, micro herbs and masago arare, if using.

PORTLAND CRAB & GRILLED PUNTARELLE ON SOURDOUGH

BY TOKLAS

SERVES 6

360g (12¾oz) white crabmeat
1 tsp crushed fennel seeds
Small pinch of chilli flakes
50ml (1¾fl oz) olive oil, plus
   extra for the puntarelle
½ bunch of dill, fronds picked
30ml (2 tbsp) lemon juice, plus
   extra for the puntarelle
½ head of puntarelle, trimmed
   (asparagus works too)
1 sourdough loaf, thickly sliced
Sea salt

Whipped Brown Crab Butter
150g (5½oz) unsalted butter
75g (2½oz) brown crabmeat
20g (¾oz) crème fraîche
1 tsp lemon juice

From the founders of Frieze art magazine and festival, Toklas restaurant and bar (and the bakery next door) is named after American food writer Alice B. Toklas, partner of Gertrude Stein, and her 1954 food memoir. The weekly-changing menu of modern European food celebrates Mediterranean and British ingredients in quietly elegant fashion. The terrace is a serene, verdant escape from the frenetic hustle of the Strand. For brunch, head to the bakery and café, which offers stellar bread, patisserie, Roman-style pizza and sandwiches; the produce is second to none.

To make the whipped brown crab butter, blend the butter in a food processor for 2–3 minutes until whipped. Add the remaining ingredients and blend briefly to combine, then taste and season with a little salt if needed.

In a bowl, toss the white crabmeat with the fennel seeds, dried chilli, olive oil, dill and lemon juice.

Bring a large saucepan of salted water to the boil, add the puntarelle and blanch quickly. Immediately drain and plunge into ice-cold water. Heat a chargrill pan over a high heat and grill the puntarelle for 5 minutes until charred. Season with salt, olive oil and lemon juice and remove the puntarelle from the pan.

Grill the sourdough bread slices until toasted, then spread with the whipped brown crab butter. Top with the marinated white crabmeat and puntarelle, then serve.

MONTGOMERY CHEESE SOUFFLÉ

BY LALEE, THE CADOGAN

SERVES 12

Marinated Apple
4 Pink Lady apples, cored and cut into matchsticks
200ml (7fl oz) apple juice
30ml (2 tbsp) lemon juice

Cheese Soufflé
200g (7oz) unsalted butter, plus extra for greasing
200g (7oz) T45 flour or other strong white flour
1.2 litres (40fl oz) whole milk
600g (1lb 5oz) Montgomery Cheddar, grated
8 egg yolks
10 egg whites
Butter, for greasing
200g (7oz) panko breadcrumbs
Sea salt and ground black pepper

Orange Mustard Dressing
3 tbsp freshly squeezed orange juice
3 tbsp extra virgin olive oil
1 tbsp Dijon mustard

To Serve
3 celery sticks, peeled and cut into matchsticks
Handful of green beans, trimmed
Caramelised walnuts
Pea shoots

The Cadogan hotel's LaLee all-day café-restaurant is named in homage to Chelsea socialite, actor and icon Lillie Langtry, whose European travels inspire the dawn to dusk menus (LaLee was the name for her luxury railway carriage). Choose to start your day in this elegant setting and you'll be treated to an extensive breakfast menu with fresh viennoiserie and continental buffet; for lunch, signature veal or chicken schnitzel and Dover sole meunière are always on the menu, and dinner is a glamorous affair.

Marinated Apple
Combine the ingredients in a sealed bag and leave to marinate for 1 hour.

Cheese Soufflé
In a saucepan over a low heat, make a roux with the flour and butter then gradually pour in the milk, stirring and cooking until thickened. Add the cheese and stir until melted and incorporated, then season with salt and pepper. Transfer to a bowl and allow to cool. Once cool, whisk in the egg yolk, then chill again.

Preheat the oven to 170°C (150°C fan/325°F/gas mark 3).

Whisk the egg whites to stiff peaks, then gently fold into the cheese sauce until completely incorporated.

Grease 12 dariole moulds, of 100ml (3½fl oz) capacity, with butter and line generously with the panko breadcrumbs. Pour the soufflé mixture into the moulds until they are three-quarters full, then transfer the moulds to a baking dish. Pour in enough boiling water to come halfway up the sides of the moulds, then transfer to the oven and bake for 20 minutes or until risen.

Orange Mustard Dressing
Whisk the ingredients together until emulsified.

To Serve
Blanch the celery in a saucepan of salted boiling water for 20 seconds. Refresh in iced water, then drain and set aside. Repeat with the green beans.

Toss the green beans, celery and marinated apple in the orange and mustard dressing, then season and divide between plates. Top with some pea shoots and caramelised walnuts, then unmould the soufflés onto the salad and serve.

COURGETTE & CHEDDAR CORNBREAD

BY SAMI HARVEY, THE LAUNDRY

Pickled Jalapeños
250ml (9fl oz) cider vinegar
100g (3½oz) caster sugar
20g (¾oz) table salt
200g (7oz) jalapeños, finely
  sliced into rounds

**Courgette & Cheddar
Cornbread**
125g (4½oz) plain flour
190g (6¾oz) cornmeal
45g (1½oz) baking powder
4 eggs
440ml (15fl oz) milk
110g (3¾oz) butter, melted
125g (4½oz) Cheddar, grated
250g (9oz) courgette
  (zucchini), grated
Sea salt and ground black
  pepper

Black Bean & Tomato Salsa
400g (14oz) can of black
  beans, drained and rinsed
300g (10½oz) cherry tomatoes,
  halved
½ red onion, finely diced
Juice of 2 limes
15g (½oz) coriander, finely
  chopped, plus extra to serve
75ml (5 tbsp) mirin

Green Goddess Dressing
150g (5½oz) mayonnaise
150g (5½oz) cream cheese
½ small garlic clove, crushed
Small handful each of chives,
  parsley and tarragon, roughly
  chopped
Juice of 1 lemon

New Zealander Melanie Brown moved to London in 2005 to work at Peter Gordon's Providores & Tapa Room and as a pastry chef at Raymond Blanc's Le Petit Blanc, going on to launch a wine-importing business championing New World wines. Fusing her wine knowledge with her culinary acumen, she opened The Laundry all-day bistro and wine shop in Brixton in 2019. Working closely with Australian-born head chef Samantha Harvey, her crowd pleasing menus are Antipodean at heart, and full of sunny flourishes: expect everything from Turkish eggs and The Laundry Fry Up to toasted banana bread with honeycomb butter.

Pickled Jalapeños
Warm the vinegar, sugar and salt in a saucepan over a low heat until the sugar and salt have dissolved. Transfer to a heatproof bowl and allow to cool completely. Add the sliced jalapeños and leave to pickle for 24 hours.

Courgette & Cheddar Cornbread
Preheat the oven to 190°C (170°C fan/375°F/gas mark 5). Line a large loaf tin with baking paper.

Combine the dry ingredients in a large bowl and the eggs, milk and melted butter in a separate large bowl. Fold the wet ingredients into the dry ingredients, then stir through the courgette and Cheddar until just combined. Season to taste, generously.

Tip the batter into the prepared tin and bake for 1 hour (cover the cornbread with foil halfway through cooking if the top is starting to brown too quickly). Leave to cool in the tin for 10 minutes, then turn out onto a wire rack.

Black Bean & Tomato Salsa
Combine the ingredients in a bowl and season to taste. Set aside.

Green Goddess Dressing
Place the ingredients in a high-speed blender and blend until smooth. Store in the fridge until needed.

To Finish & Serve
Heat a griddle pan over a high heat, cut the cornbread into thick slices and toast in the griddle pan on both sides until char marks appear.

Divide the toasted cornbread between plates and top with a large spoonful of the green goddess dressing, followed by the black bean and tomato salsa. Scatter with the pickled jalapeños and finish with extra coriander.

TEA ROOM EST. 1942

Kindness is choosing to
acknowledge and celebrate
the beauty in others.

BREAKFAST QUESADILLA

BY MALIBU KITCHEN, THE NED

SERVES 1

---

2 eggs, lightly beaten
40g (1½oz) Comté, grated
20g (¾oz) mushrooms,
  chopped and sautéed
20g (¾oz) spring onion, sliced
Knob of butter
2 flour tortillas
Sea salt and ground black
  pepper

Pico de Gallo
4 tomatoes, chopped
1 red onion, finely chopped
Small bunch of coriander,
  leaves finely chopped
Juice of 1 lime

Avocado Dip
1 avocado, mashed
Juice of ½ lime
15g (½oz) coriander, chopped

To Serve
40g (1½oz) sour cream
2 coriander sprigs
2 lime wedges

A huge operation, this grand hotel, brought to London's Square Mile by the Soho House group, is home to seven restaurants and three bars (some are members only). In the cavernous central lobby you'll find Cecconi's Venetian-style brasserie (there's a dedicated negroni menu), and then there's the Nickel Bar or the Electric Bar & Diner where you can indulge in a Stateside rendition of breakfast and brunch classics, though you may prefer Malibu Kitchen for a more virtuous start to the day.

—

'Malibu Kitchen brings Californian food to the City with a healthy menu of superfood salads, raw vegetables, cured fish and meat, flatbreads, juices and smoothies. A firm favourite on the menu is the breakfast quesadilla, a Mexican-inspired brunch dish with a southern Californian twist. The creamy, cheesy eggs are sandwiched between two fried tortillas, with fresh tomatoes and avocado on the side.'

To make the pico de gallo, combine the ingredients in a bowl and set aside in the fridge.

To make the avocado dip, in a separate bowl, stir the ingredients together with a pinch each of salt and pepper; set aside.

In another bowl, combine the eggs, Comté, mushrooms and spring onion. Season well.

Heat a frying pan over a medium heat. Add the butter and when melted add the egg mixture to the pan. Cook gently until the eggs are scrambled to your desired consistency. Season with salt and pepper to taste.

Spread the scrambled egg over one of the flour tortillas and top with the second tortilla to make a quesadilla. Gently fry the quesadilla in the same pan, until golden brown on both sides, taking care not to overcook the egg. Remove the quesadilla from the pan and transfer to a clean chopping board.

Cut the quesadilla into quarters and arrange on a plate with the pico de gallo, sour cream and avocado dip served in a bowl alongside. Garnish with the coriander sprigs and a couple of lime wedges for added freshness.

THE LONDON ROAST

BY SHAUN SEARLEY, THE QUALITY CHOP HOUSE

SERVES 8

800g (1lb 12oz) bone-in ribeye
  steak, 4cm (1½in) thick
75–125g (2½–4½oz) cold
  unsalted butter
1 large thyme sprig
2 garlic cloves, crushed
Sea salt and ground black
  pepper

Lyonnaise Onions
6 small white onions, thinly
  sliced
150g (5½oz) sliced beef fat
½ tsp thyme leaves

Yorkshire Puddings
1 cup of free-range organic
  eggs
1 cup of whole milk
1 cup of plain flour
Beef dripping, for the tin

After stints at Bistrotheque in East London and Paternoster Chop House, Shaun became head chef at historic The Quality Chop House in Farringdon, where he became renowned for his gutsy, imaginative takes on modern British food – namely the infamous beef mince on dripping toast (his confit potatoes have also become a signature dish), and his meat cookery is legendary. Open since 1869, the restaurant now also has a butchery next door.

Lyonnaise Onions
Combine the onions with the beef fat and 2 teaspoons of salt in a heavy-based saucepan and place over a low heat. Add the thyme and gently stew until the onions begin to caramelise, stirring occasionally. This takes a couple of hours to do properly. When the onions are a rich golden brown colour, remove from the heat and strain off any excess fat. If you want to store them for a few weeks, don't discard the fat but leave it covering the onions to preserve them.

Yorkshire Puddings
Whisk the eggs and milk together in a large bowl. Gradually whisk in the flour and 1 teaspoon of salt, whisking continuously. Once combined, pass the batter through a fine sieve into a jug (to make pouring easier) and leave to rest for a couple of hours.

Preheat the oven to 220°C (200°C fan/425°F/gas mark 7).

Add 1cm (½in) of beef dripping to each hole of a Yorkshire pudding tin and place in the hot oven for 3–4 minutes – we want the fat hot but not too scorching. Carefully slide the tin out of the oven, and divide enough batter between the holes until it's 2cm (¾in) from the top. Quickly return the tin to the oven and bake for 16 minutes. Have a look through the oven door before you open it – the Yorkshires should have risen nicely and be golden brown on top, with lightly golden sides. If you open the oven too early they will collapse, so be patient. They may need another few minutes. When they are ready, the walls and tops should be crisp, while the bottoms should be still a little spongy.

continued overleaf

Roast Potatoes

2.5kg (5½lb) King Edward
  potatoes, peeled and cut into
  4cm (1½in) pieces
200g (7oz) duck fat
2 garlic bulbs
Large handful of thyme
Large handful of rosemary

Honey-roast Carrots

2 bunches of leafy carrots
50g (1¾oz) beef dripping
100g (3½oz) butter
100g (3½oz) honey

To Serve

100g (3½oz) Lyonnaise onions
  (see previous page), warmed
40g (1½oz) caramelised
  walnuts, roughly chopped
Steamed purple sprouting
  broccoli
Olive oil, for drizzling

Roast Potatoes

Rinse the potatoes thoroughly in cold water while you bring a large saucepan of salted water to the boil. Add the potatoes and simmer gently for 15–20 minutes – they should be completely cooked through but still holding their shape. Carefully drain onto a flat perforated tray if you have one, to avoid piling the potato pieces on top of each other. Leave to steam dry for 10 minutes.

Meanwhile, put the duck fat in a large roasting tin and heat in the oven at 220°C (200°C fan/425°F/gas mark 7) for 10 minutes. The potatoes should now be nicely dry and cracking on the outside. Pull the tin of duck fat from the oven and carefully transfer the potatoes to the fat. At this stage, a few pieces of potato may break into smaller pieces, but don't worry; varied sizes means more texture, as the potato will cook at different times. Baste with some of the fat and season with salt. Roast for 15–20 minutes.

Break the garlic into individual cloves and crush with the back of a knife. Add to the tin with the potatoes, along with the herbs, and gently stir. Roast for another 20 minutes, stirring halfway through. Remove the tin from the oven and stir again – at this stage the potatoes should be crisp and golden brown (return to the oven for another few minutes if not). Transfer the roast potatoes and garlic cloves to a preheated serving dish and season with more salt and a little pepper.

Honey-roast Carrots

Preheat the oven to 190°C (170°C fan/375°F/gas mark 5).

Trim the carrots, leaving 3cm (1¼in) of stalk still attached. Wash the leaves and reserve. Peel and wash the rest of the carrots. Coat the carrots in the beef dripping in a small roasting tray and season with salt. Roast for 15 minutes, then add the butter and honey. Mix well and roast for another 15 minutes. You want the carrots to caramelise but still have a little bite – keep testing them with a skewer as they cook. Allow the carrots to rest.

Steak

Have the oven temperature at 90°C (190°F). Unusually, we cook ribeyes directly from the fridge rather than letting them come to room temperature first, which can quicken the cooking process but can also mean the centre of the steak cooks too quickly. Our method ensures an even cook.

Season the steak with salt and put it, standing upright and fat-side down, in a large heavy-based frying pan. Turn the heat to low. Gradually increase the heat to medium and wait for about 5 minutes until there is enough rendered fat bubbling away in the pan to caramelise the steak. Turn the steak onto its side and turn up the heat. Flip the steak after 1 minute and cook the other side for an additional 1 minute.

When both sides are nicely browned, add 75g (2½oz) of the butter to the pan. Cook the steak for another 1 minute on each side. If the butter starts to brown but the steak hasn't yet caramelised (you'll know when it has as the crust will be nut-brown and smell sweet rather than burnt), then add the remaining butter.

During the last 30 seconds of cooking, add the thyme sprig and crushed garlic to the pan, then transfer the steak to a baking tray to rest for 5 minutes.

Probe the centre of the steak with a meat thermometer; it should be just under 20°C (68°F). Transfer to the oven and cook for 25 minutes, then remove from the oven and probe the centre of the steak again – it should be between 48°C (118°F) and 52°C (125°F). If it's not, return it to the oven for a little longer. Rest the steak for 5 minutes before removing the bone from the meat and slicing.

To Serve

Get yourself a lovely sharing dish or platter and start by spreading over the warm Lyonnaise onions. Add the carrots and pour over the carrot resting juices and fats. Sprinkle with a few carrot top leaves and the caramelised walnuts. Pour over the resting juices and season with a pinch of sea salt and some black pepper. Serve the sliced steak alongside the roast potatoes, Yorkshire puddings, honey-roasted carrots and a simple side of steamed purple sprouting broccoli, drizzled with a little olive oil.

TWICE-BAKED GOAT'S CHEESE SOUFFLÉ

BY THE RITZ

SERVES 5

Onion Purée

15g (½oz) butter

500g (1lb 2oz) white onions, diced

10g (⅓oz) garlic cloves (about 2–3 cloves), chopped

1 thyme sprig

15g (½oz) sugar

500ml (17fl oz) vegetable stock

Sea salt and ground black pepper

Chervil Butter Sauce

50g (1¾oz) shallot, finely chopped

1 tbsp white wine vinegar

50ml (1¾fl oz) white wine

75ml (2½fl oz) vegetable stock

25ml (1fl oz) double cream

75g (2½oz) cold unsalted butter

½ bunch of chervil, chopped

Juice of ½ lemon

Soufflé

25g (1oz) plain flour

25g (1oz) unsalted butter, plus extra for greasing

160ml (5¼fl oz) milk

3 egg yolks

200g (7oz) Cabécou goat's cheese

125g (4½oz) breadcrumbs

50g (1¾oz) hazelnuts, toasted and ground

10 egg whites

25ml (1fl oz) lemon juice

Dining at this much-loved institution in the heart of Piccadilly is a journey of epicurean indulgence: holding fast to napery and formality, the Ritz's brigade of solicitous staff and the regal, elegant aesthetic make for a memorable meal. For breakfast, there's a budget-busting Prestige Breakfast with caviar or truffle (you can opt for simpler fare) or lunch at the sumptuous Rivoli Bar or Michelin-starred Ritz Restaurant, where Executive Chef John Williams MBE oversees a flawless and sophisticated carte of Escoffier-inspired dishes. Afternoon tea in the Palm Court is likewise a sumptuous affair.

Onion Purée

Melt the butter in a frying pan over a medium-low heat. Add the onion, garlic and thyme and sweat gently until translucent. Add the sugar and cook a little longer, then pour in the stock and stir to combine. Cover with a lid and continue to cook until the onion and garlic are soft and the stock has almost evaporated. Transfer to a blender and purée to a smooth sauce, then pass through a fine-meshed sieve into a bowl.

Chervil Butter Sauce

Place the shallots, vinegar and wine in a saucepan over a medium heat. Gently cook until the mixture has reduced to a syrup, then add the vegetable stock and continue to cook until the liquid has reduced by another two-thirds. Add the cream and stir through, then remove the pan from the heat and whisk in the butter to create a glossy sauce. Add the chervil and lemon juice, and season to taste with salt and pepper.

Soufflé

Mix the flour and butter in a saucepan with a wooden spoon over a medium heat. Once the flour has cooked out, gradually add the milk, mixing constantly, until the mixture starts to thicken. Remove the pan from the heat and crumble in half the cheese, stirring until melted. When the cheese is fully incorporated, mix in the egg yolks. Set aside.

continued overleaf

To Garnish
(use whatever seasonal
vegetables are available;
we like to use the following)
Small handful of podded peas
Small handful of podded broad
  beans, blanched
5 young asparagus spears,
  blanched and sliced into bite-
  sized pieces
5 baby carrots, steamed until
  tender then halved diagonally
Small handful of long baby
  navets (turnips), trimmed and
  halved
Small handful of radishes,
  trimmed
Small handful of pea shoots
Edible flowers

Preheat the oven to 180°C (160°C fan/350°F/gas mark 4). Line five 70ml (2¼fl oz) ramekins with butter, wiping upwards to allow the soufflé to rise, then coat with the breadcrumbs and ground hazelnuts.

Whisk the egg whites with a pinch of salt and the lemon juice to stiff peaks. Fold in one-third of the béchamel, then fold in the rest. Divide half the soufflé batter between the ramekins, then crumble in the remaining cheese. Top with the remaining soufflé mixture, then transfer the ramekins to a baking dish. Add boiling water to come halfway up the sides of the ramekins and bake for 7–8 minutes until risen. Rest for 20 minutes in the ramekins, then turn the soufflés out onto a greased baking tray and return to the oven for 5 minutes.

To Serve
Warm the onion purée and spoon in the centre of each plate. Place a soufflé on top of the purée and spoon the vegetables around the soufflé. Warm the chervil butter sauce and spoon it over the vegetables.

HESTON
BLUMENTHAL

OBE

Internationally famous for his award-
winning, 3-Michelin-starred The Fat Duck in
Berkshire, Heston Blumenthal is considered to
be one of the best and most influential chefs of
his generation. Completely self-taught, he has
pushed the boundaries of a traditional kitchen
and changed the way people cook and think
about eating. Heston has received a number of
doctorates from UK universities and is a Fellow
of The Royal Society of Chemistry as well as
The Royal Academy of Culinary Arts. In 2006 he
was awarded an OBE by Her Majesty the Queen
Elizabeth for his services to British gastronomy.

No stranger to charitable projects, Heston jumped
at the chance to be involved in the book, telling
us: 'Charity is all about supporting each other and
awareness; if you are reading this, I thank you, for
supporting those less fortunate than ourselves and
appreciating the amazing work this charity does.
I believe our relationship with food is the one thing
that can connect us to form communities, nourish
each other, and to unlock positive emotions.
OnePlate has the same outlook and goes out into
the world to make these relationships flourish.'

HESTON'S CORONATION CHICKEN

BY HESTON BLUMENTHAL, DINNER

MAKES 8 TARTS / SERVES 4

Two-Michelin starred Dinner by Heston at the plush Mandarin Oriental, Hyde Park, has been serving beautifully crafted plates of food since 2011. 'Modern dining inspired by history' is its maxim, and culinary sorcery plays out to stunning effect. 'Meat fruit' – liver parfait masquerading as a mandarin – epitomises the ultra-modern, scientific approach to reimagining historic British dishes. It's all very high-end, however the summer-only terrace offers a more casual menu.

MAKES 8 TARTS / SERVES 4

Tart Cases
125g (4½oz) clarified butter
4 sheets brick pastry

Toasted Smoked Almonds
20g (¾oz) apple wood chips
200g (7oz) peeled almonds

Curry Powder
15g (½oz) cumin seeds
6g (⅕oz) nigella seeds
10g (⅓oz) ground turmeric
30g (1oz) coriander seeds
6g (⅕oz) fennel seeds

Apricot Ketchup
Splash of grapeseed oil
150g (5½oz) white onions, sliced
50g (1¾oz) fresh ginger, peeled and sliced
20g (¾oz) garlic, sliced
500g (1lb 2oz) dried apricots, roughly chopped
5g (1 tsp) curry powder (see above)
50g (1¾oz) sugar
300g (10½oz) water
300g (10½oz) cider vinegar

Chicken Curry Oil
100g (3½oz) chicken skin, roughly cut into pieces
1 garlic clove, peeled
270g (9½oz) grapeseed oil
Zest of ½ lemon
1 thyme sprig
10g (⅓oz) curry powder (see above)
Pinch cumin seeds
2 green cardamom pods

Tart Cases

Melt the clarified butter. Place a sheet of brick pastry on the worktop and brush on a thin layer of clarified butter. Add another sheet and repeat until you have layered 4 sheets. Chill for at least 15 minutes, then cut the pastry into rounds using a 7cm (2¾in) ring and store in the fridge until needed.

To shape into cases, peel 2 layers of the pastry off and lay over an upturned fluted tart tin (a 4.5cm/1¾in brioche case). Place another tart tin on top and repeat until you have a stack of 5 layers of shell and 4 layers of pastry.

Preheat the oven to 160°C (140°C fan/325°F/gas mark 3). Bake the cases for 35 minutes until golden. Remove from the oven, then before they get too cold, remove the tart tins and trim the pastry as necessary.

Toasted Smoked Almonds

Soak the apple wood chips in water for 5 minutes, then drain. Fill the smoke box from the smoker with the soaked chips (or put the chips in a small metal cup and place this inside a large metal pot with a lid). Place the peeled almonds in a large perforated gastro tray, ensuring they are in a single layer. Place the tray in the smoker (or pot) and smoke for 50 minutes. Remove from the smoke chamber.

Preheat the oven to 200°C (180°C fan/400°F/gas mark 6) Slice the smoked almonds lengthways into slices 1mm thick. Place on a baking tray and toast for 3 minutes, stirring them every minute to ensure even toasting. Remove from the oven and place on a clean, cold baking tray. Set aside to cool completely before using.

Curry Powder

Toast the spices separately in a hot, dry pan, then set aside to cool. Once cooled, place in a spice blender (or pestle and mortar) and blend to a fine powder. Pass through a fine sieve and keep in a cool, dry place.

Chicken Curry Mayo
40g (1½oz) egg yolk
  (about 2 eggs)
40g (1½oz) Dijon mustard
10g (⅓oz) white wine or
  blended vinegar
10g (⅓oz) vegetarian kombu
300g (10½oz) chicken curry oil
  (see opposite)

Chicken & Mayo Mix
100g (3½oz) chicken curry
  mayo (see above)
20g (¾oz) sour cream
120g (4½oz) diced cooked
  chicken breast
Pinch of finely chopped
  coriander
48 golden raisins, soaked in
  boiling water for 30 minutes,
  then drained (reserve 24 for
  garnish)

To Build a Tart (for 1 tart)
1 tart shell (see opposite)
25g (1oz) chicken & mayo mix
  (see above)
3 slices of smoked almonds
  (see opposite)
3 slices red grape
6 dots of apricot ketchup (see
  opposite)
3 pieces of crispy chicken skin
  (see above)
3 coriander cress leaves
3 reserved soaked raisins

Apricot Ketchup
Heat the oil in a pan and sweat the onions, ginger and garlic until translucent. Add the apricots and cook for 10 minutes, then add the curry powder and stir well. Add the remaining ingredients, bring to a simmer and keep simmering for 20 minutes. Transfer to a blender and blend until smooth. Pass through a fine sieve and leave to cool. Store in the fridge until needed. (This will make more than you need – leftovers are great with cheese or in sandwiches.)

Chicken Curry Oil
Place the chicken skin pieces in a pan over a medium heat and, stirring continuously, cook off all the water then let the skin turn golden and crispy, with all the fat rendered. Add the garlic and oil, followed by the lemon zest, thyme and all the spices. Bring the mixture to 60°C (140°F), then stir and remove from the heat. Remove and reserve the crispy chicken skin. Let the oil cool, then pass through a fine sieve into a bowl, then again through a muslin cloth. Set to one side.

Chicken Curry Mayo
Put the egg yolks, mustard, vinegar and kombu in a blender and start to blend on a low speed, adding the chicken curry oil slowly. Keep turning up the speed setting, while slowly adding the chicken curry oil. Continue until you have used up all the oil and a thick mayonnaise has formed.

Chicken & Mayo Mix
In a bowl, combine the the mayo and sour cream. Mix well, then add the remaining ingredients and mix again.

To Assemble the Tart
Spoon the chicken and mayo mix into the tart shell, then decorate with the remaining ingredients.

CRAB, BEANS & WILD GARLIC

BY WILD BY TART

SERVES 4

Light oil, for frying
50g (1¾oz) smoked pancetta
2 shallots, chopped
1 garlic clove, chopped
1 bay leaf
Small bunch of thyme, leaves
    picked
150ml (5fl oz) white wine
250ml (9fl oz) good-quality
    chicken stock
400g (14oz) good-quality white
    beans from a jar (butterbeans
    or haricot are nice), drained
Small bunch of wild garlic,
    chopped (if in season)
Small bunch of parsley,
    chopped
Small bunch of tarragon,
    chopped
1 lemon, quartered
Sea salt and ground black
    pepper

Dressed Crab
3 tbsp mayonnaise
    (ideally homemade – with
    Dijon mustard and lots of
    lemon juice)
50g (1¾oz) brown crabmeat
50g (1¾oz) white crabmeat

Renowned catering duo Lucy Carr-Ellison and Jemima Jones met in their 20s when they both lived in New York and returned to London to launch Wild by Tart boutique catering company in 2012, creating feasts of bold, vibrant seasonal food for fashion shoots and celebrity clientele. Hot on the heels of the publication of their first cookbook, *A Love of Eating*, they opened Wild by Tart restaurant, bar and retail space in a former power station and coal store in Belgravia, where their sunny farm-to-fork ethos and killer cocktails have proved a runaway success.

Heat a little oil in a frying pan over a medium-high heat, add the pancetta and fry until golden. Reduce the heat, add the shallots, garlic, bay leaf and thyme and sauté for about 5 minutes. Add the white wine and stock and simmer for a couple of minutes, then add the beans and simmer for another 5 minutes. Add the wild garlic (if available) and most of the parsley and tarragon (keep a pinch for serving). Season to taste with salt and pepper.

Meanwhile, make the dressed crab. Ideally you want to make your own mayonnaise for this, but if you are using store-bought, jazz it up with a small dollop of mustard and a squeeze of lemon juice. Season well, then stir in the brown crabmeat and combine.

To serve, divide the herby beans between bowls and add a dollop of the crab mayonnaise. Dot with white crabmeat, squeeze over the lemon quarters and finish with a little salt and pepper and the remaining chopped herbs.

Gratitude unlocks joy.

ART NICHOLS

TRADITIONAL SODA BREAD WITH HOMEMADE BUTTER

BY DAYLESFORD ORGANIC

MAKES 1 LOAF

500g (1lb 2oz) wholemeal flour
½ tsp salt
2 tsp bicarbonate of soda
1 tsp baking powder
450g (1lb) natural yoghurt,
    kefir or buttermilk

Homemade Butter
1 litre (35fl oz) fresh cream,
    preferably unhomogenised
Generous pinch of sea salt
Any additional flavours – we
    love finely chopped roast
    garlic, grated horseradish,
    finely chopped herbs or
    freshly ground black pepper

Bringing 'a slice of the farm to the city', the Daylesford brand has opened a quartet of West London cafés in recent years, in Brompton Cross, Marylebone, Notting Hill and Pimlico.

The high-end retail operation started life as a bucolic organic farm shop and café founded by Carole Bamford at her Gloucestershire estate in 2002. Combining a steadfast commitment to organic farming and sustainable food-production projects with a luxury ethos, all four all-day cafés offer baked goods and simple please-all seasonal menus.

—

'Quick and simple, with no kneading or proving required, soda bread is the perfect loaf for those just beginning on a bread making journey.'

Preheat the oven to 190°C (170°C fan/375°F/gas mark 5) and line a baking tray with baking paper.

In a large bowl, mix together the flour, salt, bicarbonate of soda and baking powder. Once combined, pour in the yoghurt, kefir or buttermilk and mix everything together. It is really important not to overwork a soda bread, so mix gently until a dough begins to form. As soon as the dough has formed, shape into a round and transfer to your lined baking tray.

Using a knife, score the top of the dough with a deep cross and place into the oven to bake for 35–40 minutes. The bread will be cooked when a golden crust has formed and when the loaf sounds hollow when tapped on the bottom.

Transfer the bread to a wire rack to cool while you make your butter.

Pour the cream into a food processor. Turn to a high speed and wait for the cream to whip. Continue beating until the cream splits, then keep beating until a ball of butter forms in the bowl.

Transfer the butter to a sieve and strain off any residual buttermilk (reserve the buttermilk for your next loaf of soda bread). Once well strained, return the butter to a bowl and mix through your salt and any additional herbs or flavours you might like.

POTATO & GARLIC SHAKSHUKA

BY HONEY & CO.

SERVES 4

80ml (2½fl oz) olive oil
2 whole garlic bulbs, halved
 across the middle
Small bunch of thyme (tied
 with a little string)
2 onions, sliced (about
 250g/9oz)
1kg (2lb 4oz) potatoes, peeled,
 halved and sliced
2 tsp flaky sea salt
150ml (5fl oz) water
8 eggs
Freshly ground black pepper

Conviviality and a generous spirit are at the heart of all Honey & Co.'s operations. The Tel-Aviv-born founders Sarit Packer and Itamar Srulovich run a catering business as well as their London restaurants, deli and online shop – and the sleek Lamb's Conduit Street site is full of charm. Sarit makes much of the pottery that holds dips, sauces, falafel, ambrosial labneh, superlative pitta and clever evocations of the Middle East's culinary tapestry. The 'big breakfast' menu includes mezze and an expansive list of egg dishes and desserts (cake at breakfast is actively encouraged). Order bread to mop up every morsel.

Pour the olive oil into a large, deep frying pan (or sauté pan) and add the 4 garlic bulb halves, flat-side down. Place over a low heat and don't move or touch for about 10 minutes. Flip the garlic. They should be lightly golden all over the cut face. If not, let them slowly cook for another 5 minutes.

Add the bunch of thyme to the oil – it will fizz a little – and continue cooking for another few minutes before adding the sliced onion (still over a low heat). Remove the caramelised garlic halves one at a time and discard their skins.

Return the cloves to the frying pan. Cook for 10 minutes while the onions soften, then add the potatoes and salt. Mix well, cover and cook for a further 10 minutes. Mix again and repeat.

Remove the bunch of thyme (picking some leaves to set aside later), add the water and increase the heat to medium-high, so the water boils.

Boil for 5 minutes, check that the potatoes are soft (if not, cook for a little longer) then crack the eggs over the surface. Add a load of freshly ground pepper and the picked thyme leaves. Cover and cook for 5 minutes (or until the whites have set but the yolks are still runny) and serve hot.

RICK STEIN

OBE

Rick Stein's journey to culinary fame involved several twists and turns, including an English degree at Oxford, hotel management, running a disco, and setting up a nightclub in the small Cornish fishing port of Padstow. Turning the nightclub into a seafood restaurant in 1975, the self-taught chef went on to become a celebrated household name in the UK, championing the fruits of the sea and demystifying fish cookery with a series of long-running TV culinary travelogues and more than 25 cookbooks. Padstow is the hub of his family-run restaurant, hotel and cookery school business, and he also has a restaurant in London and two restaurants in New South Wales, Australia, which he runs with his wife, Sas. Head to any of Rick Stein's all-day operations and you'll find a hearty brunch (if you're lucky, a kipper and fish of the day, too).

'People thrive when they have access to good food; what OnePlate are doing is so important and I couldn't be happier to be a small part of it.'

RICK STEIN'S SMOKED SALMON & SCRAMBLED EGGS

SERVES 4

---

8 eggs
400g (14oz) smoked salmon
40g (1½oz) tiny capers
  (or use standard capers, finely
  chopped)
½ red onion, very thinly sliced
Small bunch of flat-leaf parsley,
  leaves picked
1 lemon, cut into 4 wedges
15g (½oz) butter
50ml (2fl oz) cream (optional)
Sea salt and ground black
  pepper
Toasted sourdough, to serve

Whisk the eggs together with a generous amount of salt and black pepper. Divide the salmon between plates, leaving space for the scrambled eggs. We use our own 'Rick Stein's breakfast smoked salmon' developed with our friends at The Severn and Wye smokery, but any good-quality smoked salmon will do.

Drain and rinse the capers and place them next to the salmon. Place the thinly sliced onion next to the pile of capers, then add a few parsley leaves to each plate, along with a wedge of lemon.

Heat a heavy-based pan over a medium heat for 1 minute, then add the butter. When it has melted and begun to foam (but before it colours) slowly pour the beaten eggs into the pan, stirring constantly. You can add a splash of cream at this point if desired.

Cook the eggs to your liking, moving them often; after about 1 minute they should be cooked. If you prefer your eggs more dry/firm, cook for a minute longer.

Divide the scrambled eggs between the 4 plates and serve with some toasted sourdough on the side.

QUAIL WELLINGTONS

BY ROGER OLSSON, RAFFLES AT THE OWO

SERVES 4

200g (7oz) Swiss chard, leaves blanched and drained
4 quails, breasts and legs removed
4 sheets of ready-rolled puff pastry
3 egg yolks, beaten with 1 tbsp whole milk
1 tsp thyme leaves
200g (7oz) panko breadcrumbs
Vegetable oil, for deep-frying
Flaky sea salt and ground black pepper

Chicken Mousse
400g (14oz) chicken breast, chilled in the fridge for at least 1 hour
40g (1½oz) egg white (from about 1–2 eggs)
240g (8½oz) double cream
7g (¼oz) salt

Mushrooms
50g (1¾oz) butter
70g (2½oz) shallots, finely chopped
20g (¾oz) garlic, finely chopped
2 thyme sprigs
300g (10½oz) chestnut mushrooms, finely chopped
100g (3½oz) chanterelle mushrooms, finely chopped

A combination of tradition and innovation, showcasing British food at its finest, by executive chef, Roger Olsson, of Raffles London at The OWO.

First, make the mousse. Place the chicken breast and egg white in food processor and pulse until blended and smooth, scraping the sides and bottom to ensure everything is incorporated. With the machine running, add the cream in a steady stream and blend until just combined (don't over-blend the mix as this could cause it to split). The mousse should be a shade of white (not pink). Mix in the salt at the end (to avoid cooking of the egg white), then transfer the mousse to a bowl, cover and place in the fridge immediately.

Now make the mushrooms. In a large sauté pan, melt the butter. Sweat the shallots and garlic, along with the thyme sprigs, for 5 minutes over a low heat until softening but not coloured. Add the mushrooms and cook over a medium heat, stirring frequently. When the mushrooms begin to release their moisture, turn the heat back down to low and cook, stirring occasionally, until the liquid has evaporated and the mushrooms look dry (15–20 minutes). Add salt and pepper to taste, then remove the thyme sprigs.

Mix 350g (12½oz) of the mushroom mixture with 700g (1lb 10½oz) of the chicken mousse and transfer to a piping bag. Place a sheet of cling film on your work surface then lay out a couple of blanched Swiss chard leaves flat on top. Pipe about 70g (2½oz) of mousse in a sausage shape onto the Swiss chard then place 2 quail breasts on top of the mousse. Season with a pinch of salt, then pipe another line of mousse on top of the breasts. Wrap the Swiss chard around the filling, using the cling film to help you, then seal in the cling film in a sausage shape and place in the fridge. Repeat to make 3 more quail and Swiss chard ballotines.

To construct each Wellington, lay out a sheet of puff pastry and brush it all over with the eggwash. Unwrap the first quail and Swiss chard ballotine and place it on one half of one of the sheets of pastry. Lift the over half of the pastry over the ballotine to cover it, then push down on the edge to seal, ensuring you've pushed all the air out. With a floured fork, crimp the edge of the Wellington. Brush with more eggwash, then transfer to the fridge to rest while you construct the remaining Wellingtons. Once all the Wellingtons have firmed up, brush with eggwash again and use a toothpick to score diagonal lines across the top. Sprinkle the thyme leaves on top then trim the 3 crimped edges slightly to give a sharp finish.

To Serve
4 salt-baked baby beetroots
180ml (6fl oz) port wine jus
8 medium beetroot leaves
Olive oil, for drizzling

While the Wellingtons are firming up in the fridge, bone the quail thighs. Pipe a little chicken mousse into the deboned thigh in the space where the bone was, then stretch the skin over to the other side and wrap tightly in cling film to seal. Repeat with all the thighs.

French-trim the deboned quail drumsticks, then wrap the meat very tightly in cling film, leaving the bone exposed.

Steam the thighs and drumsticks (with the cling film still in place) for 5 minutes, then place in ice-cold water. Once cold, unwrap the cling film and roll the thighs and drumsticks in the panko breadcrumbs.

Preheat the oven to 190°C (170°C fan/375°F/gas mark 5). Place the Wellingtons on a large baking tray and bake for 15 minutes. Transfer to a rack and leave to rest somewhere warm.

Fill a deep, heavy-based saucepan a third of the way up with vegetable oil and heat to 180°C (365°F). Deep-fry the thighs and drumsticks until golden. Remove with a slotted spoon and leave to drain for a moment.

Heat the port wine jus in a small saucepan with the baby beetroot. Dress the beetroot leaves with a splash of olive oil and a pinch of flaky sea salt.

Serve each Wellington with a crispy thigh and drumstick, with the beetroot in jus and beetroot leaves alongside.

SMOKED SALMON CRUMPETS, POACHED EGGS, HOLLANDAISE

BY GRIND

SERVES 2

2 crumpets (see below)
Knob of butter
60g (2¼oz) smoked salmon,
  sliced into long strips
2 poached eggs (see page 61)
30g (1oz) hollandaise sauce
  (see page 69)
Pinch of chopped chives
Pinch of radish sprouts
Pinch of mixed micro cress

Crumpets (makes about 20)
375ml (12½fl oz) warm milk
450g (1lb) plain flour
90g (3¼oz) sugar
5g (1½ tsp) dried active yeast
360ml (12fl oz) warm water
5g (1 tsp) baking powder
6g (1 tsp) salt
Vegetable oil, for greasing

An all-day dining spot and coffee brand rolled into one, Grind serves up all your brunch favourites in millnenial pink sites across the city. With sustainability at the heart of their business, you can feel like you're making a difference every time you pop by for a cup of coffee.

For the crumpets, whisk together the warm milk, flour, sugar and yeast in the bowl of a stand mixer using the dough hook, for 5–8 minutes. Add half the warm water and mix for another 3 minutes. Continue to add the water until the batter is thick and smooth, stopping when it reaches the consistency of thick cream. Add the baking powder and salt, whisk well then cover with cling film. Leave the mix in a warm place until doubled in size. When the surface is full of small bubbles, it is ready.

Lightly grease the inside of your crumpet rings and a large frying pan with some oil. Place the frying pan over a medium heat and add as many crumpet rings as will fit in the pan. When the pan and rings are hot, fill each ring with batter about halfway up the side. Cook the crumpets nearly all the way through before flipping them over, with the ring still on. Continue to cook until lightly golden and firm, then remove from the pan. You should end up with lots of holes in the crumpet once cooked.

Once cooled, store the leftover crumpets in the freezer.

In a frying pan over a medium heat, gently fry the 2 crumpets for serving with a little butter, ensuring they're toasted on both sides.

Top the crumpets with sliced smoked salmon and the poached eggs, then spoon over the hollandaise.

Finish with the chopped chives, radish sprouts and mixed cress.

FRIED SEA BASS WITH BOK CHOY & TAMARIND LIME SAUCE

BY HARVEY NICHOLS KNIGHTSBRIDGE

SERVES 1

80g (2¾oz) bok choy
Light oil, for frying
1 whole sea bass
A few spring onions, julienned
Small handful of red amaranth
Lemon wedges, to serve

Tamarind Lime Sauce
300ml (10½fl oz) rice wine
   vinegar
150g (5½oz) tamarind paste
75g (2½oz) maple syrup
400g (14oz) olive oil
150ml (5fl oz) lime juice
100ml (3½fl oz) fish sauce
25g (1oz) ginger juice
40g (1½oz) garlic
150ml (5fl oz) gluten-free soy
   sauce
1 tsp xanthan gum
1 tsp chilli flakes

Located in the heart of Knightsbridge, this luxury department store has been catering to city dwellers since its infancy in 1831. In 1975 they opened their first restaurant on the Fifth Floor to instant success and their significance as a food destination has been cemented ever since. But don't stop there – their famed Foodmarket is the stuff of dreams.

Using a blender, blend all ingredients for the tamarind lime sauce into a smooth sauce. Transfer to a saucepan and set over a medium heat to warm through.

Meanwhile, steam the bok choy until just cooked through.

To cook the fish, heat a 5mm (¼in) depth of oil in a frying pan large enough to fit the fish. Lightly sear the fish skin on both sides. Once the oil is hot but not smoking, carefully add the fish to the pan and cook for about 3 minutes until the skin is crisp and the flesh is starting to turn opaque. Flip the fish over and cook on the other side for another 3 minutes until crisp all over and just cooked through.

To plate, spread a generous amount of the tamarind lime sauce onto a platter, top with the bok choy, then place the sea bass on top. Scatter the spring onions and red amaranth over the top and serve with lemon wedges on the side for squeezing.

ONEPLATE: THE FISH FARM

MANILA

Sustainable projects that empower children and their communities are at the heart of OnePlate's vision. We want to give children, families, and entire communities the ability to grow, cultivate, catch, prepare and enjoy healthy food, now and far into the future. We want our projects to outlast us.

Our Fish Farm Project in Manila is a perfect example of a project that will live on for many years, with the potential to feed, employ and educate thousands of children and families, not only enriching diets, but enriching lives.

The development of the ponds at our fish farm was a community achievement, with local people employed to help set out and excavate the ponds and complete edge planting. Four pumps and associated valves and pipes were obtained and installed along with concrete slabs. After the ponds were filled during the rainy season, they were stocked full of healthy young fish. A nursery was also established for self-production of fingerlings.

Families like Stephen and Ladina's were invited to move to the fish farm, from the slums, and now have a home there with their three children aged 10, 6, and 2. They say this has changed their lives forever. With no way to earn a living, they spent days looking for food for their children to survive. They had no friends around them, only leaving their hut to look for food and money. Now they have plenty of organic, nutritious food for their children, a comfortable home and good friends on the farm, where everyone supports each other.

Stephen and Ladina even have a 'piggy bank' where they save a portion of their earnings every week and can buy their basic needs without borrowing money. As well as the benefit of eating the fish, they have gained valuable, lifelong agricultural skills that can be passed on to future generations.

Children in great need who benefit from the fish meals will also be formally trained in aquaculture. It's anticipated the fish farm will ultimately create five permanent full-time jobs and 35 additional full-time equivalent jobs in the community for businesses involved in the supply, transport and sale of fish products.

While the original plan was to provide fish protein for 500 children and 350 people in the community, the farm's bounty of food has exceeded expectations. Every month, there is a harvest of 1,350 fish, enough to provide 2.5 fish meals a week for 1,500 people.

Further, the sale of fish products outside the farm is directed straight back into children's education. For hundreds of local street children, paying school fees and educational resources is close to impossible. Sustainable projects like this, with abundant food and economic impact, are truly changing the future for these children.

THE AUBREY'S OKONOMIYAKI

BY EMILIANO SEBASTIAN, THE AUBREY

MAKES 1

Cured Salmon Roe
300g (10½oz) sake
200g (7oz) mirin
150g (5½oz) gluten-free soy
   sauce
½ sheet of kombu
1kg (2lb 4oz) salmon roe
50g (1¾oz) Japanese tea

**The Aubrey's 'Kewpie'
Mayonnaise**
8 eggs, at room temperature
40g (1½oz) Dijon mustard
Pinch of sea salt
14g (½oz) dashi powder
16g (½oz) Japanese sugar
90g (3¼oz) rice vinegar
65g (2¼oz) yuzu juice
1.5 litres (52fl oz) canola oil

The Aubrey's Tonkatsu Sauce
200g (7oz) Japanese sugar
170g (6oz) water
120g (4¼oz) red wine
25g (1oz) red wine vinegar
40g (1½oz) Worcestershire
   sauce
120g (4¼oz) light soy sauce
20g (¾oz) dark soy sauce
   (tamari)
10g (2 tsp) yuzu juice
125g (4½oz) rice vinegar
20g (¾oz) white wine vinegar
1 onion, chopped
1 carrot, grated (unpeeled)
1 apple, grated (unpeeled)
1 peach, stoned and chopped
   (unpeeled)
4 dates, chopped
2 bay leaves

Befitting its Knightsbridge postcode, the aesthetic at The Aubrey in the Mandarin Oriental is one of unabashed opulence. Named after Aubrey Beardsley, the 19th century English illustrator and author whose creations were influenced by the Japonism movement in Western art and Art Nouveau, the restaurant is styled as an 'elevated, eccentric izakaya' (late-night Japanese booze and snack joint). They've had fun with the weekend brunch, with Japanese-style iterations of brunch classics – try lobster tamogoyaki scrambled egg, Tokyo eggs royale or French toast – or there's the signature wagyu sando.

—

'Each element of The Aubrey's Okonomiyaki is sequenced below. Following these steps will give you all the components you need to build one okonomiyaki to serve one hungry adult, or is perfect as a table centrepiece to share. The kewpie mayonnaise and Tonkatsu sauce will make more than you need – store the leftovers in jars in the fridge.'

The Aubrey's 'Kewpie' Mayonnaise

Put the eggs in a saucepan with cold water to come about 2.5cm (1in) above the eggs, and heat over a medium heat until the temperature reaches 60°C (140°F). Maintain that temperature for 3 minutes, either by lowering the heat slightly or adding a little cold water (you don't want the temperature to go above 61°C (142°F) or the eggs will begin to cook). Transfer the eggs to the iced water and leave until completely cool.

Next, separate the yolks from the whites. Put the yolks in a blender or a big mixer with the mustard, salt, dashi and sugar. Start processing, slowly adding the oil until emulsified, then finish by adding the yuzu juice and vinegar, adjusting to taste.

The Aubrey's Tonkatsu Sauce

Put the sugar and water in a pot and cook over a medium heat until thick and a dark caramel colour. Deglaze the pot with the remaining liquid ingredients, then add all the remaining ingredients and simmer for about 30–60 minutes. Remove from the heat and let it cool down. Remove the bay leaves, transfer to a blender, blend and then strain.

Dashi

Put the water and kombu in a pot, bring to the boil, then take off the heat and add the katsuobushi. Set aside for 20 minutes before straining into a bowl.

¼ tsp grated nutmeg
¼ tsp ground cloves
200g (7oz) tomato paste

Dashi
1 litre (35fl oz) water
20g (¾oz) kombu
30g (1oz) katsuobushi

Cabbage
1 green cabbage
Sunflower oil, for deep-frying
Salt

Okonomiyaki Pancake
130g (4¾oz) plain flour
¼ tsp salt
¼ tsp sugar
¼ tsp baking powder
160g (5¾oz) peeled and
   grated nagaim
175ml (6fl oz) dashi
   (see above)
4 large eggs, plus 2 extra egg
   whites, beaten
½ cup tenkasu tempura scraps
2 packets of shimeji
   mushrooms, roots removed,
   mushrooms separated

To Assemble
1 Okonomiyaki pancake
   (see above)
The Aubrey's 'kewpie'
   mayonnaise (see opposite)
The Aubrey's tonkatsu sauce
   (see opposite)
8 slices (cold) smoked salmon
Bonito flakes (katsuobushi)
Spring onions, green parts
   only, finely sliced
Dried shredded seaweed
   (kizami nori)
Cured salmon roe
   (see opposite)

Cabbage
Remove and discard the outer leaves. Discard. Cut the cabbage in half and finely chop it. Place in a bowl, add a good amount of salt and let it sit for 2 hours. After 2 hours, wash and dry the cabbage. Press with a tea towel to remove excess water.

Heat enough oil for deep-frying in a deep-fat fryer, to 160°C (320°F), or heat a 3cm (1¼in) depth of oil in a frying-pan over a medium heat. Add the cabbage and fry until golden. Remove the cabbage from the oil and set aside on kitchen paper to soak up the excess oil.

Okonomiyaki Pancake
In a bowl, combine the flour, salt, sugar and baking powder. Add the grated nagaimo and dashi, and mix it all together until combined. Cover the bowl with cling film and let it rest in the fridge for 1 hour or more.

Remove the batter from the fridge, add the eggs and tenkasu, and mix until combined. Add the cabbage to the batter, then the mushrooms.

In a large pan, heat the oil over a medium heat. When hot, carefully spoon in the batter, forming a circle on the pan, around 2cm (¾in) thick. Using a spatula, carefully lift up a side to check the colour of the bottom; if it is getting a nice golden-brown colour, flip the pancake over. Gently press your spatula on the okonomiyaki to compress and keep it binding together. Cover with a lid and cook for another 5 minutes. Flip it over one last time and cook, uncovered, for 2 minutes.

To Assemble
Place the cooked pancake on a large round plate. Drizzle the 'kewpie' mayonnaise back and forth in fine lines. Drizzle with the tonkatsu sauce. Decoratively fold or twist each slice of smoked salmon, fanning it out around all of the pancake, leaving a space in the middle.

In the centre, place a heap of bonito flakes and spring onion and top with kizami nori. Finish with the salmon roe, dropping it around the bonito flakes. Serve immediately.

BOUDIN NOIR, FRIGGITELLI PEPPERS, FRIED EGG & ESPELETTE PEPPER

BY BRAWN

SERVES 6

800g (1lb 10oz) can of
  Christian Parra Boudin Noir
Olive oil, for frying
30 Friggitelli peppers
  (capsicums), long stalks
  trimmed
12 large eggs (Cacklebean
  or similar)
Lemons, for squeezing
Espelette chilli pepper
Flaky sea salt and ground black
  pepper

Billing itself as a neighbourhood restaurant – if you're a local, consider yourself truly blessed – Brawn is lauded as one of the best purveyors of casual produce-led food in the city. The corner spot on East London's Columbia Road (home of the famous flower market) is run by chef-restaurateur Ed Wilson and partner Josie Stead, who focus on acquiring exceptional native and European produce and celebrating it in its truest form with seasonally attuned dishes and a stunning roster of wines majoring on natural and biodynamic producers. Their coastal sister restaurant, Sargasso, in Margate, is worth a trip out of town.

Preheat the oven to 160°C (140°C fan/325°F/gas mark 3).

Preheat 2 heavy cast-iron or non-stick frying pans over a very high heat. You need them to be very hot but not smoking.

Using a can opener, open both ends of the boudin noir then carefully push the boudin noir out of its casing using one of the metal lids. It should come out in one large piece. Using a sharp knife, cut the boudin noir into 6 large discs (dipping the knife in warm water and cleaning after every slice helps).

Add a 5mm (¼in) depth of olive oil to one of the pans and, when starting to smoke, add the slices of boudin noir, turn the heat down to medium and fry until crisp, then flip and fry until crisp on the other side (you may want to do this in batches). Transfer the boudin noir to a baking tray, season with salt and pepper and place in the oven to keep hot while you prepare the rest of the dish.

In the other pan add another 5mm (¼in) depth of oil and wait until smoking hot. Add the peppers and fry until brown, keeping them moving to colour on all sides – be careful as the pan may spit. Once the peppers are coloured and soft (don't overcook, a little bite is good), tip them into a large mixing bowl and season well with salt, Espelette chilli and lemon juice, tossing to ensure they are evenly coated.

Wipe out the pan with kitchen paper and place back over a medium heat. When the pan is hot, add a glug of oil and fry the eggs until slightly crisp on the edges but still with runny yolks.

Place a slice of boudin noir on each plate and spoon some peppers alongside. Top with 2 fried eggs, then season with more flaky salt and a dusting of Espelette, some black pepper and a drizzle of olive oil. Serve immediately (with a cold beer if the time is right!).

Sweet

BANANA BREAD WITH VANILLA MASCARPONE, BERRY COMPOTE & WHITE CHOCOLATE CRUMB

BY WILLOWS

SERVES 8

Banana Bread
100g (3½oz) butter, softened
225g (8oz) caster sugar
4 very ripe bananas, mashed
100ml (3½fl oz) buttermillk
   or Greek yoghurt
1 tsp vanilla extract
2 large eggs, lightly beaten
250g (9oz) plain flour
1 tsp bicarbonate of soda
1 tsp ground cinnamon
Pinch of fine sea salt
100g (3½oz) chopped walnuts

Vanilla Mascarpone
400g (14oz) mascarpone
300ml (10½fl oz) double cream
40g (1½oz) icing sugar
1 tsp vanilla extract

Berry Compote
400g (14oz) forest berries
50g (1¾oz) caster sugar
50ml (1¾fl oz) lemon juice
20g (¾oz) cornflour

White Chocolate Crumb
100g (3½oz) granulated sugar
20g (¾oz) light brown sugar
90g (3¼oz) plain flour
20g (¾oz) cornflour
1 tsp baking powder
1 tsp fine sea salt
40ml (1½fl oz) rapeseed or
   other neutral-flavour oil
10ml (2 tsp) vanilla extract
40g (1½oz) white chocolate,
   melted

Sharing is what brunch is all about, whether food or good conversation, and that's an ethos that Willows embraces. With Scandi-style smörgåsbord platters and considered produce, this restaurant in Clapham is thoughtfully curated. Enjoy a little fika moment with their elevated banana bread.

Banana Bread
Preheat the oven to 180°C (160°C fan/350°F/gas mark 4). Grease a loaf tin and line with baking paper.

Cream together the butter and sugar in a large bowl. Add the banana, buttermilk or yoghurt, vanilla and egg and mix well, then sift in the flour, bicarbonate of soda, cinnamon and salt and fold through. Add the walnuts and fold through, then pour the batter into the prepared tin and bake for 1 hour or until a skewer inserted into the centre comes out clean.

Vanilla Mascarpone
Place the ingredients in a large bowl and beat until firm peaks form.

Berry Compote
Combine the berries, sugar and lemon juice in a saucepan and cook over a medium heat until the berries release their juices. Add the cornflour and stir until glossy (do not let the compote boil), then remove from the heat.

White Chocolate Crumb
Preheat the oven to 150°C (130°C fan/300°F/gas mark 2).

Combine the sugars, flour, cornflour, baking powder and salt in a mixing bowl. Add the oil, vanilla and melted chocolate and stir through, then spread the mixture evenly on a baking sheet and bake for 15 minutes or until golden. Let the crumbs cool completely before storing in an airtight container.

To Serve
Cut the banana bread into chunky slices and dollop a large tablespoon of vanilla mascarpone, followed by a large tablespoon of the berry compote over the top. Sprinkle with a generous amount of the white chocolate crumbs and serve immediately.

MAPLE GLAZED BANANA PANCAKES WITH WHIPPED BUTTER

BY SAM'S KITCHEN

MAKES ABOUT 10 LARGE PANCAKES

2 eggs
125g (4½oz) sugar
65g (2¼oz) butter, melted and
  cooled, plus extra for frying
500g (1lb 2oz) buttermilk
3 large, ripe bananas, mashed
375g (13¼oz) T55 flour
5g (1 tsp) bicarbonate of soda

Whipped Butter
250g (9oz) butter, softened
1 tsp ground cinnamon
A few slices of treacle-cured
  bacon (we use HG Walter's),
  cooked and very finely
  chopped
1 tbsp walnut praline

London-born Sam Harrison, a restaurateur for whom hospitality is his lifeblood, worked in Sydney and Canada before returning to his home city to team up with colleague Fanny Stocker and open Sam's Riverside in 2019. Overlooking the Thames, the dining room offers something for everyone – seafood is a specialism, especially the oyster and seafood platters – and the seasonal, modern European menu is vocal in its support for welfare-driven producers. Sam's Larder café and grocer/deli in Chiswick is a popular pit-stop, too.

Place the eggs and sugar in a bowl and whisk until pale and fluffy. Add the melted butter and stir until completely combined, then add the buttermilk and mashed banana and whisk until combined. Add the dry ingredients and whisk until there are no lumps, then cover and leave to rest for 30 minutes.

Meanwhile, make the whipped butter. Place the butter in the bowl of a stand mixer and beat until light and fluffy. Add the remaining ingredients and mix again until incorporated. Place to one side while you cook the pancakes.

Lightly butter a frying pan and place over a medium heat. When hot, add a generous amount of pancake batter to the pan. Fry the pancake until the underside is lightly golden, then flip it over and fry on the other side. Remove from the pan and keep warm. Repeat with the remaining batter.

Serve stacked on plates with a dollop of whipped butter on top.

Without love, deeds,
even the most brilliant,
count as nothing.

SAINT THÉRÈSE OF LISIEUX

PORRIDGE WITH CANDIED NUTS, FIGS & GRAPE PURÉE

BY 26 GRAINS

SERVES 1

Candied Walnuts & Hazelnuts
25g (1oz) butter
10g (⅓oz) walnuts, broken
  into pieces
10g (⅓oz) hazelnuts, chopped
  into chunks
2 tsp honey
2 tsp sugar
Pinch of salt

Grape Purée
500g (1lb 2oz) red grapes
100g (3½oz) caster sugar
100ml (3½fl oz) water

Porridge Base
50g (1¾oz) rolled porridge oats
20ml (1½ tbsp) water
80ml (2½fl oz) oat milk
Pinch of salt

To Serve
1 fig, quartered
1 mint leaf
Grated lemon zest
Fig oil (optional)

A calm and cosy spot in the heart of Neal's Yard, 26 Grains knows how to do breakfast well. Founder of 26 Grains, Alex Hely-Hutchinson, is a lover of all things Danish – particularly the Danes' commitment to seasonal eating and their fondness of porridge. It's no surprise then that their menu centres around both sweet and savoury porridge, just like this delicious bowl.

Candied Walnuts & Hazelnuts
Preheat the oven to 160°C (140°C fan/325°F/gas mark 3). Line a baking tray with baking paper.

Melt the butter in a large saucepan over a medium heat. Add the nuts, honey, sugar and salt, and cook for 5 minutes, then spread out on the prepared tray, transfer to the oven and bake for 15 minutes. Remove from the oven, allow to cool, then roughly chop.

Grape Purée
Combine the grapes, sugar and water in a saucepan and place over a medium heat. Simmer for 7–10 minutes until soft. Use a hand blender to purée the mixture until smooth, then pass the purée through a fine-meshed sieve into a bowl. Discard the grape seeds and skins. This makes more than you need for one serving.

Porridge Base
Combine the ingredients in a saucepan and place over a medium heat. Cook, stirring occasionally, until thickened, then stir more frequently until you reach your desired consistency. Remove from the heat.

To Serve
Place the porridge in a bowl, drizzle over some grape purée (store the rest in the fridge) over one side and sprinkle the candied nuts over the other side. Place the fig quarters on top of the nuts and finish with the mint leaf, a little lemon zest and a drizzle of fig oil, if desired.

ONEPLATE: AGROFORESTRY PROJECT

THE FRUIT & NUT ORCHARD, MANILA

Dave and Fiona, the generous owners of Warran Glen Café nestled within a beautiful garden centre in Australia, are passionate about delivering a beautiful atmosphere for their customers and making an impact through food.

When they heard about OnePlate's dream to fund a large Fruit and Nut Orchard to provide a reliable and nutritious food source for hundreds of street children, they were excited to partner with us to bring this vision to life. But they didn't want to just make a contribution. Inspired by the beautiful natural surroundings of their own business and the joy it brings them and their patrons, Dave and Fiona committed to funding the entire Fruit and Nut Orchard project, bringing similar beauty and nourishment to the lives of the children we serve.

It was simple. One dollar from every plate of fish and chips sold at the café was directed straight to the OnePlate Agroforestry Project. Warran Glen Café patrons were delighted to know that simply through enjoying a delicious meal they were making a difference.

The Warran Glen Café quickly raised enough for OnePlate to fund the entire project, plant the orchard and begin establishing a nutritious food source for over 500 children.

More than 1,500 trees were planted, including mango, guyabano, rambutan, jackfruit, grapefruit, star apple, banana, lemon, tamarind and mulberry, plus nut trees, like pili nut, coconut, pecan and walnut.

The Fruit and Nut Orchard in Manila now supports the health and wellbeing of street children every week; children like 21-year-old Kiram, who was rescued from the streets 10 years ago. At seven, Kiram was sleeping on the pavement and scavenging through garbage, until he was found by a wonderful caring organisation, given food and access to education.

Now his life has taken a 180-degree turn. Thanks to his dedication and natural abilities, Kiram gained a job at the Fruit and Nut Orchard at 18, learned welding, driving, machinery management and construction, and took on a leadership role as a 'big brother' for the younger boys. He has learned how to budget, study hard, deal with people, make sound decisions and solve problems. Kiram now dreams of owning a piece of land, just like the orchard, for his future family.

This is one of OnePlate's most diverse and abundant projects. The combination of both fruits and nuts is bringing extraordinary nutritional value to underprivileged children, and we are so grateful to Warran Glen Café for their passion, belief in the joy of food, and their sustainable impact.

'There is a seed inside of every tree and a tree inside of every seed.' Matshona Dhliwayo

MISO, DARK CHOCOLATE & HAZELNUT COOKIES

BY BURNT PROVISIONS

MAKES 12

100g (3½oz) caster sugar
165g (6oz) dark brown sugar
30g (1oz) miso
115g (4oz) cooled melted
  butter
1 large egg
155g (5½oz) plain flour
1 tsp salt
1 tsp bicarbonate of soda
50g (1¾oz) crushed roasted
  skinless hazelnuts
170g (6oz) dark chocolate
  (80% cocoa), broken into
  small pieces

The menu at this all-day café and restaurant in Shepherd's Bush is driven by what's in season and at its best – it punches way above your average neighbourhood coffee shop. Serving brunch all week, with Dusty Knuckle pastries and their own creative seasonal bakes – don't miss the miso, dark chocolate and hazelnut cookies – husband-and-wife team Finlay Logan and Honor Powley hit the sweet spot with hot smoked salmon kedgeree, 'nduja Turkish eggs, and a humongous salt beef, sauerkraut, mustard and cheddar croque madame.

In a large bowl, combine the sugars, miso and cooled melted butter. Add the egg and use a wooden spoon to cream until pale. Sift in the flour, salt and bicarbonate of soda and stir well, then stir through the hazelnuts and chocolate. Set the mixture aside in the fridge for a minimum of 2 hours, or overnight.

Preheat the oven to 175°C (150°C fan/325°F/gas mark 3). Line a baking tray with baking paper.

Divide the cookie mixture into 12 balls, each 65g (2¼oz), then place on the prepared tray with space in between for spreading. Transfer to the oven and bake for 12 minutes. Remove from the oven, leave to rest on the tray for 5 minutes, then enjoy.

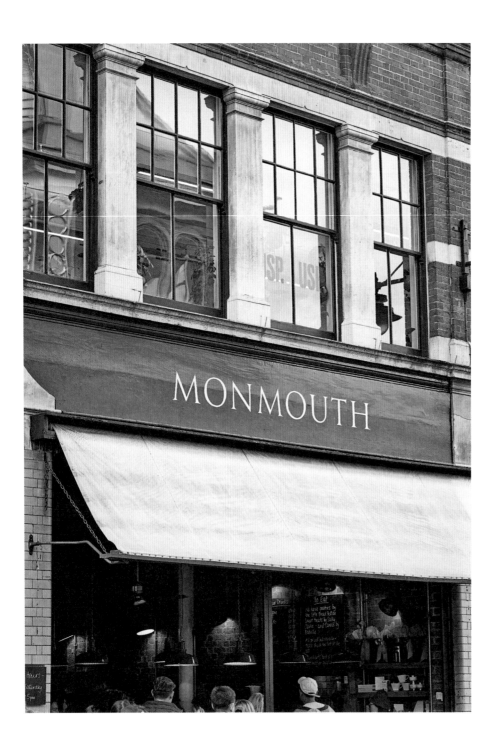

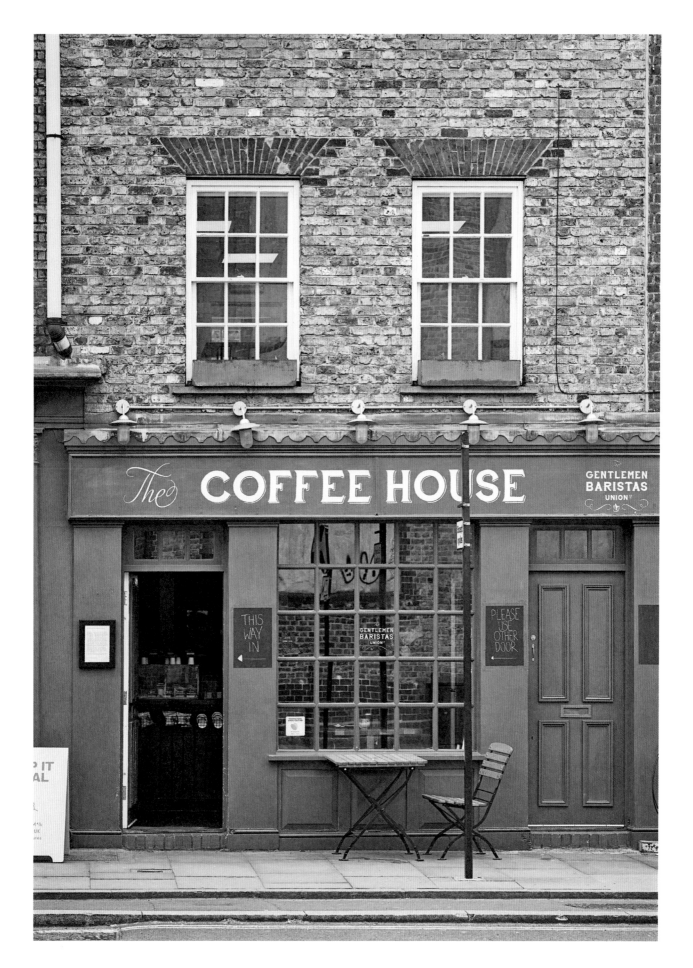

ESPRESSO COOKIES

BY KAFFEINE

MAKES 20

230g (8oz) butter
400g (14oz) caster sugar
2 eggs
1 tsp vanilla bean paste
Pinch of sea salt
200g (7oz) cocoa powder
170g (6oz) plain flour
1 tsp bicarbonate of soda

**Cream Cheese Frosting
(optional)**
150g (5½oz) icing sugar
100g (3½oz) softened butter
2 tbsp freshly made espresso
  coffee
1 tsp vanilla bean paste
500g (18oz) cream cheese

As their name suggests, coffee is pretty important at this café and espresso bar. Inspired by the coffee culture in Australia and New Zealand, Kaffeine now has two locations in the pretty neighbourhood of Fitzrovia. Their delicious cookies pack a punch – perfect for a weekend pick-me-up. This recipe makes 40 single cookies or 20 sandwich cookies.

In a stand mixer with the whisk attached, beat the butter and sugar on high speed for 2–3 minutes until pale and fluffy. Add the eggs and vanilla and beat together until well combined, then add the dry ingredients and continue to beat until the dough comes together (scrape the base of the bowl from time to time). Transfer the mixture to a plastic container and set aside in the fridge for 2 hours.

Preheat the oven to 170°C (150°C fan/325°F/gas mark 3). Grease and line a baking tray (either use one tray and bake the cookies in batches, or use several trays).

Weigh and shape the dough into 28g (1oz) balls, then space them out on the prepared tray. Bake for 12 minutes, then allow to cool completely. Store in an airtight container for up to 1 week.

If making sandwich cookies, make the cream cheese frosting. Using a hand whisk, beat together the icing sugar, butter, coffee and vanilla. Add the cream cheese in 3 batches, whisking well after each addition (do not overmix or the frosting will be too liquidy). Transfer the frosting to a large piping bag and chill in the fridge for at least 1 hour.

Pipe or spoon the cream cheese frosting onto half of the cookies and sandwich together with the remaining cookies.

PHILIP KHOURY

Renowned pastry chef Philip Khoury grew up in the western suburbs of Sydney and his Lebanese-born parents were great cooks, with a particular talent for creating ludicrously lovely sweet things. With a design degree under his belt, Khoury went on to study patisserie, cutting his teeth at Peter Gilmore's iconic Quay restaurant and going on to become head of research and development for pioneering Australian pâtissier Adriano Zumbo. Now head pastry chef at Harrods, London's luxury department store, he is reformulating classics of the genre. He describes vegan pastry as 'the last frontier' of plant-based cuisine and, in his début book *A New Way to Bake,* he puts to bed the conception that vegan pastry will always be subordinate to its traditional counterparts.

Provenance matters to Khoury, and OnePlate's commitment to connecting sustainable food sources to those most in need is one he shares: 'understanding where our food comes from is imperative if we're to reduce our impact on the planet, and OnePlate's dedication to investing in this should be celebrated'.

PHILIP KHOURY'S BANANA BREAD

400g (14oz) peeled, very ripe
  bananas
125g (4½oz) brown sugar
  or caster sugar (unrefined
  sugars also work)
75ml (2½fl oz) light-flavoured
  oil
225g (8oz) plain flour
2 tsp baking powder

Optional, but recommended
2 tsp ground cinnamon
Pinch of fine sea salt
100g (3½oz) walnuts or
  chocolate chips

To Serve (optional)
Nut butter
Sliced banana
Vegan honeycomb

This is an easy staple recipe that can be whipped up in one bowl, is made from pantry essentials and is quite adaptable (any oil, any sugar, and easy to jazz up with chocolate chips). It is naturally/accidentally plant-based. Just make sure you're using browning ripe bananas – this can't be cheated (trust me, I've tried!). It's a perfect way to rescue bananas that are past the point most people would like to eat them.

Preheat the oven to 190°C (170°C fan/375°F/gas mark 5). Line a 20 x 10cm (8 x 4in) loaf tin with baking paper.

Mash the banana really well in a mixing bowl until it starts to turn to a liquid (some small chunks are fine). Add the sugar and oil and whisk well to combine.

Sift the flour, baking powder, cinnamon and salt, if using, into a large bowl and stir with a fork.

Add the flour mixture to the banana mixture and gently fold; don't overmix or the loaf will be tough! Add the walnuts or chocolate chips at this stage, if you like, and fold through.

Scrape the batter into the prepared tin and smooth the top. Transfer to the oven and bake for 40 minutes or until a skewer inserted into the middle comes out clean.

I know it's hard, but wait until the banana bread has cooled completely before cutting!

Wrap well or store in an airtight container in the fridge for up to 1 week.

For a delicious treat, top the banana bread with your favourite nut butter, slices of fresh banana and some vegan honeycomb.

VANILLA BRIOCHE FRENCH TOAST

BY CLARIDGE'S

SERVES 4

6 slices of brioche, crusts
  removed
6 eggs
100ml (3½fl oz) whole milk
80g (2¾oz) icing sugar
1 vanilla pod, split lengthways
  and seeds scraped
Pinch of ground cinnamon
20g (¾oz) best-quality salted
  butter

To Serve
120ml (4fl oz) maple syrup
  (we use Vermont or Quebec
  syrup)
200g (7oz) clotted cream
200g (7oz) berries of your
  choice

There's something timeless about Claridge's, the opulent hotel in Mayfair which manages to simultaneously epitomise old-school glamour and stay impeccably up to date. What began as a one-house hotel in the 1800s soon expanded into an Art Deco sensation, favoured by royalty and heads of state since Queen Victoria's visit in 1860. With its stunning ballrooms Claridge's was the place to party, and from the 1920s onwards it was frequented by stars of Hollywood, from Audrey Hepburn to Cary Grant. It goes without saying that a lavish breakfast at Claridge's is the ultimate London treat (apparently The Queen Mother's favourite table in the restaurant was always decorated with sweet peas).

Cut each brioche slice in half to make 2 triangles. In a large bowl, whisk together the eggs, milk, icing sugar, vanilla seeds and cinnamon.

Melt half the butter in a large frying pan over a medium-high heat. Dredge the brioche triangles in the egg mixture. When the butter is foaming, reduce the heat to medium and fry 6 of the triangles (make sure you drain off any excess egg mixture before adding the brioche to the pan) on both sides until golden brown. Set aside and keep warm. Repeat with the remaining butter and brioche triangles.

Serve the French toast immediately with the maple syrup, clotted cream and your choice of berries.

CINNAMON BUNS

BY E5 BAKEHOUSE

MAKES 12

Dough
100g (3½oz) plain flour, plus extra for dusting
245g (8½oz) stoneground white bread flour
5g (1 tsp) fine sea salt
50g (1¾oz) unrefined caster sugar
160ml (5¼fl oz) whole milk
1 medium egg (50g/1¾oz), plus extra egg, for eggwash
4g (1 tsp) active dried yeast
50g (1¾oz) unsalted butter, softened
Demerara sugar, for sprinkling (optional)

Cinnamon Filling
80g (2¾oz) unsalted butter
100g (3½oz) light muscovado sugar
2 tsp ground cinnamon

Sugar Syrup
75g (2½oz) unrefined caster sugar
75ml (2½fl oz) water

TIP —*This recipe does make extra sugar syrup. You can use the leftovers for sweetened drinks and cocktails, or for other pastries and desserts. It will keep in a jar in the fridge for about a month.*

e5 Bakehouse emerged in 2010 when Ben MacKinnon hand built a wood fired bread oven in the corner of a railway arch in Hackney. Inspired by the principles of permaculture, and following the mantra 'small is beautiful', the bakehouse organically grew in response to its community and the team of dedicated bakers and chefs, who began exploring sourdough techniques and natural fermentation. They run training courses for refugees in collaboration with The Refugee Council, have a certified organic farm in Suffolk, and have an in-house stone mill where they mill heritage wheat from their farm on a daily basis. Underpinning the company is a commitment to ecological sustainability, producing bread, cakes, pastries and lunches which are nourishing and in harmony with nature.

—

At e5 Bakehouse we make our cinnamon buns and babka using a semi-sourdough recipe. The sourdough starter is stiff, low in hydration and is the leaven that is inside our very popular Hackney Wild loaf. The decision to add a bit of sourdough starter to the bun dough is mostly for flavour. We've kept yeast in our recipe for a little extra insurance – to make sure the buns rise, and to ensure the end result is light and fluffy. This home baking recipe does not contain any sourdough starter, but if you're an experienced baker you can reduce the yeast and replace it with a stiff leaven.

You can use fresh yeast, dried yeast, instant dried yeast or osmotolerant yeast in this recipe. All of these yeasts have different ways of being activated. Osmotolerant yeast is what we use at the bakery. It has been developed to survive in recipes containing lots of sugar and helps to speed up fermentation in sugary enriched doughs. Do use whatever yeast you can find; just make sure it hasn't expired.

It is fun and interactive to make dough by hand. It allows you to take the time and notice what is truly happening to the dough. We have simplified our e5 Bakehouse recipe so it's easy to do at home without extra work or the need for a stand mixer.

Using your hands, mix the dough ingredients except the demerara sugar together in a large bowl until a cohesive dough forms and all the flour and butter have been fully incorporated. This will take about 4 minutes. Place a very damp tea towel over the bowl and set aside to rest in a warm place for 45 minutes.

continued overleaf

The stretch and fold technique employed here will do all the work for you. Gluten is developed when hydrated and left to rest. All you need to do is help the dough become stronger by stretching it out and folding it over itself. As you fold the dough, it should start to feel pillowy and begin to hold its shape. You should be able to feel the development of the gas over time. The dough will feel lighter, stronger and look more round as air is being trapped inside.

Complete your first stretch and fold: pull up one side of the dough and fold it over the opposite side. Work your way around the bowl, stretching and folding as you go. Cover and rest for 30 minutes, then repeat the stretching and folding, followed by 30 minutes of resting. The dough is now ready for shaping. Alternatively, cover the bowl well so no air gets in and place in the fridge overnight, ready for shaping the next morning.

To make the cinnamon filling, soften the butter by letting it come to room temperature or by popping it in the microwave for a few seconds. Once soft, mix in the sugar and cinnamon and stir until well combined and smooth. Set aside.

To make the sugar syrup, combine the ingredients in a small saucepan and bring to the boil for 1 minute, then remove from the heat and let sit until ready to use.

Grease and line a 33 x 23cm (13 x 9in) baking tin with baking paper.

Dust your dough lightly with flour and press the air out. With a rolling pin, roll the dough into a 40 x 34cm (15 x 13in) rectangle. Spread the cinnamon butter filling over the dough with the help of a dough scraper, leaving a 2cm (¾in) border at the base. Starting from the side furthest to you, roll up the dough into a tight log.

Divide the log into quarters, then cut each quarter into 3 equal pieces. Place the buns, swirl side up, in the baking tin, then cover with a tea towel and set aside to rise in a warm spot. Depending on the temperature of the room this will take 30–45 minutes. You want the buns to almost double in size. They will look swollen and be soft to touch when they're ready to bake.

Meanwhile, preheat the oven to 175°C (155°C fan/350°F/gas mark 3½).

When your buns have finishing proofing, brush gently with the eggwash. For texture, you can sprinkle the tops lightly with some coarse demerara sugar, if desired. Put the tin in the oven and bake the buns for 12 minutes. Turn the tin and bake for another 5 minutes or until the cinnamon buns are golden and caramelised. When the buns come out of the oven, glaze them with the sugar syrup. Allow to cool, then tear off a bun and enjoy.

ESPRESSO MARTINI

BY H. R. HIGGINS

MAKES 1

25ml (1fl oz) Kahlua
25ml (1fl oz) Espresso
  (we recommend H.R. Higgins
  Brazil Daterra Bruzzi or 1942
  Blend)
50ml (2fl oz) vodka

A family-run specialist coffe and tea merchant based in the heart of Mayfair, H. R. Higgins has been supplying the great and the good with speciality beans and leaves since 1942. The emporium was the brainchild of Harold Rees Higgins, whose grandson David now runs the business from the HQ at 79 Duke Street, supplying connoisseurs the world over, running coffee tasting masterclasses, and serving the finest brews with selections of freshly baked cakes and pastries in a dedicated coffee lounge below the shop. Awarded the highly prized Royal Warrant in 1979, H. R. Higgins became the official coffee and tea merchant for the Royal Household, a coveted accolade in a crowded market. London's coffee scene is playing a strong game, with the innovative third-wave scene fully established into the mainstream and a proliferation of cafés selling specialty coffee (H. R. Higgins were forerunners by a good few decades). And this scene is on an upward trajectory, with new roasteries and brewers popping up all over the city to please the capital's die-hard coffee-lovers. When it comes to partnering coffee and food, H. R. Higgins's espresso martini – sophisticated at any time of day, of course – might just top the chart as the perfect brunch pick-me-up, a libation that rights all wrongs and goes down like a dream after a spot of gustatory overindulgence.

—

'Invented by barman Dick Bradshaw in the 1980s when he was asked to create a drink to 'wake me up'. It has since become one of the most popular coffee cocktails, and we like to serve it at the start of our coffee-tasting masterclasses to cleanse the palate.'

Combine all ingredients into a cocktail shaker and fill generously with ice. Shake vigorously and then pour into a chilled glass and decorate with a few coffee beans.

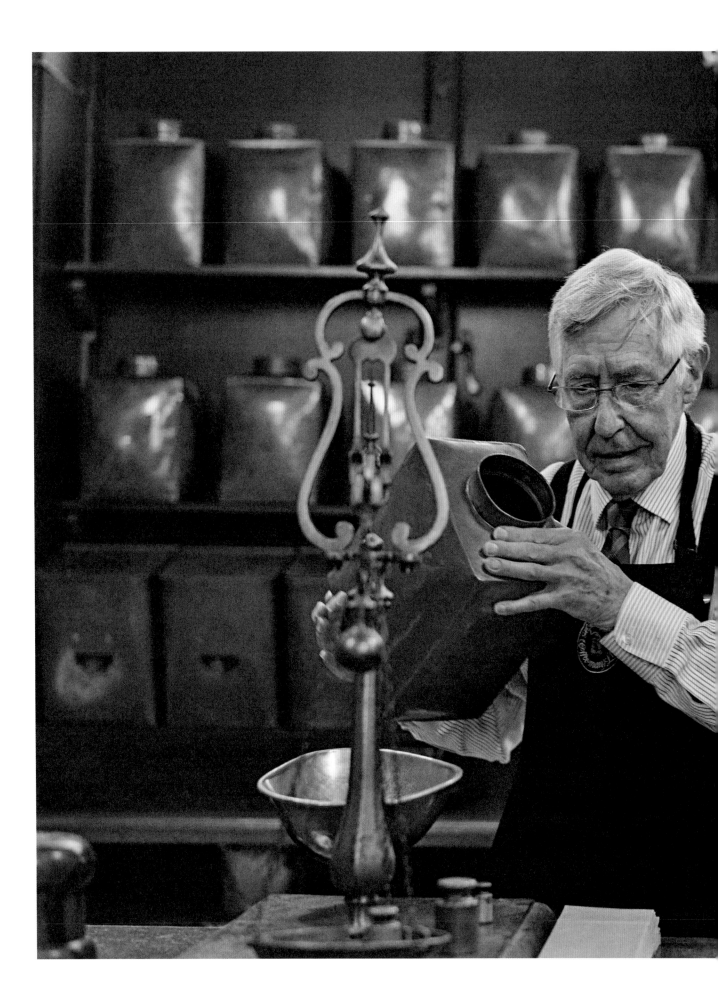

WELSH CAKES

BY FORTNUM & MASON

MAKES 20

425g (15oz) plain flour, plus
extra for dusting
1 tsp baking powder
¼ tsp ground allspice
Pinch of salt
120g (4¼oz) unsalted butter,
at room temperature, cut into
cubes, plus extra for frying
120g (4¼oz) lard or vegetable
shortening, cut into cubes
175g (6oz) caster sugar
120g (4¼oz) raisins
2 eggs, beaten
30ml (2 tbsp) whole milk

The epitome of elegance and glamour, Fortum & Mason department store in Piccadilly is a British institution, even having been mentioned by Charles Dickens. First founded in 1707, they have been providing extraordinary food ever since, and deliver a sense of pleasure to anyone who walks through their legendary doors. The ice cream parlour, afternoon tea salon and world-class collection of teas are iconic, and there's an abundance of riches for breakfast and brunch lovers too.

—

Known as 'picau ar y maen' in Welsh, meaning 'cakes on the stone' (they were originally cooked on a heated bakestone), these are incredibly easy to make (perfect for children too), endlessly versatile and deeply delicious. You can serve them hot or cold, with butter, jam or ice cream, as a mid-morning snack, or as a stand-alone pudding. Welsh cakes will never let you down.

Sift the flour, baking powder, allspice and salt together into a large mixing bowl. Add the butter and lard or shortening to the flour mixture and rub together your fingertips for 5–7 minutes until the mixture resembles breadcrumbs. Stir in the sugar and raisins and combine.

Mix the eggs and milk together, then pour into the flour mixture and stir until it forms a stiff dough. Bring the dough together with your hands in the mixing bowl until it forms a ball. Turn the dough out onto a lightly floured surface and roll it out to a thickness of 12cm (4¾in). Dip a 6cm (2¼in) round cutter in flour and cut 20 rounds from the dough.

Melt a knob of butter in a heavy-based frying pan over a medium heat and fry the dough rounds in batches for 3–4 minutes on each side, until crisp and golden. Serve warm, or keep in an airtight container for up to a week and reheat gently before serving.

BIRCHER MUESLI

BY HIDE

300ml (10½fl oz) apple juice
25g (1oz) porridge oats
25g (1oz) chia seeds
50g (1¾oz) dried sour cherries, halved
25g (1oz) golden raisins
25g (1oz) dried apricots, quartered
1 apple, such as Braeburn or Pink Lady, coarsely grated, avoiding the core
250g (9oz) Greek yoghurt, strained
75g (2½oz) pistachios, lightly toasted
Zest and juice of ½ lemon
5 tbsp pomegranate seeds
5 tbsp blueberries

To serve
5 tbsp mixed berries
3 tbsp pistachios, lightly toasted and chopped
4 mint sprigs, leaves picked

Ollie trained at Le Manoir aux Quat'Saisons and did stints at a multitude of Michelin-starred kitchens, winning critical acclaim as the head chef of Texture in London for his technical innovation and exquisite flavour combinations, before opening his eponymous restaurant, Dabbous, in 2012. In 2018 he launched Hide in Piccadilly as chef-patron, winning it a Michelin star within months of opening. Hideaway boutique café and wine bar in nearby Mayfair is adored for its breakfasts, ice cream, croque monsieur, lobster rolls, pizza bianca and exquisite pastries.

Mix together the apple juice, oats, chia seeds, sour cherries, golden raisins and apricots in a bowl. Set aside overnight for the fruit to plump up.

The next day, stir the remaining ingredients through the bircher. Keep in the fridge until needed.

To serve, divide between bowls, top with the berries, pistachios and mint leaves, and enjoy.

Use your voice for kindness, your ears for compassion and your heart for love.

FRENCH TOAST WITH HONEY CARAMEL

BY LANGAN'S BRASSERIE

SERVES 6

1 litre (35fl oz) double cream
200ml (7fl oz) whole milk
2 vanilla pods, halved
  lengthways and seeds
  scraped out
100g (3½oz) egg yolks
  (from about 5–6 eggs)
200g (7oz) caster sugar
1 brioche loaf, sliced 3.5cm
  (1½in) thick
100g (3½oz) clarified butter
  (see page 242)
3 bananas, sliced 2cm (¾in)
  thick
Icing sugar, for dusting

Honey Caramel
125g (4½oz) caster sugar
200ml (7fl oz) double cream
1 vanilla pod, halved
  lengthways and seeds
  scraped out
50g (1¾oz) English blossom
  set honey

To Serve
100g (3½oz) strawberries,
  hulled and halved
100g (3½oz) blueberries,
  halved
100ml (3½fl oz) double cream,
  semi-whipped
100g (3½oz) (3½fl oz) maple
  syrup

If only walls could talk. Adored by the cognoscenti and an endless cohort of celebrities since its doors were first opened in 1976 by Peter Langan and Sir Michael Caine, this brasserie enjoyed a singular reputation for glamour and delicious scandals. With acclaimed Graziano Arricale at the helm, the venerable three-storey Mayfair restaurant was reborn in 2021 after a serious dose of TLC, and remains proudly anachronistic, describing its all-day culinary offering as 'British elegance respecting French tradition': restoration has seen the installation of a raw seafood bar, but you can still expect classics, from beef tartare prepared tableside to Caesar salad and signature spinach soufflé.

Pour the cream and milk into a saucepan and add the vanilla seeds. Bring to the boil, then immediately remove from the heat and leave to infuse for 30 minutes.

Return the cream mixture to the boil. In a large heatproof bowl, beat together the egg yolks and sugar, then add the boiling cream mixture, whisking constantly until well combined. Pass the mixture through a fine-meshed sieve into a deep-walled container and set aside in the fridge for about 1 hour until chilled.

Add the brioche slices to the chilled custard and leave to soak for 15 minutes on each side. Once soaked, drain the brioche slices on a wire rack with kitchen paper underneath to catch excess liquid.

Meanwhile, to make the honey caramel, place the sugar in a saucepan over low heat and allow to melt and form a golden caramel. In a separate saucepan, heat the cream and vanilla seeds until hot. As soon as the sugar turns golden brown, very slowly add the hot cream mixture, whisking constantly. Once all the cream mixture has been added, whisk in the honey until smooth. Pour the mixture through a fine-meshed sieve into a bowl and leave to cool.

Preheat the oven to 180°C (160°C fan/350°F/gas mark 4).

Heat a frying pan over a medium-high heat and add some of the clarified butter. Working in batches if necessary, add the soaked brioche and cook for 3–4 minutes on each side until golden. Place the French toast on a baking tray and finish cooking in the oven for 8–10 minutes.

While the French toast is in the oven, warm the honey caramel in a saucepan over a low heat, add the banana slices and leave for 30–60 seconds until the banana is caramelised.

Divide the French toast between plates and dust icing sugar over the top. Finish with the caramelised banana slices and serve with the strawberries, blueberries, whipped cream and maple syrup on the side.

LEMON & OLIVE OIL CAKE

BY LINA STORES

SERVES 8

200g (7oz) whole almonds
50g (1¾oz) polenta
50g (1¾oz) plain flour, sifted
5g (1 tsp) baking powder, sifted
100g (3½oz) unsalted butter
140ml (4¾fl oz) extra virgin
  olive oil
50ml (2fl oz) milk
4 medium eggs, at room
  temperature
200g (7oz) caster sugar
Zest of 2 lemons
Juice of 4 lemons
Icing sugar, for dusting

TIP — *Drizzle our Lina Stores oregano-infused limoncello over the top of the cake, instead of dusting with icing sugar, for an extra flavour kick.*

First opened in 1944 by Lina, a formidable lady from Genoa, Lina Stores is London's most iconic Italian delicatessen and restaurant with multiple locations around London. Over 80 years later, Lina Stores is still known for its high-quality, authentic produce from regional Italy, including fresh, handmade pasta and homemade dolci, as well as cured meats and cheeses. You might simply fancy a cannolo and espresso to go, but it would be an oversight not to pick up some homemade pasta while you're there or settle in at the restaurants for breakfast to try the signature truffle scrambled eggs with sourdough or pancetta and fried egg panino.

Preheat the oven to 160°C (140°C fan/325°F/gas mark 3). Grease a 20cm (8in) round cake tin and line with baking paper.

Grind the almonds in a blender or food processor to a coarse breadcrumb-like consistency. Transfer to a large bowl and add the polenta, flour and baking powder, stirring to combine.

Melt the butter in a saucepan over a low heat, then remove from the heat and add the olive oil and milk.

Whisk the eggs and sugar in a large bowl until light and fluffy, then slowly add the butter mixture to the egg. Add the dry ingredients, followed by the lemon zest and juice, and slowly mix to combine. Pour the batter into the prepared tin and bake for 45 minutes or until the centre is still slightly underdone, when tested with a skewer.

Allow the cake to cool to room temperature, then remove from the tin and dust with icing sugar. Cut into slices and serve.

SWEET POTATO PANCAKES WITH YOGHURT & DATE SYRUP

FROM *NOPI: THE COOKBOOK*, BY YOTAM OTTOLENGHI AND RAMAEL SCULLY

SERVES 4–6

2 medium sweet potatoes,
  unpeeled (700g/1lb 8½oz)
200g (7oz) plain flour, sifted
2 tsp baking powder
1 tsp grated nutmeg
1 tsp ground cinnamon
1½ tsp salt
3 eggs, separated
150ml (5fl oz) whole milk
50g (1¾oz) unsalted butter,
  melted, plus an extra 80g
  (2¾oz) diced, for frying
1 tsp vanilla extract
1 tbsp runny honey

To Serve
160g (5¾oz) Greek yoghurt
60g (2¼oz) date syrup
1 tsp icing sugar, for dusting

At NOPI, Ottolenghi's version of fine dining is an elegant operation, where you can expect a riot of bold, complex flavours that head Far East one moment, to the Middle East the next. Vegetable dishes come first – perhaps maple roasted carrots with chermoula, St James ricotta and preserved lemon – though there's plenty for carnivores too. If it's brunch you're after, head to one of his five London café-delis, where the spotless white spaces are filled with an abundance of alchemic salads and sweet treats.

—

'As with most things sweet potato, pancake or brunch related, the addition of some grilled rashers of bacon will never be unwelcome, so do add if you wish. You can make the pancake batter a day ahead, if you like, up to the point just before the egg whites are whisked and stirred through.'

Preheat the oven to 240°C (220°C fan/475°F/gas mark 9). Line a small baking tray with baking paper.

Place the sweet potatoes on the tray and roast for 1 hour until completely soft and browned. Remove from the oven, set aside to cool, then peel off the skin. Place the flesh in the middle of a clean piece of muslin or J-cloth. Draw up the sides, roll into a ball and squeeze out any liquid that is released from the flesh. The drained weight of the sweet potato should be around 320g (11oz). Reduce the oven temperature to 180°C (160°C fan/400°F/gas mark 4).

Mix together the flour, baking powder, nutmeg, cinnamon and salt in a medium bowl. Place the egg yolks, milk, melted butter, vanilla and honey in a separate bowl and whisk well to combine. Fold into the dry ingredients before adding the sweet potato flesh. Whisk well until completely smooth.

Place the egg whites in a separate bowl and whisk until stiff: this should take 3–4 minutes if whisking by hand, or 1–2 minutes if using an electric whisk. Gently fold into the sweet potato mixture and set aside.

When ready to serve, put 20g (¾oz) of the diced butter into a large frying pan and place over a medium heat. When the butter starts to foam, ladle 2 heaped tablespoons of the pancake batter into the pan – you should be able to cook 3 pancakes at a time. Cook for 3–4 minutes, turning once halfway through, when the edges of the pancake are brown and the mixture starts to bubble in the middle. The pancakes are quite soft, so be careful as you turn them over. Transfer to a baking tray lined with baking paper and set aside while you continue with the remaining mixture, wiping the pan clean before adding 20g (¾oz) more butter with each batch. You should have 12 pancakes. Place in the oven for 5 minutes, just to warm everything through.

To serve, place 2 or 3 pancakes in the middle of each plate and dollop with the yoghurt. Drizzle with the date syrup, dust with the icing sugar and serve.

ELLA MILLS

Ella Mills is an award-winning author and founder of the plant-based brand Deliciously Ella. Following her own experience of ill health in 2011, she set about changing her diet in a bid to improve her health, and wrote about it online, chronicling her journey and recipes. Deliciously Ella was born, and she swiftly amassed a huge readership and media attention: her debut cookbook, published in 2015, was a global bestseller and led to a food and lifestyle empire that includes London restaurant Plants, a hugely successful food range, and a wellbeing app. 'Healthy should feel good', she says, 'and should never feel like a compromise.' For Ella, mealtimes have always been 'a way to connect and a way of bringing people together and nourishing every part of yourself'. She has a particular fondness for brunch, as 'it tends to signify lovely lazy days with nowhere to go and nothing to do.'

Her collaboration with OnePlate attests to the importance of food in all our lives and 'knowing that it also has the power to make a meaningful difference in the world, instigating change where it's needed most, is very inspiring.'

DELICIOUSLY ELLA GRANOLA

MAKES ABOUT 650G (23OZ)

100g (3½oz) pecans
100g (3½oz) flaked almonds
100g (3½oz) oats
100g (3½oz) pumpkin seeds
120g (4¼oz) sunflower seeds
3 tbsp coconut oil
1 tsp ground cinnamon
3 tbsp maple syrup
150g (5½oz) raisins

This was one of the first recipes I ever made. It's a simple granola made with an oat, pecan, almond and seed base, with sweet notes of maple, cinnamon and coconut. I used to make it for my friends and family – I even made it for my now parents-in-law the first time I went to stay with them!

Preheat the oven to 160°C (140°C fan/325°F/gas mark 3). Line a baking sheet with baking paper.

Roughly chop the pecans and almonds. You can do this either with a kitchen knife, or by placing them in a food processor and pulsing several times. Tip the nuts into a large bowl and add the oats, pumpkin seeds and sunflower seeds.

Melt the coconut oil, cinnamon and maple syrup in a small saucepan over a medium heat, then pour over the dry ingredients and stir well until all the ingredients are coated.

Spread the granola mixture evenly across the baking sheet and bake for 35–40 minutes, stirring every 15 minutes to ensure nothing burns. Once cooked, remove from the oven and mix in the raisins.

Once cooled, place the granola in an airtight container, such as a jar or Tupperware, for storage. It keeps well for up to 1 month.

BERRIES & BRIOCHE FRENCH TOAST

BY PEGGY PORSCHEN

SERVES 4

50g (1¾oz) egg yolks (from about 2–3 eggs)
50g (1¾oz) caster sugar
½ tsp ground cinnamon
100ml (3½fl oz) whipping cream
100ml (3½fl oz) whole milk
½ vanilla pod, split lengthways
100g (3½ oz) mascarpone
Zest of ½ lemon
4 thick slices of brioche
2 tbsp butter
2 tbsp vegetable oil
1 banana, sliced into long pieces
1 tbsp brown sugar

To Serve
Mixture of blueberries (halved), blackberries, raspberries and strawberries (hulled and quartered)
Freeze-dried raspberry dust
Lemon balm leaves
Edible viola flowers
Maple syrup

Being commissioned to create 500 chocolate Fabergé eggs for Elton John's White Tie & Tiara Ball in 2003 was a career high for Peggy, who dreamt from childhood of becoming a cake designer. Born near Cologne, Germany, she left her flight attendant job to train at Le Cordon Bleu London, working as a pastry chef and cake decorator before opening her first luxury café, Peggy Porschen Parlour, in Belgravia (then a second site in Chelsea), becoming renowned for her distinctive fairy-tale, powder-pink aesthetic and flawless cakes and confectionary (and all-day brunch).

Whisk the egg yolks, caster sugar and cinnamon together in a bowl.

Place the cream, milk and vanilla pod in a saucepan and bring to a simmer. Pour the warm cream mixture over the beaten egg yolk mixture, stirring constantly. Return the mixture to the saucepan and cook over a medium-low heat, stirring, for about 5 minutes until you have a thin, smooth custard. Allow to cool slightly. Discard the vanilla pod.

Combine the mascarpone and lemon zest in a small bowl, then move to the fridge to chill and set.

Place the brioche in a large shallow bowl and pour the custard over, soaking both sides thoroughly.

Heat the butter and oil in a frying pan over a medium heat until foaming. Add the brioche and fry for about 3 minutes on each side until golden brown.

While the brioche is frying, sprinkle the banana slices with the brown sugar and caramelise the tops using a blowtorch (or place under a very hot grill for a few seconds).

Cut each slice of French toast diagonally in half and place on plates. Using a small teaspoon, quenelle the lemon mascarpone and place on top of the French toast. Arrange the banana slices and fresh berries on the plates and sprinkle with a little freeze-dried raspberry dust. Finish with lemon balm and edible viola flowers and serve with maple syrup on the side. Enjoy!

GLUTEN-FREE CARAMELISED BANANA PANCAKES

BY VICTORIA SHEPPARD, QUEENS OF MAYFAIR

SERVES 2

150g (5½oz) gluten-free
  self-raising flour
30g (1oz) sugar, plus extra
  for sprinkling
5g (1 tsp) gluten-free baking
  powder
5g (¾ tsp) fine sea salt
185ml (6¼fl oz) whole milk
1 large egg
2 tbsp neutral-flavoured oil
  (sunflower, vegetable),
  plus a little extra to cook
  the pancakes
2 bananas, cut in half
  lengthways
100g (3½oz) crème fraîche
Maple syrup, for drizzling
Candied nuts and a mint sprig,
  to serve (optional)

Run by sisters Grace and Victoria Sheppard, this ever so elegant all-day café and bar is a boon for Mayfair brunchers. With backgrounds in PR, marketing and interior design, Grace and Victoria have combined an upmarket aesthetic with a great instinct for appetites – they have every brunch whim and wish covered, from fancy fry-ups and speciality coffees to bottomless brunch favourites with royal monikers, perhaps the 'Queen's Bakery Basket', 'The Duchess' vanilla pancakes with a seasonal compote, or a sharing shakshuka.

Combine the flour, sugar, baking powder and salt in a bowl. In a separate bowl, whisk together the milk, egg and oil. Pour the wet ingredients into the flour mixture and whisk until you have a smooth batter. Set aside to rest for 10 minutes.

Sprinkle enough sugar to cover a small plate and roll the bananas in the sugar to coat.

You can either use a blowtorch or your grill to caramelise the bananas. If using your grill, set it to medium heat.

Lightly oil a large frying pan over a medium heat. Ladle in the batter (you should get 8 pancakes in total; cook them in batches if necessary) and cook for 3 minutes on each side. When you turn the pancakes over, put the bananas under the grill for about 2 minutes until golden, or use a blowtorch to gently crisp the tops.

Stack 4 pancakes on each plate, adding a thick layer of crème fraîche and a dash of maple syrup between each pancake. Pour a generous drizzle of maple syrup over the top pancake and top with the caramelised bananas. Finish with a scattering of candied nuts and a sprig of mint, if desired.

To do small things with
great love is a great thing.

BANANA, CHOCOLATE & RYE LOAF

BY SKYE GYNGELL, SPRING

MAKES 1 LOAF

70g (2½oz) spelt flour
70g (2½oz) rye flour
2 tsp baking powder
1 tsp bicarbonate of soda
½ tsp ground cinnamon
½ tsp fine sea salt
200g (7oz) banana (firm but
  ripe), mashed
80ml (2½fl oz) kefir buttermilk
80g (2¾oz) rye sourdough
  starter
60g (2¼oz) black treacle
1 vanilla pod, split lengthways
  and seeds scraped out
80g (2¾oz) unsalted butter,
  softened
80g (2¾oz) sugar
2 eggs
80g (2¾oz) walnuts
130g (4¾oz) Medjool dates,
  pitted and chopped
180g (6¼oz) shaved dark
  chocolate
90g (3¼oz) millet
20g (¾oz) muscovado sugar

Poolish
125g (4¼oz) warm water
⅛ tsp fast action dried yeast
125g (4¼oz) plain flour

Skye Gyngell, whose innovative Mediterranean-inflected approach to seasonal cooking at the bucolic Petersham Nurseries in Richmond won Petersham its first Michelin star, opened Spring at Somerset House in 2014 in one of the most breathtakingly beautiful dining rooms in London. A self-proclaimed 'cook' (she avoids the term 'chef'), Australian-born Skye's produce-first ethos means ingredients are second to none, and her impassioned commitment to reducing food waste and championing sustainable food systems is widely admired. She is also chef-patron at Heckfield Place, a country house hotel, restaurant and farm in Hampshire.

To make the poolish, combine the ingredients in a bowl, cover and set aside in the fridge overnight.

The next day, preheat the oven to 170°C (150°C fan/325°F/gas mark 3). Grease a loaf tin with butter and line with enough baking paper to overhang the edges by 2.5cm (1in).

Combine the flours, baking powder, bicarb, cinnamon and salt in a large bowl.

In a separate large bowl, whisk together the mashed banana, kefir buttermilk, rye starter, treacle, vanilla seeds and poolish.

In another large bowl, or using an stand mixer, beat the butter until smooth, then add the sugar and whip until fluffy. Slowly add the eggs, one at a time, until emulsified. Alternating between the dry and wet ingredients, slowly incorporate both mixtures into the batter, starting and ending with the dry ingredients. Add the walnuts, dates, chocolate and millet and fold through.

Pour the batter into the prepared tin and sprinkle generously with the muscovado sugar.

Bake on the middle shelf of the oven for 40 minutes or until a skewer inserted into the thickest part of the cake comes out clean.

Cool the loaf in the tin before turning out onto a wire rack. It will keep in an airtight container for up to 2 days.

PANCAKES WITH STRAWBERRIES, POACHED RHUBARB & CRÈME ANGLAISE

BY THE SAVOY

SERVES 4

Oil, for greasing
150g (5½oz) Kent strawberries,
  hulled and sliced, to serve

Pancake Batter
130g (4½oz) plain flour
10g (⅓oz) caster sugar
1½ tsp baking powder
Pinch of fine sea salt
35g (1¼oz) yoghurt
1 egg
120g (4¼oz) whole milk
20g (¾oz) unsalted butter,
  melted

Vanilla Crème Anglaise
125ml (4¼fl oz) whole milk
125ml (4¼fl oz) whipping
  cream
1 vanilla pod, split lengthways
  and seeds scraped out
60g (2¼oz) egg yolks
  (from about 3–4 eggs)
40g (1½oz) caster sugar

Poached Yorkshire Rhubarb
300ml (10½fl oz) water
50g (1¾oz) caster sugar
20g (¾oz) grenadine syrup
  (optional)
1 vanilla pod
200g (7oz) Yorkshire rhubarb,
  trimmed and cut into
  segments

A home-from-home for a rollcall of Hollywood grandees, heads of state and royalty, Britain's first luxury hotel was opened by hotelier and theatre impresario Richard D'Oyly Carte in 1889 (he went on to buy Claridge's). Pass through the famous gilded revolving doors and you'll find the food offering is befittingly sumptuous. Gordon Ramsay's name has been above the door for decades and he operates all three restaurants, the all-day River Restaurant, your best bet for brunch, the Savoy Grill, and Restaurant 1890. This dish, from executive pastry chef Nicolas Houchet, is a celebration of British summer fruits.

Pancake Batter
The day before you plan to make the dish, blend the batter ingredients in a blender or a food processor. Transfer to a bowl, cover and leave to rest in the fridge overnight.

Vanilla Crème Anglaise
Heat the milk, cream and vanilla seeds in a saucepan over a medium heat until steamy. Whisk the egg yolks and sugar in a large bowl until smooth.

Whisking constantly, gradually add the hot milk mixture to the beaten egg and sugar until completely incorporated, then pour the mixture back into the saucepan and heat, whisking, to 82°C (180°F) on a kitchen thermometer. As soon as the temperature is reached, immediately strain the mixture into a heatproof bowl. The crème anglaise will keep in an airtight container in the fridge for up to 2 days and can be served hot or cold.

Poached Yorkshire Rhubarb
Place the water, sugar, grenadine syrup, if using, and vanilla pod in a saucepan and bring to a simmer. Add the rhubarb and simmer gently for about 5–6 minutes until the rhubarb starts to soften but is still holding its shape. Remove from the heat and keep warm.

Pancakes
Lightly grease a frying pan and an 8cm (3¼in) cake ring with oil. Heat the frying pan over a medium heat and add the cake ring. Pour a 1cm (½in) depth of pancake batter into the cake ring and cook for 2 minutes, then remove the ring and, using a flat spatula, carefully flip the pancake. Cook for a further 2 minutes or until the underside is golden brown. Remove to a plate and repeat to make 8 pancakes.

Spoon some crème anglaise onto each plate and top with 2 pancakes. Add some rhubarb and sliced strawberries to the top of each and serve.

FRENCH TOAST WITH MAPLE SYRUP

BY THE TABLE CAFÉ

SERVES 2

---

2 tbsp clarified butter
  (see page 242)
2 large eggs
2 tsp granulated sugar,
  plus extra for sprinkling
¼ tsp fine sea salt
Pinch of ground cloves
Pinch of ground mace
Pinch of ground nutmeg
¼ tsp ground cinnamon
Finely grated zest of ½ lemon
  (optional)
2 tsp plain flour
2 slices of good-quality
  brioche, 2cm (¾in) thick
Toppings of your choice
  (e.g. yoghurt, sliced apple
  and blackberries)
Maple syrup, for drizzling

Award-winning food that champions local suppliers is the order of the day at The Table café. With two sites south of the river in Battersea and Southwark, this all-day-dining spot has all your brunch needs covered.

Melt 1 tablespoon of the clarified butter and set aside.

Beat the eggs in a wide, shallow bowl, then whisk in the melted butter, sugar, salt, spices and lemon zest, if using. Stir a little of this mixture into the flour to make a paste, then beat it back into the egg mixture until smooth.

Heat the remaining clarified butter in a frying pan over a medium-high heat. Soak the brioche in the egg mixture for about 30 seconds each side until soft but not floppy. Transfer to the hot pan and cook, undisturbed, for about 2 minutes until golden and crisp. Turn the brioche over and cook for another minute or so, then transfer to plates, sprinkle with extra sugar and serve with indecent haste.

Top the French toast with your favourite toppings and drizzle with maple syrup to finish.

AÇAI BOWL

BY FARM GIRL

½ packet (50g/2oz) frozen açai
6 pieces of frozen banana
200ml (7fl oz) almond milk
1 tbsp chia seeds
Handful of shaved coconut

To serve
Seasonal fruit of your choice
Shaved coconut
Edible flowers

Inspired by Californian café culture, co-founder of Farm Girl, Rose Mann, opened her first breakfast and brunch café in Notting Hill in 2015 with her husband Anthony Hood. The 'farm girl' grew up on a rural dairy farm near Melbourne, Australia, and her all-day holistic, health-focused cafés are now a permanent fixture on the London café scene, with two more in South Kensington and Soho. Needless to say, the coffee is superlative.

Place the ingredients in a blender and blitz until smooth.

Transfer the açai mixture to a bowl and top with seasonal fruit of your choice, shaved coconut and edible flowers.

RICOTTA HOTCAKES WITH HONEYCOMB BUTTER

BY GRANGER & CO.

SERVES 6–8

If anyone understands how to deliver the ultimate brunch repertoire, it's 'brunch king' Bill Granger. The Australian self-taught cook, restaurateur and food writer is the brainchild behind the laid-back all-day operation Granger & Co., which has five branches across London. Bill opened his first café in Sydney and 30 years on his eclectic Antipodean menus continue to take in culinary influences from far and wide, and bright, colourful, joyful food is his trademark.

Honeycomb
Light-flavoured oil, for greasing
150g (5½oz) caster sugar
75g (2½oz) golden syrup
1½ tsp bicarbonate of soda

Honeycomb Butter
250g (9oz) unsalted butter, softened
2 tbsp runny honey
90g (3¼oz) honeycomb (see above, or use store-bought)

Hotcakes
300g (10½oz) ricotta
175ml (6fl oz) whole milk
4 eggs, separated
125g (4½oz) plain flour
1 tsp baking powder
Pinch of salt
50g (1¾oz) butter

To Serve
Icing sugar, for dusting
1 banana, thickly sliced on an angle

Honeycomb

Lightly oil a 20cm (8in) cake tin. Put the sugar and golden syrup in a heavy-based saucepan over medium-low heat. Swirl the pan to dissolve the sugar, then stir with a spatula until dissolved – this might take 10–15 minutes. Do not let the mixture bubble at this stage. Increase the heat and use a sugar thermometer to monitor the mixture until it registers 155°C (311°F) and forms a dark amber caramel. Remove from the heat and quickly stir in the bicarbonate of soda until golden and foaming. Be careful not to over-stir: you want to retain as much air in the mixture as possible.

Carefully pour the mixture into the prepared cake tin. Leave to cool and harden for about 1½ hours, then break into chunks using a rolling pin. You will need about half the amount to make the honeycomb butter, so store the rest in an airtight container at room temperature for up to 2 weeks. You can dip it in melted chocolate and sprinkle it over ice cream. Or make double the amount of honeycomb butter and freeze the leftovers.

Honeycomb Butter

Blend the ingredients in a food processor until smooth. Roll the butter into a log, wrap in baking paper and chill in the fridge for 2 hours.

Hotcakes

Mix together the ricotta, milk and egg yolks. Sift the flour, baking powder and salt into another bowl. Add the ricotta mixture and stir to combine.

Whisk the egg whites in a clean, dry bowl until stiff peaks form. Fold into the batter in two batches, using a large metal spoon.

Melt a little butter in a non-stick frying pan over medium-low heat. Add 2 tablespoons of batter per hotcake, and cook, in batches, for 2 minutes or until golden underneath. Turn and cook the other side until golden.

To Serve

Serve the hotcakes, dusted with icing sugar, topped with the sliced banana and generous amounts of the honeycomb butter.

ONEPLATE: THE BEE PROJECT

KENYA

Until they witness the miracle of fruit and vegetables grown from seed, or the beauty of glistening honeycomb built by hundreds of tiny bees, the children we serve have no foundation for healthy, nutritious food. They do not know where it comes from, or how good it tastes.

This is why OnePlate is so passionate about innovations like The Bee Project, where children have the opportunity to understand the amazing process of how honey is made and to enjoy the sweet produce. For these children, for whom food is scarce and rarely healthy, providing access to fresh honey and honey products is a simple way to immediately improve diet and wellness.

Funded with the help of our partner organisation, our Bee Farm in Kenya has been transformational for so many children and communities. Expanding to 300 beehives and over 1,300 tree and flower seedlings, this project has created a complete eco-system for a new bee population.

Calliandra trees, bottle brush, sunflowers and sesbania plants have been planted to attract the bees and encourage pollination, along with *Moringa oleifera*, commonly known as the 'miracle' tree. Every part of

the nutrient-rich Moringa tree – seed pods, fruits, flowers, roots and bark – is edible, offering unlimited social enterprise opportunities from sale of tree products including leaves and pods for food, cattle feed and biofuel.

The Bee Farm and the forage that has been created is dependent on the success of the beautiful OnePlate Avocado plantation nearby (page 134), where the bees can access the nectar and pollen-bearing plants they need to make honey. African bees prefer avocado, mangoes, banana, eucalyptus, coffee, orange and acacia. Along with these sweet sources of nectar, sunflowers and lavender bushes have been planted to maximise the nectar and pollen resource.

With thousands of bees per hive, each hive will produce an amazing 16kg (35lb) of honey per year, which will be eaten and enjoyed by the children as well as sold to re-invest in the farm. Along with improved nourishment through the generation of honey as well as the pollination of plants on the property, The Bee Project is ensuring increased production of essential medicine and natural therapies, employment and new commercial opportunities, and funds invested towards schooling for the children.

JAMES, JULES & THE GIANT PEACH

BY UTTER WAFFLE

SERVES 4

Small handful of shelled
  pistachios
100g (3½oz) caster sugar
20g (¾oz) ground cinnamon
415g (14oz) can of peach
  halves in juice

Waffle Batter
410g (14½oz) gluten-free flour
20g (¾oz) baking powder
5 eggs
460ml (16fl oz) milk
125g (4½oz) butter, melted

Spiced Peach Liquor
Juice from the can of peaches
  (see above)
1 rosemary sprig
½ tsp ground cinnamon
½ tsp ground allspice

To Serve
200g (7oz) mascarpone
Handful of strawberries,
  hulled and halved
Handful of blueberries

We are Utter Waffle, a South London-based food truck, restaurant and events catering company specialising in... you guessed it, waffles! Our waffles are a little different to those found at regular waffle joints, with most being savoury and combining high-end toppings and flavour combinations to create the perfect breakfast, brunch, lunch or dinner.

Named after owners James and Jules, this dish is our take on an American brunch, elevating it with a touch of British sophistication. In our restaurant we pair this with a vanilla cheesecake mousse, but for ease at home we've swapped it out for mascarpone.

So, first things first – the waffle batter! Grab a decent-sized bowl and combine the flour and baking powder. Whisk the eggs and the milk into the flour mixture until smooth, then add the melted butter and mix until thoroughly combined. (Top tip: don't stop whisking if the butter is sitting on the surface of the batter – it'll solidify and create really uneven waffles.)

Next up, you can't have a James, Jules and the Giant Peach without the giant peach! So, open up your can of peaches and strain the peaches through a colander, catching the juice in a small saucepan. Add the rosemary, cinnamon and allspice to the juice, and stir to combine, then place over a medium heat. Bring to the boil and cook until the juice has reduced by half, or you have a viscous, dark liquor. Remove from the heat and set aside.

Finely chop the pistachios or, if you're feeling a little lazy, pop them in a food processor and pulse a few times into a chunky crumb.

Combine the sugar and cinnamon in a small bowl. Pop your peaches (one half per person, or whatever you fancy) flat-side up on a baking tray and dust with some of the cinnamon sugar. If you're a budding chef, blowtorch the peach halves until the sugar has melted and they're shiny and brûléed. If, like most of us, the greatest mod-con you have in your kitchen is the kitchen roll holder, pop them under a hot grill, and watch like a hawk so they don't burn! You're looking for a lovely golden colour, but not black!

We're almost ready to assemble our dish... once we've made our waffles. If you've got a waffle machine, then you'll probably know how to do the rest. If you haven't, we suggest using our signature batter to make pancakes instead, as it works equally well in this dish.

Divide the waffles between plates and sprinkle with the remaining cinnamon sugar. Top with the mascarpone, 2 caramelised peach halves, some pistachio crumbs and a few fresh strawberries and blueberries. Finish with a drizzle of our sticky, spiced peach syrup.

CHOCOLATE CROISSANT BREAD PUDDING

BY VIOLET BAKERY

SERVES 8

Butter, for greasing
4 chocolate croissants
300ml (10½fl oz) double cream
900ml (30fl oz) whole milk
Pinch of sea salt
1 vanilla pod, split lengthways
   and seeds scraped
230g (8oz) caster sugar
7 eggs
2 tbsp cocoa powder
50g (1¾oz) dark chocolate
   (70% cocoa solids), broken
   into bite-sized pieces

This low-key Californian-style bakery-café in East London might be diminutive in size but the impact of its owner Clare Ptak on the UK's baking scene can't be overestimated. One of London's best-loved bakeries, Violet Bakery is unrivalled for its flavour-focused, seasonal cakes made with organic and low-intervention ingredients. The daytime café menu of things on toast, toasties and daily quiche, alongside counter treats of season-led bakes, is a brunch-lover's dream, particularly if you're lucky enough to nab al fresco seating.

Preheat the oven to 180°C (160°C fan/350°F/gas mark 4) and butter a deep baking dish, 20 x 30cm (8 x 12in). Find another baking dish that is large enough to hold the buttered baking dish and a water bath (you will be making a bain marie later to gently cook the custard).

Tear the croissants into pieces and place on a baking tray. Toast in the oven for about 10 minutes, turning the pieces over halfway through, until crunchy.

Pour the cream and milk into a large, heavy-based saucepan. Add the salt and vanilla seeds, along with the pod itself. Place over a medium-low heat and, just before the mixture starts to simmer, or when it starts to 'shiver', remove from the heat.

Meanwhile, in a clean bowl, whisk your sugar and eggs into frothy ribbons. When the milk is ready, pour one-third of it into the sugar and egg mixture, whisking constantly. Add the remaining milk mixture and whisk in the cocoa powder. Strain the mixture into a bowl or jug.

Place the toasted croissants in the buttered baking dish, then pour enough of the chocolate custard over the top to cover the croissants. Leave to soak for 30 minutes.

Pour the remaining custard over the pudding and scatter the chocolate pieces on top. Place the baking dish inside the larger dish and place in the oven. Use a jug to pour water into your bain marie so that it comes at least halfway up the sides of the dish. Bake for about 30 minutes until just set.

RESTAURANT & CAFÉ DIRECTORY

26 GRAINS
1 NEAL'S YARD, COVENT GARDEN
WC2H 9DP

45 JERMYN ST
45 JERMYN STREET, ST. JAMES'S,
SW1Y 6DN

**ALEX DILLING AT THE HOTEL
CAFÉ ROYAL**
10 AIR ST, MAYFAIR, W1B 5AB

AMAZONICO LONDON
10 BERKELEY SQUARE, MAYFAIR,
W1J 6BR

THE AUBREY
MANDARIN ORIENTAL HYDE
PARK, 66 KNIGHTSBRIDGE,
KNIGHTSBRIDGE, SW1X 7LA

BALANS
60–62 OLD COMPTON STREET, SOHO,
W1D 4UG

—KENSINGTON, SHEPHERDS BUSH,
SOHO, STRATFORD

THE BARBARY NEXT DOOR
16A NEAL'S YARD, COVENT GARDEN,
WC2H 9DP

BARE BREW
7 HIGH ST, WANSTEAD, E11 2AA

THE BEAUMONT HOTEL
8 BALDERTON STREET, BROWN
HART GARDENS, MAYFAIR, W1K 6TF

THE BERKELEY
WILTON PLACE, KNIGHTSBRIDGE,
SW1X 7RL

BERNERS TAVERN
10 BERNERS STREET, MARYLEBONE,
W1T 3NP

BOBO & WILD
1 POOLE STREET, SHOREDITCH,
N1 5EE

—CLAPHAM COMMON, REDBRIDGE

BOURNE & HOLLINGSWORTH
42 NORTHAMPTON ROAD,
CLERKENWELL, EC1R 0HU

BRAT
4 REDCHURCH STREET,
SHOREDITCH, E1 6JL

— LONDON FIELDS

BRAWN
49 COLUMBIA ROAD, BETHNAL
GREEN, E2 7RG

BREAD BY BIKE
30 BRECKNOCK ROAD, CAMDEN,
N7 0DD

BRINDISA KITCHEN BAR
UNIT 51 JUBILEE, WINCHESTER
WALK, BOROUGH MARKET, SE1 9AG

THE BULL & LAST
168 HIGHGATE ROAD, HIGHGATE,
NW5 1QS

BURNT PROVISIONS
163 ASKEW RD, HAMMERSMITH,
W12 9AU

CAFE MURANO
33 ST. JAMES'S STREET, ST. JAMES'S,
SW1A 1HD

—BERMONDSEY, COVENT GARDEN

THE CAMBERWELL ARMS
65 CAMBERWELL CHURCH STREET,
CAMBERWELL, SE5 8TR

CARAVAN
EXMOUTH MARKET, CLERKENWELL,
EC1R 4QD

—CANARY WHARF, THE CITY,
COVENT GARDEN, FITZROVIA,
KING'S CROSS, LONDON BRIDGE

CARMEL
23-25 LONSDALE ROAD, QUEENS
PARK, NW6 6RA

CAVITA
56–60 WIGMORE STREET,
MARYLEBONE, W1U 2RZ

CHARLOTTE STREET HOTEL
15–17 CHARLOTTE STREET, SOHO,
W1T 1RJ

CLARIDGE'S
BROOK STREET, MAYFAIR, W1K 4HR

DAISY GREEN COLLECTION
20 SEYMOUR STREET, MARYLEBONE,
W1H 7HX

—BISHOPSGATE, BROADGATE
CIRCLE, MAYFAIR, PADDINGTON,
GRAND UNION CANAL, ST JOHN'S
WOOD, SOHO, VICTORIA

DAYLESFORD ORGANIC
76–82 SLOANE AVENUE, CHELSEA,
SW3 3DZ

**DINNER BY HESTON
BLUMENTHAL**
MANDARIN ORIENTAL HYDE
PARK, 66 KNIGHTSBRIDGE,
KNIGHTSBRIDGE, SW1X 7LA

DISHOOM
12 UPPER MARTIN'S LANE, COVENT
GARDEN, WC2H 9FB

—BATTERSEA, CANARY WHARF,
CARNABY, KENSINGTON, KING'S
CROSS, SHOREDITCH

THE DORCHESTER
53 PARK LANE, MAYFAIR, W1K 1QA

DRAKE & MORGAN
6 PANCRAS SQUARE, KINGS CROSS,
N1C 4AG

—BISHOPSGATE, CANARY WHARF,
CITY, DEVONSHIRE TERRACE,
ISLINGTON, REGENT'S PARK,
SHOREDITCH

DUCKSOUP
41 DEAN STREET, SOHO, W1D 4PY

DUSTY KNUCKLE
ABBOT STREET CAR PARK,
DALSTON, E8 3DP

—HARINGEY

E5 BAKEHOUSE
396 MENTMORE TERRACE,
HACKNEY, E8 3PH

FAIRMONT WINDSOR PARK
BISHOPSGATE ROAD, ENGLEFIELD
GREEN, EGHAM TW20 0YL

FARM GIRL
59A PORTOBELLO ROAD,
NOTTING HILL, W11 3DB

—SOUTH KENSINGTON

FORTNUM & MASON
181 PICCADILLY, ST. JAMES'S, W1A 1ER

THE GORING
15 BEESTON PLACE, BELGRAVIA,
SW1W 0JW

GRANGER & CO.
175 WESTBOURNE GROVE, NOTTING
HILL, W11 2SB

—CHELSEA, CLERKENWELL, KING'S
CROSS, MARYLEBONE

GREENBERRY CAFÉ
101 REGENT'S PARK ROAD, PRIMROSE
HILL, NW1 8UR

GRIND
213 OLD STREET, SHOREDITCH,
EC1V 9NR

—CITY, COVENT GARDEN,
LIVERPOOL STREET, LONDON
BRIDGE, GREENWICH, SOHO,
WATERLOO

GROUCHO CLUB
45 DEAN STREET, SOHO, W1D 4QB

HARRODS
87–135 BROMPTON ROAD,
KNIGHTSBRIDGE, SW1X 7XL

HARRY'S DOLCE VITA
27–31 BASIL STREET,
KNIGHTSBRIDGE, SW3 1BB

HARVEY NICHOLS
109–125 KNIGHTSBRIDGE,
KNIGHTSBRIDGE, SW1X 7RJ

HELMA
13C DOWNHAM ROAD,
HAGGERSTON, N1 5AA

HIDE
85 PICCADILLY, MAYFAIR, W1J 7NB

HIDEAWAY LONDON
100 MOUNT STREET, MAYFAIR,
W1K 2TG

HONEY & CO.
54 LAMB'S CONDUIT STREET,
BLOOMSBURY, WC1N 3LW

—FITZROVIA

HOPPERS LONDON
49 FRITH STREET, SOHO, W1D 4SG

—KING'S CROSS, MARYLEBONE

H.R.HIGGINS
79 DUKE STREET, MAYFAIR, W1K 5AS

IDA
167 FIFTH AVENUE, MAIDA VALE,
W10 4DT

THE IVY ASIA
20 NEW CHANGE, ST PAUL'S,
EC4M 9AG

—CHELSEA, MAYFAIR

THE IVY
1–5 WEST STREET, COVENT GARDEN,
WC2H 9NQ

KAFFEINE
66 GREAT TITCHFIELD STREET,
FITZROVIA, W1W 7QJ

—2ND FITZROVIA LOCATION

KURO EATERY
5 HILLGATE STREET, NOTTING HILL,
W8 7SP

KAPARA
JAMES COURT, MANETTE STREET,
SOHO, W1D 4AL

KILN
58 BREWER STREET, SOHO, W1F 9TL

LA FROMAGERIE
2–6 MOXON STREET, MARYLEBONE,
W1U 4EW

—BLOOMSBURY, HIGHBURY

THE LALEE
THE CADOGAN, 75 SLOANE STREET,
CHELSEA, SW1X 9SG

LANGAN'S BRASSERIE
STRATTON STREET, MAYFAIR,
W1J 8LB

THE LAUNDRY
374 COLDHARBOUR LANE, BRIXTON,
SW9 8PL

LINA STORES
51 GREEK STREET, SOHO, W1D 4EH

—THE CITY, CLAPHAM, KING'S
CROSS, MARYLEBONE

LINNAEAN
EMBASSY GARDENS, 2 NEW UNION
SQUARE, NINE ELMS, SW11 7AX

LLEWELYN'S
293–295 RAILTON ROAD, HERNE HILL,
SE24 0JP

LUCKY & JOY
95 LOWER CLAPTON ROAD,
CLAPTON, E5 0NP

LULU'S
291 RAILTON ROAD, HERNE HILL,
SE24 0JP

MALIBU KITCHEN, THE NED
27 POULTRY, THE CITY, EC2R 8AJ

MARKSMAN
254 HACKNEY ROAD, BETHNAL
GREEN, E2 7SB

M RESTAURANT
60 THREADNEEDLE STREET,
THE CITY, EC2R 8HG

MILK BEACH
19–21 LONSDALE ROAD, QUEEN'S
PARK, NW6 6DH

—SOHO

MINNOW
21 THE PAVEMENT, CLAPHAM
COMMON, SW4 0HY

MURANO
20 QUEEN STREET, MAYFAIR, W1J 5PP

NATOORA
5 ELGIN CRESCENT, NOTTING HILL,
W11 2JA

—BERMONDSEY, CHISWICK,
FULHAM, MARYLEBONE, SLOANE
SQUARE

NESSA
86 BREWER STREET, SOHO, W1F 9UB

NOBU LONDON
19 OLD PARK LANE, MAYFAIR,
W1K 1LB

—PORTMAN SQUARE, SHOREDITCH

NOPI
21–22 WARWICK ST, SOHO, W1B 5NE

OREN
89 SHACKLEWELL LANE, DALSTON,
E8 2EB

OTTOLENGHI
ROVI RESTAURANT, 59 WELLS
STREET, FITZROVIA, W1A 3AE

—CHELSEA, HAMPSTEAD, NOTTING
HILL, ISLINGTON, MARYLEBONE,
SPITALFIELDS

PAVILION BAKERY
130 COLUMBIA ROAD, BETHNAL
GREEN, E2 7RG

PEGGY PORSCHEN
116 EBURY STREET, BELGRAVIA,
SW1W 9QQ

PETERSHAM NURSERIES
OFF CHURCH LANE, PETERSHAM
ROAD, RICHMOND, TW10 7AB

—COVENT GARDEN

PERILLA
1–3 GREEN LANES, NEWINGTON
GREEN, N16 9BS

PLANTS
18 WEIGHHOUSE STREET, MAYFAIR,
W1K 5AH

POPHAMS
110A LAURISTON ROAD, VICTORIA
PARK, E9 7HA

—ISLINGTON, LONDON FIELDS

RICK STEIN
THE TOWPATH, PETERSHAM ROAD,
RICHMOND, TW10 6UX

—BARNES, KINGSTON

THE QUALITY CHOP HOUSE
92–94 FARRINGDON ROAD,
FARRINGDON, EC1R 3EA

QUEENS OF MAYFAIR
17 QUEEN STREET, MAYFAIR, W1J 5PH

RAFFLES AT THE OWO
57 WHITEHALL, WHITEHALL,
SW1A 2BX

THE RITZ
150 PICCADILLY, ST. JAMES'S, W1J 9BR

SALT THE RADISH
45 BLACKSTOCK ROAD,
FINSBURY PARK, N4 2JF

SAM'S KITCHEN
1 CRISP WALK, HAMMERSMITH,
W6 9DN

—BRENTFORD, CHISWICK

THE SAVOY
THE STRAND, STRAND, WC2R 0EZ

SEABIRD
40 BLACKFRIARS ROAD,
SOUTHWARK, SE1 8NY

SMOKING GOAT
64 SHOREDITCH HIGH STREET,
SHOREDITCH, E1 6JJ

SONS & DAUGHTERS
UNIT 119A COAL DROPS YARD,
KINGS CROSS, N1C 4DQ

SPRING
SOMERSET HOUSE, STRAND,
WC2R 1LA

ST. JOHN RESTAURANT
26 ST JOHN'S STREET, FARRINGDON,
EC1M 4AY

—ISLINGTON, MARYLEBONE,
BANKSIDE

SUNDAY IN BROOKLYN
98 WESTBOURNE GROVE, NOTTING
HILL, W2 5RU

THE TABLE CAFÉ
83 SOUTHWARK STREET, BANKSIDE,
SE1 0HX

TOKLAS
1 SURREY STREET, TEMPLE,
WC2R 2ND

UTTER WAFFLE
119 DULWICH ROAD, HERNE HILL,
SE24 0NG

VIOLET BAKERY
47 WILTON WAY, DALSTON, E8 3ED

WILD BY TART
3–4 ECCLESTON YARDS, BELGRAVIA,
SW1W 9AZ

WILLOWS
11 THE POLYGON, CLAPHAM, SW4 0JG

THE TEAM

Harriet Webster
Project Manager

With over 8 years' experience in the publishing industry commissioning and producing high-quality, award-winning, illustrated books, Harriet is a freelance project manager specialising in food and lifestyle.

Georgia Gold
Photographer

Georgia is a food and lifestyle photographer who has shot with some of the industry's biggest names across the UK and Australia. Her background in creative direction has a strong influence on her work – she focuses on storytelling and finding the beauty within each individual project.

Dean Hobson
Photographer

Dean Hobson, a renowned British photographer based in Australia, excels in travel and documentary photography, focusing on capturing genuine human emotions and moments. His extensive travels and diverse creative skills deeply inform his work, notably his striking documentation of life in Africa.

Emily Ezekiel
Food & Prop Stylist

Having worked with some of the biggest names in the food industry, Emily is a food writer, stylist and art director based out of her creative space, Narroway Studio, in the heart of East London.

Joseph Denison Carey
Assistant Food Stylist

Professional chef, Joseph often appears on our television screens and runs The Bread + Butter Supper Club.

Michelle Mackintosh
Designer

Michelle Mackintosh is a multi-award-winning book designer and illustrator. She designs lifestyle and cultural books for a clientele of global publishers. She has also written four books: *Snail Mail*, *Sustainable Gifting*, *Care Packages* and *Pretend you're in Tokyo* and co-written 10 books on Japan.

Claire Rochford
Designer

Claire is a freelance designer and art director based in the UK with 20 years experience working in illustrated book publishing.

Sally Somers
Copy Editor

Sally Somers is a freelance editor specialising in cookery. She lives with her family in Frome, UK, where she tends her various vegetable plots and beehives.

Thérèse Nichols

OnePlate Co-founder & Director

Regina Wursthorn

OnePlate Co-founder. Finance & Operations

Joshua Lanzarini

OnePlate Co-founder. Technical

Katarina Kelekovic

OnePlate Co-founder. Projects

Nick Woods

OnePlate Ambassador & Legal

Ben Whattam

OnePlate Global Brand Ambassador

Lysbeth Fox

OnePlate Ambassador & PR

Marcus Watson

OnePlate London Business Development Partner

THANK YOU

We would like to express our heartfelt gratitude to the wonderful individuals who contributed to the making of this cookbook and bringing it to life. Your unwavering support, creativity, and dedication has enriched these pages into a culinary masterpiece. We are profoundly grateful for your expertise, time, and enthusiasm. Each recipe, story, and piece of advice you shared has not only enriched this cookbook but also the lives it will touch. We would also like to express our deepest appreciation to our readers and supporters. Your purchase of this cookbook will not only bring joy to your table but will also make a significant difference in the lives of those in need. It is because of your kindness and generosity that together we can make a positive impact in the world. Thank you.

Particular thanks to:

Harriet Webster, Georgia Gold, Dean Hobson, Emily Ezekiel, Joseph Denison Carey, Michelle Mackintosh, Claire Rochford, Sally Somers, Wendy Hobson, Donna Tyler, Jamie Robinson and Chris Singleton at F1 Colour, Lee Stuart, Anne George, Laura Nickoll, Lucy Heaver, Nina Bosanac, Nick Woods, Tristan McLindon, Ben Whattam (Co-Founder & CEO RisingGen), Lysbeth Fox (Founder & CEO Fox communications), Marcus Watson (Adoreum co-founder & Chairman), Rosalie Deighton, Courteney Levy-Collins, Jamie Angus, Richie Notar, Victoria Shepherd, Maryanne Mooney, Neville Waterman, Dahlia Sable, Geoff Belleville, Fiona and Toby Hall, Kevin Bailey, David Leahy, Michael Murphy, Robert Toone, Tristan Velasco, Lindsay Rogers, Dylan Jones, Skye Gyngell, Jamie Oliver, Yotam Ottolenghi, Anna Jones, Heston Blumenthal, Angela Hartnett, Diana Henry, Claire Ptak, Melissa Hemsley, Rick Stein, Philip Khoury, Ella Mills. Narroway Studio.

A thank you to our incredible patrons:

Kitty Kay-Shuttleworth, Susanne Guthrie, Nikesh Patel, Romane Howsam and Sophie Rushton-Smith.

OUR GENEROUS SPONSORS

INDEX

BRUNCH IN LONDON

OnePlate Co-founder & Director: Thérèse Nichols

Project Manager: Harriet Webster

Copy Editor: Sally Somers

Designers: Michelle Mackintosh & Claire Rochford

Photographers: Georgia Gold & Dean Hobson

Prop Styling: Emily Ezekiel

Food Styling: Emily Ezekiel & Joseph Denison Carey

First published in 2024 by OnePlate.

OnePlate

OnePlate is a registed charity with the Australian Charities and Not-for-profits Commission.
ABN: 18612478501

ISBN: 978-0-646-88789-0

Printed in China on FSC certified paper with soy inks.

Recipe on page 128 kindly provided from *Veg* by Jamie Oliver, published by Penguin Random House © Jamie Oliver Enterprises Limited (2019 *Veg*).

Recipe on page 138 kindly provided from *The Dusty Knuckle* by Max Tobias, Rebecca Oliver & Daisy Terry, published by Quadrille, Hardie Grant Publishing (2022).

Recipe on page 378 kindly provided by Ottolenghi Ltd from *NOPI:The Cookbook*, published by Ebury Press (2015)